TRAVEL AND IMAGINATION

Current Developments in the Geographies of Leisure and Tourism

Series Editors:

Jan Mosedale, University of Applied Sciences HTW Chur, Switzerland and **Caroline Scarles**, University of Surrey, UK in association with the Geographies of Leisure and Tourism Research Group of the Royal Geographical Society (with the Institute of British Geographers).

Tourism and leisure exist within an inherently dynamic, fluid and complex world and are therefore inherently interdisciplinary. Recognising the role of tourism and leisure in advancing debates within the social sciences, this book series, is open to contributions from cognate social science disciplines that inform geographical thought about tourism and leisure. Produced in association with the Geographies of Leisure and Tourism Research Group of the Royal Geographical Society (with the Institute of British Geographers), this series highlights and promotes cutting-edge developments and research in this field. Contributions are of a high international standard and provide theoretically-informed empirical content to facilitate the development of new research agendas in the field of tourism and leisure research. In general, the series seeks to promote academic contributions that advance contemporary debates that challenge and stimulate further discussion and research both within the fields of tourism and leisure and the wider realms of the social sciences.

Other titles in the series:

Lifestyle Mobilities
Intersections of Travel, Leisure and Migration
Edited by Tara Duncan, Scott A. Cohen and Maria Thulemark

Mediating the Tourist Experience
From Brochures to Virtual Encounters
Edited by Jo-Anne Lester and Caroline Scarles

Travel, Tourism and Art
Edited by Tijana Rakić and Jo-Anne Lester

Narratives of Travel and Tourism
Edited by Jacqueline Tivers and Tijana Rakic

Travel and Imagination

Edited by

GARTH LEAN, RUSSELL STAIFF and EMMA WATERTON
University of Western Sydney, Australia

Taylor & Francis Group

LONDON AND NEW YORK

First published 2014 by Ashgate Publishing

2 Park Square, Milton Park, Abingdon, Oxon OX14 4RN
711 Third Avenue, New York, NY 10017, USA

Routledge is an imprint of the Taylor & Francis Group, an informa business

First issued in paperback 2016

British Library Cataloguing in Publication Data
A catalogue record for this book is available from the British Library

The Library of Congress has cataloged the printed edition as follows:
Lean, Garth.
 Travel and imagination / by Garth Lean, Russell Staiff and Emma Waterton.
  pages cm. – (Current developments in the geographies of leisure and tourism)
 Includes bibliographical references and index.
 ISBN 978-1-4724-1025-2 (hardback)
1. Travel–Psychological aspects. 2. Tourism–Psychological aspects.
3. Imagination. I. Title.
 G155.A1L413 2014
 910'.019–dc23

                                                                            2013032315

ISBN 978-1-4724-1025-2 (hbk)
ISBN 978-1-138-24853-3 (pbk)

Contents

List of Figures   *ix*

Notes on Contributors   *xi*

Acknowledgements   *xvii*

Prelude: Transit   1
Simone Lazaroo

1   Reimagining Travel and Imagination   9
    Garth Lean, Russell Staiff and Emma Waterton

PART I   MOBILE IDENTITIES

2   Embodied Travel: In Search of the Caribbean Self in Tropical
    Places and Spaces   25
    Jennifer D. Adams

3   The Jealous Imagination: Travels *in* my Mind and *out* of my Body   39
    Harriet Bell

4   Travel-as-Homemaking   53
    Gordon Waitt and Patricia Macquarie

PART II   TALES OF THE IMAGINATION

5   The Imagination in the Travel Literature of Xavier de Maistre and its
    Philosophical Significance   75
    Guy Bennett-Hunter

6   The Prominence of the Railroad in the African American
    Imagination: Mobile Men, Gendered Mobility and the Poetry of
    Sterling A. Brown   89
    Michael Ra-shon Hall

7   Tourist Imagination and Modernist Poetics:
        The Case of Cees Nooteboom   103
        Odile Heynders and Tom van Nuenen

8   Making Spain: The Spanish Imaginary in Travel Writing since
        the Second World War   119
        Steve Watson

PART III   VISUAL, MEDIA, REPRESENTATION

9   'Where all the Lines of the Map Converge': Werner Herzog's
        Ekstatic Imagination and Performative Thresholds   139
        Gabriella Calchi-Novati

10   Toys on the Move: Vicarious Travel, Imagination and the Case of
        Travelling Toy Mascots   149
        Shanna Robinson

11   MT Promises: Science Fictional Travel Technologies and the
        Making and Unmaking of Corporeal Identity   165
        Sean Williams

PART IV   UNSETTLING IMAGINATIONS

12   'It's Still in Your Body': Identity, Place and Performance in
        Holocaust Testimonies   181
        Steven Cooke and Donna-Lee Frieze

13   Ready for Takeoff? Lacerated Fantasies of Caribbean Paradise in
        the *Décollage* Art of Andrea Chung   197
        Marsha Pearce

14   Venice, Desire, Decay and the Imagination: Travels into the
        'Dark Side'   213
        Russell Staiff

A FINAL WORD

15   Travel and Imagination: An Invitation   229
        Garth Lean and Emma Waterton

Index *241*

List of Figures

3.1 Reproduction of diary page with scales distorted according to
     imagined embodied response   44

4.1 The Illawarra Escarpment looking north towards Stanwell Park
     from McCauley's Beach, Thirroul   55

6.1 Interior view of Pullman car with porters waiting to serve passengers,
     1920 or before   92
6.2 Pullman porter standing on rear platform of train car preparing for
     departure, August 1896   95

10.1 A popular anthropomorphizing technique observed was having the
     toy gaze at a view or landscape   155
10.2 Skipper at the main square in Antwerp   156
10.3 This photo from user Discret_incognito78 is characterized by
     considerable attention to framing, photographic skill and a sense
     of creative aestheticism   157

13.1 Andrea Chung, *Cut Yai*, 23 × 30.5 cm (9 × 12 inches), magazine
     décollage, 2009   198
13.2 Andrea Chung, *The Good Life*, 46 × 30.5 cm (18 × 12 inches),
     magazine *décollage*, 2009   206
13.3 Andrea Chung, *Eastern Hideaway*, 46 × 30.5 cm (18 × 12 inches),
     magazine *décollage*, 2009   206
13.4 Andrea Chung, *Dry Yaye*, 23 × 30.5 cm (9 × 12 inches), magazine
     décollage, 2008   208

Notes on Contributors

Jennifer D. Adams is an Associate Professor of Science Education at Brooklyn College and The Graduate Center, CUNY. Her research focuses on STEM teaching and learning in informal science contexts including place-based education. Travel is one of her passions and her journeys have provided her a lens to explore sense of place and place-based education for students of the Caribbean Diaspora in Brooklyn, New York, through autobiographical and ethnographic research where she draws on cultural geography, Caribbean studies and environmental thought to inform her work. Most recently she has embarked on a journey of integrated arts and science education for understanding the natural world with secondary students on the Caribbean island of Barbuda and in central Brooklyn, New York.

Harriet Bell worked in building conservation for nearly 15 years before starting a PhD at the University of Sheffield. This explored the articulation of values in the conservation and regeneration of listed, post-war public housing. She became disabled during the course of her research as a result of multiple sclerosis (MS) and has become increasingly interested in how people with disabilities experience and negotiate urban space, and the historic environment in particular. Most recently she has been working on a research project for the University of Leicester with the City Council: 'Valuing Leicester's Historic Core'.

Guy Bennett-Hunter is a Research Fellow in Philosophy in the School of Divinity, History and Philosophy at the University of Aberdeen in Scotland, UK. He was educated by the Universities of Durham and Cambridge, taking his PhD in 2011, and has held teaching and research positions in philosophy at Durham University and the University of Edinburgh. Dr Bennett-Hunter's main research interests are in the philosophy of religion, phenomenology and existentialism, pragmatism and aesthetics. He is currently working on a research project which critically engages with theological appropriations of scientific and philosophical theories of emergence. His other current work applies pragmatist and Wittgensteinian philosophical approaches to the concept of religious certainty.

Gabriella Calchi-Novati received a BA magna cum laude in Letters and Philosophy, an MA (honours) in Public Relations from Università Cattolica del Sacro Cuore (Milan) and an MPhil. (first) in Irish Drama and Film from Trinity College Dublin. Her main area of research is 'performance philosophy' and her work has appeared in *Performance Research, Performance Paradigm, About Performance and Cinema: Journal of Philosophy and the Moving Image*; and in edited collections. Calchi-Novati holds a PhD awarded with distinction for her thesis *Performativities of Intimacy in the Age of Biopolitics*. She lectures in Performance Studies and Critical Theory in the Drama Department, Trinity College Dublin.

Steven Cooke is a Lecturer in Cultural Heritage at Deakin University, Melbourne, Australia. His background is in cultural and historical geography and he has published widely on issues relating to the memorial landscapes of war and genocide, museums and national identity and maritime heritage and urban redevelopment. He worked in senior positions in the heritage sector for a number of years before moving to Deakin where he is Course Director for the Cultural Heritage and Museum Studies postgraduate programs and Deputy Director of the Cultural Heritage Centre for Asia and the Pacific.

Donna-Lee Frieze is a Visiting Fellow at the Alfred Deakin Research Institute in Melbourne and a Senior Fellow at the Center for Jewish History in Manhattan who has taught a graduate unit on Genocide Studies for over 10 years at Deakin University, Melbourne. In 2009 she was joint consulting scholar for a conference on Raphael Lemkin and sole consulting scholar for a six-month exhibition on Lemkin, both at the Center for Jewish History in New York City. She has published widely on genocide studies. Her teaching and research areas include genocide studies, film and philosophy she is the editor of Raphael Lemkin's autobiography, Yale University Press, 2013.

Michael Ra-shon Hall is an interdisciplinary scholar and PhD candidate (ABD) at the Graduate Institute of Liberal Arts (ILA), Emory University, USA. His areas of research and teaching include twentieth century and contemporary American and African American literature, visual culture and cultural histories of travel within and beyond the African Diaspora. Hall holds a BA in English (with minors in History and Spanish Language and Literature) from Southeastern Louisiana University, a Master of Professional Studies in Africana Studies (with foci in African American Studies and American Art) from Cornell University and an MA in Interdisciplinary Studies in Culture and Society from Emory University. His dissertation project, *Beyond Freedom and Confinement: Travel and Imagination in African American Cultural History, Arts and Letters, ca. 1900–1970*, examines the impact of travel and tourism on the critical works and creative expressions of African American artists.

Odile Heynders is a Professor of Comparative Literature in the Department of Culture Studies at Tilburg University, The Netherlands. She has published books and articles on strategies of reading, European poetry and the history of literature studies in the Netherlands. Her recent research project is on literary authors as European public intellectuals: *Voices of Europe*. Heynders is Head of the Research Programme: *Literature and Visual Art in the European Public Sphere*.

Simone Lazaroo is a Senior Lecturer in Creative Writing at Murdoch University in Perth, Western Australia, and writer of four published novels, three of them prize-winning and all of them shortlisted for international or national awards. Her short stories have been published in the USA, England and Australia. She has judged various literary prizes, including the Commonwealth Writers' Prize (Australia – New Zealand – South East Asian region), and was awarded the David TK Wong Fellowship in 2000 for writing at the University of East Anglia, England. She has been a recipient of Australia Council Literature Board and Western Australia Department of Culture and the Arts grants, and will be a European Commission Erasmus Mundus Visiting Scholar in Spain in 2014. Her fifth novel, *Lost River – Three Albums*, will be published in early 2014. She is currently working on a collection of short stories exploring travel, cities, homelessness, consumerism and migration.

Garth Lean is a researcher and teacher in the School of Social Sciences and Psychology at the University of Western Sydney. He holds an applied science degree in environmental management and tourism, an honours degree in tourism management and an interdisciplinary PhD in travel/tourism. Garth has also worked in tourism planning and marketing with local and state governments. His research interests include: travel, tourism, mobile identities, imagination, transformation, cultural heritage, visual methods, online research, the alternative presentation of travel and tourism research, multicultural education and carbon governance. He has published a variety of papers on travel and, in addition to this book, is currently developing the edited volumes *Travel and Transformation* (Ashgate) and *The Poetics of Travel* (Berghahn Books) with Russell Staiff and Emma Waterton, and the sole authored book *Transformative Travel* (CABI). He is a member of the Geographies of Leisure and Tourism Research Group with the Royal Geographical Society.

Patricia Macquarie is a postgraduate student in the School of Earth and Environmental Sciences at the University of Wollongong. She was awarded a PhD in 2013 for her thesis entitled *Valuing Landscape, Performing Landscape: A Case Study of the Illawarra Escarpment*. In this study Patricia applied her background in the humanities, and employment background in a university environmental science administration context, to the theoretical and methodological issues involved in assessing the everyday social value of particular landscapes.

Marsha Pearce has recently completed her doctoral research in Cultural Studies. She is based at the University of the West Indies, St. Augustine Campus, Trinidad, where she teaches in the Department of Creative and Festival Arts. Her research interests include: visual culture, visual narratives of travel and tourism and the intersections of art, Caribbean identity and representation.

Shanna Robinson is currently undertaking a PhD with the Institute for Culture and Society at the University of Western Sydney. Her research focuses on the infusion of experimentalism and creativity in touristic experience, with a particular focus on intersections of power, imagination and embodied practice. Shanna also teaches at UWS College and her broader research interests include: cultural theory, mobilities, travel, media and ethics.

Russell Staiff holds a doctorate in art history from the University of Melbourne and is a member of the Institute of Culture and Society within the University of Western Sydney where he researches the interface between cultural heritage, tourism and communities with a special focus on Southeast Asia. He has recently co-edited a volume on *Heritage and Tourism* for Routledge and the monograph *Re-imagining Heritage Interpretation* published by Ashgate in 2014.

Tom van Nuenen is a PhD candidate at the Culture Studies department of Tilburg University, where he is performing research into online travel discourses. He holds an MA in Culture Studies (cum laude, top 1 per cent). In 2011 he was part of a research programme funded by KNAW (the Royal Netherlands Academy of Arts and Sciences). He has worked for several years as a copy editor, and blogs on music and video games.

Gordon Waitt is Professor of Human Geography at the University of Wollongong. He has contributed feminist perspectives to leisure and tourism studies. He encourages scholars to engage with ideas that investigate the spatial imperatives of the sensuous body to explore how people make sense of place, self, and collectives. With Christine Metusela he recently co-authored *Tourism and Australian Beach Culture: Revealing Bodies* (Channel View Publications). In 2006, with Kevin Markwell, he co-authored *Gay Tourism: Culture and Context* (Haworth Publications).

Emma Waterton is based at the University of Western Sydney, in the Institute for Culture and Society. Her interests include: unpacking the discursive constructions of 'heritage'; explorations of tourism, heritage and affect; thanatourism; visuality; and explorations of innovative methodologies. She has over 30 publications since 2005, including one authored (*Politics, Policy and the Discourses of Heritage in Britain* (Palgrave Macmillan 2010)) and two co-authored monographs (*Heritage, Communities and Archaeology* (with Laurajane Smith, Duckworth 2009) and *The Semiotics of Heritage Tourism* (with Steve Watson, Channel View Publications, 2014)), six co-edited volumes (with Routledge, Ashgate, Oxford University Press and Cambridge Scholars Publishing) and three guest edited special issues. She has served on the Editorial Board for *Sociology* (2008–2010), and is currently part of the Editorial Board for the *Journal of Heritage Tourism* (2012–ongoing) and the *International Journal of Heritage Studies* (2013–ongoing). She was Assistant Editor for the *International Journal of Heritage Studies* from 2009–2013.

Steve Watson is Principal Lecturer in Tourism at York St John University in the UK. His research is focused on the ways in which heritage is constructed and understood in tourism and the way that tourism acts as a vector for various social and cultural meanings. He has published widely in the field of heritage tourism and recent co-edited books include: *The Cultural Moment in Tourism* (with Laurajane Smith and Emma Waterton) and *Heritage and Tourism, Place, Encounter Engagement* (with Robyn Bushell and Russell Staiff). His other research interest is in Spanish travel writing, particularly the way that this is used in the construction of cultural imaginaries of place. He is currently preparing a book on this topic.

Sean Williams is a professional writer whose lifelong interest in the critically neglected trope of the matter transmitter has resulted in a series of novels called Twinmaker and a PhD from the University of Adelaide.

Acknowledgements

We would like to thank our contributors for all of their time and hard work. Throughout the course of this volume's production, they offered us not only their intellectual input but responded with speed and patience to what must have seemed an endless string of requests. We are keenly aware that this process will at times have been testing and are grateful to each of them for their generosity and support.

We also acknowledge, with gratitude, the help and guidance provided by Jan Mosedale and Caroline Scarles, Series Editors of the Current Developments in the Geographies of Leisure and Tourism series within which this volume finds its place. Thanks, too, to the Geographies of Leisure and Tourism Research Group of the Royal Geographical Society. We extend our appreciations to Katy Crossan, our Commissioning Editor at Ashgate, for her continuous advice and support. Finally, we would like to acknowledge the support of the School of Social Sciences and Psychology at the University of Western Sydney.

As for the volume's shortcomings – we claim them entirely for ourselves.

Prelude

Transit

Simone Lazaroo

In her twilit suburban apartment on the outskirts of the most isolated city in the world, as the sprinkler hissed under the Hills Hoist and football players yelped on the oval across the road, Sheila Jones searched the internet for travellers' bargains in that bigger, more sophisticated city on the far side of the globe. She'd yearned most of her adult life to visit Manhattan, but hadn't felt wealthy enough since her divorce a decade before. Now, it wasn't just the scarcity of economy class seats, her dwindling sick leave or the nearness of her fiftieth birthday that made her fear time was running out.

'The incision's healing nicely. Take a holiday', her oncologist had suggested, 'before your chemotherapy begins in four weeks'.

'Will the chemo cure me for good?'

'You have about a fifty–fifty chance of the cancer recurring'.

Fifty–fifty. It could mean a fair chance. It could mean not fair enough.

'And then? What happens if it recurs?'

'New drugs are being trialled all the time'. His pale manicured hand smoothing the sheet. 'But once cancer reaches that secondary stage, the chances of patients' long-term survival diminish somewhat'.

Could she ever really escape from such a prognosis? Images of Manhattan shimmered like a mirage on her computer screen: skyscraper windows gilded by the sun setting over Central Park's autumn leaves; Times Square; insouciant couples in evening dress in a chandeliered bar; the Statue of Liberty at dawn; yellow taxis speeding past glittering store window displays. Unlimited promise.

Shopping week, following Thanksgiving on November 24, is the best time to bag a bargain in Manhattan, the website read. Only a fortnight away! She could buy herself some stylish clothes to conceal her newly lopsided chest, some elegant shoes, maybe even give herself a total makeover. At the very least, she'd forget for a while the grey routine of her secretarial life and the precariousness of her mortality.

The horizon on the ocean side of the football oval had darkened to cobalt, her favourite blue. Maybe she'd find clothes that colour in the Manhattan sales. Finally, encouraged by more reports of the strong Australian dollar on the television news, she bought the last available economy Singapore Airlines ticket and booked a room in the cheapest hotel near Central Park. She could just afford to escape for five days.

* * *

She arrived in Manhattan in a yellow taxi the day after Thanksgiving, but most of the autumn leaves in Central Park had already fallen. After checking into her beige room in the Comfort Inn, she ignored her jetlag, showered and pulled on her clothes and leather walking shoes.

Avoiding the hot dog vendors leaning on their white trailers under the park's bare elms, Sheila followed her Lonely Planet NYC Guide map towards the midtown department store sales. She paused every now and then to photograph glass towers and enormous Christmas trees in chandeliered lobbies, until she was suddenly interrupted by something less lofty.

A gaunt old woman's outstretched hand, clawed and scaly as a crow's foot.

'Gotta few dollars for a cawfee?' she rasped.

'I don't lie like her! I need a beer', grinned a red-faced man leaning against a Starbucks window, his incisors missing, a rolled up sleeping bag at his feet.

Sheila pulled her handbag closer to her ribs and hurried along Broadway. She couldn't really afford to donate, what with the need for clothes to conceal her uneven chest and goodness knows what other expenses ahead of her. None of the Manhattan tourist websites had shown people begging. There were more of them on the following blocks, some of them silent and huddled behind handwritten signs. 'Out of luck, work, and accommodation', one young man's cardboard sign read, 'please help'. His face was downturned, as if he was ashamed to be seen. His long lashes and narrow chest, the fine down on his pimply chin. She guessed he was about 16.

And another beggar, and another. More than she'd seen her whole life. The further she walked, the more of them asked her directly for money. *Why's it so embarrassing? Because you feel too poor to give them anything, yet you're wealthy enough to be holidaying here? How'd you decide which ones to give to, anyway?* She hid her camera in her bag and fastened the safety catch.

The next block seemed abruptly full of tourists, their faces upturned to some higher spectacle. Sheila looked up to multi-storeyed electronic screens shimmering with advertisements. Times Square, no doubt. This was the Manhattan she'd expected, not all those beggars. Countless streamlined images lighting up the grey day: consumer goods, logos, desirable bodies in designer clothes, lots of cleavage. A sudden dull ache beneath her mastectomy scar.

Bright green digital news headlines circled like sharks underneath the advertisements:

UNEMPLOYED FIGURES INCREASE ... OCCUPY WALL STREET PROTESTORS FORCED OUT ... 4000 CITY WORKERS TO LOSE JOBS.

But the glow from the product images outshone the bad news, illuminated the congregation's faces, softened her ache.

Fortified by the signs of capitalism's endurance, Sheila continued down Broadway to Macy's department store. On the street corner next to Macy's enormous illuminated white Christmas tree, a dark-skinned man in a tuxedo jacket sang *Guess the Lord Must be in New York City*, his voice swelling in waves above the din of traffic, his hands pressed together under his chin like a little shelter. He looked handsome enough, despite his yellowed teeth and stained *VOTE OBAMA – YES WE CAN* t-shirt. As he finished his song, she accidentally kicked over the paper McDonald's cup half full of coins next to the sleeping bag at his feet. His big toes protruded from holes in grimy canvas sneakers. Retrieving the coins, she noticed him glancing at her chest. Her open coat had tugged her shirt to her breastless left side, unfastening the top few buttons. He whistled softly. He'd seen her mastectomy scar. Mortified, Sheila buttoned her shirt, pulled her coat closed over it and stepped back.

'Say, you wanna sing with me?' He smiled gently. 'See the fortune I got to share with you? I got food stamps, too', he winked.

'Haven't got the voice for it', she mumbled, hurrying into Macy's, her heart hammering home her humiliation.

Inside, gold Christmas wreathes hung from the ceilings under red star-spangled signs: *BELIEVE*. She took the escalator up. On the third floor, cleavage-displaying evening dresses shimmered. She'd never have the body to wear anything like that again, unless she could find the money for breast reconstruction. Down on the next floor, most of the garments were for old women; overpriced Crimplene trousers with elasticized waists, voluminous pastel cardigans. A wave of panic: her life could be finished soon, decades before she was ready to wear those kinds of clothes.

BELIEVE. Believe in what?

* * *

Sheila spent most of the following days queuing for hours to see the museums near Central Park, the Empire State Building, the Statue of Liberty. Yet she still felt she hadn't experienced the real New York. And she hadn't found new shoes or a scrap of cobalt blue clothing anywhere, not even amongst the designer garments in Bloomingdale's and Bergdorf's. Outside Bergdorf's, dispirited by the supercilious smirks of sales assistants as she'd checked price tags, Sheila almost collided with a bleach-blonde transvestite wearing impeccable make-up, a five o'clock shadow and a fur coat.

'What the fuck *you* starin' at?', the transvestite snapped at her, throwing a Macy's catalogue onto a bus stop bench and teetering in her stilettos to a taxi. As the taxi sped away, Sheila picked the catalogue up and flicked through it. Their prices were certainly bargains compared to Bergdorf's. She headed back to the beacon of Macy's Christmas tree, glad the singing homeless man wasn't there.

She took the escalator back to the second floor. She found a few rayon blouses and double-knit trouser suits for career women in a corner she'd overlooked the first time, but they were all made in China like the Myer stock back home, and none of them were as cheap.

'Excuse me', she asked the young dark-suited man at the information desk near the escalator. 'Where are the discounted clothes for ... someone like me?'

He glanced dismissively at her. 'The bargains for senior citizens are in the basement, Ma'am', he replied, his teeth and cufflinks gleaming.

* * *

In the basement she stocked up on cheap oversized shirts to conceal her chest for the office, pyjamas for chemotherapy. Made in China, but at least she could say she'd bought them in New York. *BELIEVE,* exhorted the red slogan on her star-strewn Macy's plastic shopping bags. They didn't feel heavy enough as she left the store, considering the money she'd paid.

'Hi again, Sugar'. That deep lilting voice. Damn. Because he wasn't singing, she hadn't noticed the homeless man on the footpath outside until too late.

'Oh. Hi'. She barely glanced at him. He certainly wasn't the New York experience she'd hoped for.

'You from Awstralia?'

'Yeah'. At least he didn't smell.

'You talk so cool'.

'Well. I reckon you do, too', replied Sheila.

'*Ar reckon*. See what I mean? Cool!' His stained teeth. 'Plenny Awzies comin' here now, what with your strong dollar 'n' all'. He gestured surreptitiously towards her chest, lowered his voice. 'I seen your scar the other day. Why you come all this way so soon after an operation like that?'

'A holiday I guess'. She pulled her coat tighter around her.

He lowered his voice. 'Mastectomy, right? Wife had one'.

'You have a wife?'

'Had. Long time ago'.

'I'm sorry'.

'S'okay. She just moved on'.

Sheila wondered if that was his euphemism for death. Had his wife died of breast cancer?

'Actually, I also came to look for clothes to conceal my ... chest', Sheila explained. 'The sales, you know. I fly back late tonight'.

'You want bargain clothes? You should go to the Goodwill thrift shop on 25th. Got my tux there'. He stroked the shiny lapels proudly.

'Really'. The frayed cuffs, the moth holes.

'Where you stayin'?'

'Comfort Inn'.

'Opposite Central Park? Any chance of me goin' back with you to get a nice hot shower?'

Her pulse skipped a beat. She couldn't read his expression.

'I've already checked out', she lied hastily.

'Where's your stuff then?'

'Locked up in their luggage room'. She glanced back through Macy's glass doors. At the closest counter, a blonde cosmetician wearing a white technician's coat beckoned her adamantly with a plump blusher brush. 'Must've left something behind', Sheila lied again. The doors glided open mercifully fast as she turned back.

'He hittin' on you?' the cosmetician smiled sympathetically. Her bleached white teeth.

'Pardon?'

'That panhandler. He asking you for money?'

'Sort of'.

'You sound like an Aussie, right? Those panhandlers can spot the tourists. Best ignore 'em. Free makeover with quality product?'

'How much do I have to buy?'

'Zilch. No strings attached. Sit right here'. Sheila sat on the high chrome chair like an infant while the cosmetician tied a large black bib around her neck and cleaned her face. 'Sure look like you could do with some colour'.

Sheila could only just hear the homeless man outside, singing *Happy Holiday*.

'I've been ill'.

'*He-e-ey*! That's too *bad*. But you're an Aussie, *right?* Not as tough as New Yorkers, but tough enough. We'll fix you *rr-ight* up'. The cosmetician brushed some beige liquid over Sheila's face in a loose cross, like a blessing. 'This foundation is from our ultra-sheer translucent hypo-allergenic range'.

The glass doors hissed open and closed, admitting customers, shutting out snatches of the homeless man's song. The cosmetician anointed Sheila's eyelids and cheeks with coloured powders, loaded her lashes with mascara.

'That blusher and shadow give you a real warm winter's glow'. The cosmetician stepped back, held up a mirror. 'Sure look radiant, honey', she concluded, unfastening the large bib with a flourish.

'Could do with some of that foundation. Sorry I don't have money to buy some'.

'Don't worry. And just ignore the panhandlers, right? Have a nice day!'

'Thank you', Sheila clambered off the stool, 'so much'. She sidled away from the counter.

'Safe journey!' The cosmetician waved her blusher brush.

Sheila sprayed herself with DKNY perfume from the sample bottles on the way out, tiptoed behind the homeless man as he concluded another song, but he heard the rustle of her shopping bags and turned around.

'Singin' my heart out for a dime', he smiled at her as people rushed past, 'but they all too busy shoppin' or gettin' home'. She pulled out her purse, kept her greenbacks hidden, dropped a few coins into the empty McDonald's cup at his feet. The bank back home wouldn't buy foreign coins, anyway. 'Thanks Sugar. You thought I was tryin' a hook up with you before, din' you? Just wanted a shower, that's all. Hope you always have hot showers and a soft bed. Hope you had a real good holiday here. Safe journey back, Sugar. I never bin for a holiday anywhere, y' know. Scuse me'. He brushed her cheek suddenly with his hand. She suppressed a scream, felt her new foundation smear, stepped back and snapped her purse shut. 'Just seeing if you still real', he said. 'Say, look at that'. He looked at the pale pigment marking his dark hand. 'A face full of product'.

Sheila looked him directly in the eyes for the first time. There, she saw another immense city whose surfaces she'd barely touched. Averting her eyes to the street behind him, she glimpsed the southern horizon deepening to cobalt. Almost unbearable, the thought of returning home.

'Well, you know, it was free', she murmured. 'And I've lost a lot lately. I had to do *something* to cheer myself up'.

'Sure. Gotta do somethin' to rise above it all. I bin there, Sugar', the homeless man said, 'Why you think I sing? I bin there, too'.

* * *

Five in the morning Singapore time, after her plane had chased a lost day across multiple time zones. After choosing between Eastern and Western meals and downing a few Singapore slings served by the exotically uniformed air hostesses, Sheila had slept only a few hours, dreaming of the homeless man singing in the shower of her Comfort Inn suite.

At first the transit area of Changi Airport's Terminal 3 seemed to her a replica city, its carpeted arcades of global brand shops hushed and blessedly beggar-free. She dragged her Macy's bags past Starbucks and a rotund Stetson-wearing American lolling at the counter of Dunkin' Donuts; almost collided with two brightly dressed Japanese toddlers sitting astride their small pink ride-on suitcases pulled by jetlagged parents.

In the twilit lounge behind the food court, travellers slept on faux suede couches, yesterday's newspapers or scarves covering their faces. No couch for her to rest, and all the Western designer shops looked closed. But a shop named *Old Singapore* was already open, one wall papered with an enlarged sepia-hued photographic print of an English colonial couple in a trishaw pedalled by a malnourished Chinese man. Sheila scrutinized the familiar navy blue-patterned sarong kebayas hanging from a bamboo rack near the entrance.

'Special price on authentic Singapore Airlines' hostess uniforms designed by Christian Dior', called the young Chinese shop assistant, hurrying towards her. Sheila turned and walked away quickly, too exhausted to distinguish between the genuine article and fakery. And what was really Eastern, and what was Western? On her way to the lavatories, she fingered and bruised the petals of real oriental orchids in pseudo-Grecian urns; but her touch left no mark on plastic ferns around a slate-edged pool. There, giant orange koi fish rolled their toy-like eyes and thrashed hungrily. Beyond them, butterflies hanging from palm trees in a glass atrium might've been artificial, dead or just sleeping until the sun rose over the runways.

Behind the pristine lavatories with their Royal Doulton fixtures designed for squatting in some cubicles and sitting in others, Sheila noticed more signs: *Prayer Room. Meditation Room.* Her pulse hastened as she made her way towards them. At last. Space for finding herself, or to rest, at least!

The meditation room was furnished with nothing but grey carpet, a chrome shoe-rack and a few tortured willow branches spray-painted white, uniformly cut and held in place by a chrome bar against the Laminex wood-grain wall. Otherwise empty, the room was only the size of her walk-in wardrobe at home. The sign on the wall between the two rooms read:

> *Please remove your shoes.*
> *Please observe solemness.*
> *Please board your flight on time.*

Not enough space to meditate. She turned towards the prayer room. Small chrome icons identical to the ones on the lavatories' exterior walls indicated the women's prayer cubicle to the left, the men's to the right. Only a curtain and a chrome luggage rack divided them. In the men's cubicle, an Asian man in a sarong knelt on the grey carpet facing the laminated wall. A burqua-clad woman knelt in the women's cubicle. Their bowed heads reminded Sheila of the homeless man. Finishing her prayer, the woman in the burqua glimpsed her, placed her hands together under her chin, smiled and bowed to Sheila. Sheila couldn't return the gesture, for her hands were too full of shopping.

As her *BELIEVE* bags snagged the luggage rack on the way out, it occurred to Sheila that those people in the prayer room and the homeless man outside Macy's had something she lacked. *What did they show me? What have I learned?* Something to do with their hands pressed together like a little shelter, but jetlag fogged her glimpse of clarity. She only just heard the final boarding call for her flight, muffled by the rustle of her shopping bags.

* * *

Lying in her hospice bed two years after her return to the most isolated city in the world, Sheila places her hands together on her chest and closes her eyes. Though it's a warm early summer evening, she can't stop shivering. Her shoeless feet feel especially cold. Then she hears a man singing from a great distance away, glimpses a cobalt blue horizon. *Not just a line between earth and sky. A place between living and dying. A way of letting go. All this heavy baggage.*

Her breathing slows, her heartbeat gathers her in. There's no final boarding call this time. She's surprised that departure should feel so stress-free and such a blessing. The streets and boundaries of the suburbs recede as she begins her journey towards that distant, truer city. Floating in the monsoonal air past the confusion of East and West in Singapore's transit lounge, she breaks into a sweat, but in three blinks of her eyes she finds herself shivering outside Macy's

Manhattan store. *Those days spent searching for the place of my dreams. Where did the time go?*

She hovers above the homeless man singing his songs of hope and longing; feels his hand on her cheek again; sees in his eyes that other city she'd never really know. She empties everything in her pockets into his cup, hums the last few lines of his song with him, though she's not sure which song he's singing.

The horizon to the rest of the world goes on forever. She merges with air, clouds, flight paths. There, beyond the boundaries of cities, nations and commerce, she enters real radiance. *My final departure. All my memories and baggage are released. More is seen and heard than can be understood. Do all our journeys finish like this?*

Chapter 1
Reimagining Travel and Imagination

Garth Lean, Russell Staiff and Emma Waterton

When an individual embarks upon a journey they do so in possession of a unique subjectivity informed by a multitude of experiences leading up to that particular moment in time. They usually, though not always, depart from a 'home environment' in which they have been travelling in various ways (physically, virtually, communicatively, imaginatively) from birth, albeit to varying degrees (Lean 2012a). As such, each individual traveller carries with them a quite unique experiential baggage, which can spark, inform and limit their imaginings in innumerable and unpredictable ways. This becomes even more complex when one considers that the spaces, places and landscapes through which we travel are themselves mobile, shaped by various flows of people, information, ideas, representations and objects, both historical and contemporary (Leed 1991, Rojek and Urry 1997). This multitude of catalysts may resonate with the traveller in a variety of ways, linking with past experiences and memories, to inform and stimulate the traveller's imagination. What is more, places are in a constant state of flux (Coleman and Crang 2002, Cresswell 2002, Bærenholdt et al. 2004). Both familiarity and difference abound, and while the physical journey may be somewhat easy to map, the mental voyage is a rather more unpredictable and unbounded affair.

A traveller's imagination during a travel experience (and, for that matter, their performances, relationships and motivations, which in turn influence their imaginings) may be informed, both before and during any given physical travel experience, by: relationships with significant and less-significant others (both before and during travel), movies, books (both fiction and non-fiction, including guidebooks), documentaries, television programmes, conversations, studies (both formal and informal), previous physical (and non-physical) travels, various roles/performances (work, family, parental) and objects given, acquired and carried, to name only a few. This list could include just about anything that stimulates the senses or triggers an affective response. Indeed, the mind has no real need of a physical stimuli at all, and can simply, though complexly, head in innumerable directions of its own accord (McGinn 2004). In addition, an exploration of travel and imagination must also acknowledge that one's imagination does not cease after any given physical travel experience, but can become intimately entwined in ongoing lived experience, again, to varying degrees (Lean 2012b). Added to this, an investigation of travel and imagination needs to look beyond the individual to representations and understandings of the imagination, along with observing imaginaries that are constructed and undergoing continual alteration. While the imagination itself is slippery, complex and impossible to understand, in the context of physical travel, it becomes doubly so.

The imagination, of course, is not a new topic of enquiry. Nor, for that matter, is travel. Both are themes that have captured the interest of a wide range of disciplines for some time. The notion of the imagination, for example, has been held in focus by disciplinary lenses that include, but are not limited to: history, geography, cultural studies, heritage studies, visual studies, cinematic studies, the arts, literary studies, philosophy, psychology and the mind sciences more broadly. The work that has tumbled forth from these fields has dealt with a plethora of topics and debates, including: the nature of reality, reason, faith/belief, objectivity/subjectivity, creativity, dreams, make-believe, fantasy, memory and remembering, perception, the 'mind's eye', understanding, world-views, learning and story-telling, to name an incomprehensive few. While it would not be possible to summarize such wide ranging debates in this chapter (this would require a multivolume set), it remains the case that many of these themes will be touched upon and explored throughout the volume's chapters.

Given this book's location within a series on leisure and tourism geographies, it is particularly important to acknowledge the body of work that has observed the geographical imagination over the last half century (see for example: Lowenthal 1961, Daniels 1992, Gregory 1994, Schwartz and Ryan 2003, Cosgrove 2006, 2008, Daniels et al. 2011). Not only is this a body of scholarship with close correlations to themes congruent with travel (for example, our knowledge, interpretation, visions and representations of, and interactions with, people, cultures, spaces, places and landscapes), its recent popularity highlights the currency of the theme both within and beyond geography. This was exemplified by Stephen Daniels (2011) setting the 'geographical imagination' as the theme for the 2011 conference of the Royal Geographical Society and Institute of British Geographers.

As highlighted above, the imagination, and imaginaries, are a central part of corporeal travel experiences and, as such, have been frequently observed and commented upon within tourism and travel (and related) scholarship (for just a few examples, see: Kaplan 1996, Rojek and Urry 1997, Osborne 2000, Dann 2002, Roberson 2002, Bærenholdt et al. 2004, Minca and Oakes 2006, Ruoff 2006, MacCannell 2011, Urry and Larsen 2011, Picard and Robinson 2012, Smith et al. 2012 – some of these works are explored throughout the book). Scholarship looking directly at the imagination in relation to travel, however, has been somewhat limited and tourism-centric. While the works developed provide important considerations, they address a restricted range of subtopics from a narrow collection of disciplinary perspectives. For example, Crouch et al. (2005) offer a multidisciplinary analysis of the nuanced relationship between media and tourism under the broad theme of the imagination. Few of the contributions, however, allowed their focus to fall primarily upon the notion of 'the imagination'. Again, looking at the influence of the media in informing both host and guest imaginaries, Reijnders (2011a) examined the role of popular films, television shows and books in developing place imaginaries and in motivating travellers (Light 2009 and Reijnders 2011b also explore this in their respective papers on Dracula and Transylvania). Similarly, Salazar (2010) drew upon two in-depth anthropological studies of tour guiding in Tanzania and Indonesia to explore how guiding practices are informed by 'tourism imaginaries' which are fuelled by media representations, and how these in turn inform tourist expectations. Building upon the 'expectation' theme, and within the same anthropological book series, Salazar et al's (2011) volume sought to look at the relationship between tourist expectations and the imagination, from both host and guest perspectives. There have also been recent attempts to look more broadly at tourism imaginaries (see Gravari-Barbas and Graburn 2012, Salazar 2012), again predominantly from anthropological perspectives. While these represent important contributions to an understanding of travel and the imagination, it has left open the need for perspectives that stretch beyond imaginaries to a more holistic view upon the imagination. Thus, building on the initial work of scholars such as Benedict Anderson (1983) and, more recently, Charles Taylor (2004), we argue here that imaginaries are a component of the broader notion of the imagination. We also highlight the need to take a wider focus than observing tourism alone, and propose an encapsulation of the expansive mobilities landscape, along with taking multi- and inter-disciplinary perspectives. Indeed, while not an academic work per se, one of the more interesting explorations of travel and imagination, and possibly the most frequently cited, was offered in de Botton's (2002) *The Art of Travel*. de Botton draws upon a variety of literary, historical, art and philosophical case-studies looking at tourists, explorers, long-term visitors, drivers, walkers, domestic travellers and even bedroom travellers (see Bennett-Hunter's expansion on the work of Xavier de Maistre in Chapter 5) to explore travel and tourism practices. While not directly focused upon the imagination, it provided one of the richest explorations of the general theme in relation to travel to date.

It is the contestation of this volume that, rather than being treated as a surreptitious and peripheral component of the physical travel experience, the imagination is a facet of travel that warrants careful examination in its own right. Given the rich history of multidisciplinary enquiry, and the sheer breadth of elements the theme of the imagination touches upon, this exploration should not, however, be led solely through the lens of tourism. Following calls from scholars such as Franklin and Crang (2001), Franklin (2007) and Robinson and Jamal (2009), we argue that the disciplinary scope of tourism is too narrow to adequately conceptualize travel and the imagination, quite simply as physical travel encompasses such a broad array of mobilities. This is especially so if travel is conceptualized beyond the physical, to encompass any form of movement in which the conscious, or unconscious, mind may embark. This is well captured by Lazaroo in the Prelude to this volume, where she positions travel on a spectrum that spans from physical movement through to, and beyond, the life journey itself. This need to look beyond tourism becomes even more pronounced when we acknowledge that 'the imagination' itself is a notion that is best investigated from a variety of disciplinary and interdisciplinary perspectives. It was with this in mind that this volume invited a multidisciplinary authorship to ruminate upon the themes of travel and imagination. While this volume does not represent a comprehensive exploration of the two (this would be an arguably impossible task), it nonetheless represents an invitation to scholars to explore this fascinating, yet complex, area of inquiry in all of its wonderful colour, slipperiness, mystery and intrigue. The book intends to provide a catalyst for thinking, discussion, research and writing, with the vision of generating a canon of scholarship on travel and the imagination that is currently absent from the literature.

Themes or Not? Tendrils of Connectivity

In the initial call for chapters we expressed an interest in several aspects of the imagination/travel dyad: imagination as pertaining to a constellation of phenomenon (dreams, make-believe, fantasy, memory and remembering, perception, the 'mind's eye', understanding, world-views, learning, story-telling and so on) and linked to a variety of modes of travel (embodied corporeal travel, travel through representations, travel in the mind). We requested authors not feel limited to the travel experience itself but to any temporal and spatial boundaries they chose; to open up new and innovative explorations that ranged across everything from the fantasies prompted by representations (fiction, cinema, art, maps, virtual travel and so forth), creativity, 'escape', science fiction as a genre, desire and the libidinous, people, events, places (travel as a way of anchoring the imagination in physical destinations, pathways, routes) and so forth. We anticipated the contributions would not be limited by a disciplinary-based ontology and would be multidisciplinary in approach.

And so it has come to pass. Collectively, the chapters are not only diverse in their various explorations of travel and imagination, they suggest, simultaneously, two things: (1) a continual opening out of the possibilities of thinking the relationship and (2) coherently intertwined thematic currents that are iterated and re-iterated in a number of heterogeneous registers of analysis (and across a number of manifold temporalities, spatialities and contexts). In other words, the 'opening out' suggests complexity that, unsurprisingly, makes easy generalization about travel/imagination impossible and yet the thinking displayed in the chapters resides under a particular analytic description that, despite the immense assortment of contexts/circumstances (Spain, the Caribbean, Edinburgh, southeast Australia, New York, Auschwitz-Birkenau, Venice, Antarctica, trains, bedrooms, airports, prayer rooms, department stores, cinemas, museums, galleries, 'the mind', books, the internet, science fiction, art, poetry, cinema, toy mascots and travel literature), works through identifiable elements of contemporary cultural and social theory (evinced by descriptors like embodiment, mobility, performance, representation/ non-representation, gender, sexuality, race, affect, ideology, reflexivity).

Nevertheless, when it came to identifying themes in the chapters, we were quite delighted to find that 'themes' really meant sinuous strands of investigation, illumination, elucidation that, at times, cohered across the chapters but at other times were sufficiently muscular to be relational and powerful in proximity rather than relational and powerful in conjunction or in synthesis. What follows, therefore, is a series of musings that arise from our readings of all the authors represented in the collection.

Place

'Place' is a prominent idea that is critical to most of the commentaries, a much needed anchor, it seems, in thinking the travel/imagination dyad. Therefore, the notion of 'place', in the context of imagination and travel, is quite interesting because of its ineluctable conceptual role, a necessary structural/linguistic abstraction to bring legibility and/or focus to travel/imagination. The physical space of objects and surfaces is, in every chapter herein, conjoined with dynamic processes: mobility of objects, bodies and imaginings (all entangled); a vast array of representations (created and received/consumed); embodied desire, anticipation, experience, somatic co-existence, emotional interactions, reckonings with self, identity formations and performances; historical, ideological, post/ colonial, artistic, literary, ecological, conceptual and performed renderings and inscriptions of landscapes. All of these processes are fluid, substantial and insubstantial at the same time. Such observations render 'place' as anything but solid or fixed or, indeed, requiring a physical manifestation other than a mental indexical correspondence that may have only a tenuous connection to the 'real', often no more than an echo or temporary imprint of the physical. Science fiction 'worlds' are the obvious example. 'Place-making' would seem to be the best way of describing how place is considered and '*in* place' as the way travel/imagination is conceptualized, whether those places are 'real' or not.

Travel

One of the most striking and intriguing features of the chapters is to do with the word 'travel'. No one assumes this is anything but an intricate, and perhaps even inadequate, descriptor of particular kinds of movement. The use of the term 'mobility' begins to assuage the problematics the word 'travel' poses, but not entirely of course. The way many writers qualify 'travel' is intrinsically alluring. There has been a long history in Anglophonic discourse that pits 'travel' against 'tourism', but this is essentially a matter of categorization and, often, socio-cultural distinctions. None of the writers in the present volume entertain this bifurcation, other than in passing. We suspect that the very travel/imagination dyad immediately presupposes a different kind of thinking about travel because of the embodied implications, the 'inner world' and 'outer world' connotations (even when such binaries are overridden in the analysis) and the *a priori* assumption that one cannot conceive of the one without the other.

Predictably, therefore, 'travel' throughout the book has many guises. At times it is corporeal, bodies moving through space and time. However, this is never in isolation from emotional 'journeys', somatic experiences along the way, desire and anticipation before, during and after, travels in the mind, journeys within represented 'worlds' (art, poetry, tourism images, photography, cinema, travel literature and casual conversations), the entangled and powerful links between representations and bodily journeys, the inescapable connections to the symbolic order, the relationships with other mobile entities (transport, companions, communications, crowds, food, the weather and other environmental dynamics, and representations themselves in their yielding plasticity). In the accounts of the authors 'mobile subjects' may be a description that gets closer to the intricacies, but not entirely. The figure of 'travel' therefore inevitably keeps receding as the caveats and elaborate workings crowd the foreground of explication. In a mobile world, we ask, what gives 'travel' legibility? Like 'place', travel is something both substantial and insubstantial, an entity that 'others' itself in its signification. One thing the writers in this collection make very clear, context is pivotal, so 'travel' draws meaning from its surrounding conditions, along with those experiencing and observing it, and not from itself.

Imagination

Imagination is an even more elastic term than travel and for good reason. It is a slippery notion, because while its referent is clearly understood by everyone, its manifestations are multiple in the extreme. Across the chapters imagination relates to memory, representations, day-dreaming, social imaginaries, manufactured cultural constructions that reveal/conceal, fantasy, narratives, conjuring the absent, rediscovering the known, aesthetic mental images/feelings like romanticism, the picturesque and the sublime, creativity, transcending clock-time, idealism, ideological formations and transfiguring the habitual.

As many of the authors point out explicitly, or imply, a critical domain of imagination is the image (and thus the etymology of the word), a mental visualization of some kind. Although in making this observation, there is a wariness to be too explicit because of the 'shape-shifting' character of the imagination and the acknowledged complexity of the phenomenon. As McGinn (2004) makes clear, there is enormous diversity in Western thought about imagination because of the intricate inter-relationship between mental performances, the notion of an 'inner life', the entanglement with perception, the relationship to external physical objects (or commonsense/naive realism), the intentional versus unprompted activation by subjects and the way imagination is linked to ideas/thought/remembering. McGinn prefers the term 'mindsight' as a way of negotiating this interesting quandary: we all know what imagination is but beyond this recognition being more explicit is extremely difficult because of the many manifestations listed above. Mental images seem to be similar to physical objects but, at the same time, they are not the same at all. And their spatial configurations are radically divergent from perceptions of time/space in the external world of physical objects. More importantly, to the writers in this collection, imagination is not a philosophical predicament requiring explication but an entity that has a powerful role in the ways they think, experience and write about travel (however conceived). In other words, the Gordian/translucent quality does not prevent meaningful exploration and examination.

What is analytically exhilarating is the diversity of the 'application' of the term imagination to so many different travel contexts and its interpretative capacity. The following list is indicative of the range of elucidations undertaken in this collection. Imagination is portrayed as a font for the desire to travel and as inextricably fused to corporeal travel, represented travel and travel memories with complex flows between the 'inner' and 'outer' states of bodily movement. Imagination is considered a mode of structuring the social as liquid where ontological distinctions have no weight and where 'place' is both material and immaterial. Imagination is crucial to travel narratives and to the way subjectivities are positioned within narratives and in the telling. Imagination is equally crucial to the identity of the traveller, to the experience of travel and to the way travellers conceptualize these experiences for themselves and others.

The distinction between imagination and the imaginary allows for the extension of the inner world of mind-sight to a consideration of imagination as culturally and socially constituted, as a process of formation that is deeply connected to cultural affiliations and the way imaginations are unavoidably and inescapably linked to other cultural productions (that, in turn, are the coalescing of imaginations): art, literature, cinema, music, performance, architecture, design and so forth. However, cultural inscription is only one dimension. The imaginary also refers to a collective social construction into which the 'self' inserts itself, becomes a co-producer and an agent of the continuous circulation of manufactured imagined images/ideas of the social. In this way the imaginary becomes political: an ideological rendering that exerts itself through political regimes and the maintenance and operation of power. The consideration of travel in the context of formidable shared imaginings of East/West, occidental/oriental, colonial/postcolonial, nation-state/cosmopolitan, home/away, rural/urban, socio-economic class, race/ethnicity, sexuality and so on, and the various 'struggles' and contestations these involve, indicates the profound effect (and affect) of such social imaginaries.

A key discursive current running through the chapters (and the energy metaphor is apt) is indicated by a clutch of terms: disruption, gaps, transfiguration, transgression, transformation and subversion. While the context of the use of such words is quite varied, they point to a much written about phenomenon: the constant calibration of the 'inner world' of the imagination and the 'outer world' of bodies bound by time and space/place and the ways that one can affect the other and vice versa. For terms like 'disruption', 'gap' and 'transfigure' (and so on) to work requires a conceptualization of mind-sight as different to the experience of bodies in place and in time. This gesture towards a dependant-autonomy of the imagination (drawing on the 'real' but also able to act, somehow, independently of 'real' time/space embodied experience) allows many of the authors to explore what happens when 'reality' doesn't match the imagined, when the imagined is revealed to be a type of misconception, a hoax, an ideal, a romantic illusion, a way of papering over and disguising much less palatable 'realities'. We are reminded of the words of T.S. Eliot (1969) in *The Hollow Men*: 'Between the idea and the reality/ Between the motion/ And the act/ Falls the shadow'. What is illuminating is the authors' need to provisionally rely on the *distinction* between imagination and physical reality to get at the vigorous understandings arising from a perceived 'gap'. But at the same time, they invariably argue for an understanding that goes beyond such binary thinking, that sees no separation between self, nature, culture, technology, knowing, feeling, corporeal travel, virtual travel and so on. It is, we think, why one of the filaments across the chapters is a focus on bodies. Embodiment, for many of the authors, is a crucial concept in writing travel/ imagination, and for a number of reasons, but one of them is that it stands as a considerable caveat, or counter-weight, to the imagination versus physical reality, to the 'inner world'/'outer world' binary opposition in their analyses (see below).

Because imagination in Western thought is so tied up with 'image', creativity (being imaginative), fiction/fantasy (make-believe), re-creation and representation, it is not unexpected that many writers have turned to art and aesthetics in their investigations. This is a complex arena of engagement. On the one hand it relates to an exploration of creative outputs induced by travel as symbol or as experience (across many genres) and, on the other hand, it is about the way the imagination/travel dyad fosters an imaginative interaction that is partly a cultural (re-)inscription (informed by representations), partly a performance, partly a poetic transformation. Not only are the authors juggling various dimensions of the aesthetics/imagination/travel interface, they are also ever conscious of the widely accepted idea that aesthetics is itself a historical and culturally informed invention laid over material and imagined objects/places/landscapes (Eco 2004). Further, in contemporary culture aesthetics is much less to do with a 'discerning eye' and much more to do with the emotional and the somatic, a process of *naming* and *knowing* feelings and emotional responses or about the cultivation of particular social and economically inscribed tastes. The retrieval and replication of Western aesthetic categories like the picturesque, the romantic, the sublime, the rural, the urban (when applied to landscapes), the modern in the context of travel/imagination is not just about responding to both corporeal journeys and travels in the imagination (carnal responses), but a way of doing so, a mode of travelling/imagining. Many of the writers, perhaps following the lead of de Botton (2002) in his attempt to flesh out these associations (and he is oft-quoted in this volume), explore the poetic/aesthetic in highly individual ways but, nonetheless, never too distant from Western taxonomies. What is instructive in this collection is the seeming impossibility of thinking the travel/imagination dyad without also strongly evoking other domains of the imagination: poetry, cinema, photography, the visual arts, performance and fiction, all of them pertaining to the 'world' as represented, not just the 'world' as imagined or the 'world' as experienced.

Bodies

Bodies and embodiment are both theme and analytic throughout the book. As suggested above, the body and embodiment allow most writers to bring together a number of ideas germane to their discussions and to provide a conceptual architecture that avoids the binary thinking that is almost unavoidable when considering the imagination with 'inner worlds' and 'outer worlds' being the most obvious example. But analytical strategies are not the only motivation here. Most writers are insistent that the travel/imagination entanglement only makes sense in terms of bodies/embodiment of both travel/mobility (corporeal, virtual, fantasies and so on) and imagination (which is always embodied). The body of the subject is as crucial as place is to *thinking* travel/imagination. Indeed, bodies *in* and *of* place (performing place) are the irreducible conditions for knowing/feeling/ experiencing the entwined idea of travel/imagination.

What are the implications of the body as the locus of travel/imagination? The assumptions the authors make – sometimes explicitly and sometimes not – arise from a position that is familiar territory in social and cultural theory: bodies are not neutral surfaces/entities. Bodies are deemed to be situated, marked/mediated by discourses (history, culture, gender, class, sexuality and so on); they are performative (identity, mobility, somatic, desiring, sexual, gendered and so on); and they have co-production roles with space/place, technology, knowledge practices and so forth. Bodies have agency, are empowered to have effects and are affected; they can be contained/restrained or they can be transgressive/excessive. Unlike the travel writing of the nineteenth and early twentieth centuries, the authors in this volume strongly resist erasing the seeing/somatic/emoting/knowing/imagining/ narrating body. In fact, quite the opposite.

By concentrating on the body, the writers bring together a number of elements into their critical 'cartography': memories, emotions, the politics of affect, the senses, technology, time, biography and identity, anxiety, fear, danger, pain, death, transfiguration, corporeal travel, imagination, the imaginary and imagined travel, the physical act of writing/creating, events, places, people and relationships. It is a long list but an impressive display of how in the twenty-first century the travel/ imagination dyad cannot be disembodied. It makes no sense. And analytically it signals a refusal to easily entertain unsustainable binaries.

Structuring Travel and the Imagination

Given the messiness, complexity and interconnections of themes we have identified above, it may now seem somewhat contradictory for us to report on the ways in which we have divided the chapters in this volume. There is of course no way that we could hope to propose a handful of Parts that could wholly absorb and somehow make sense of that messiness. That said, we nonetheless feel it is necessary to provide some form of structure to help readers navigate their way through the chapters collected together here. In reviewing the chapters, we thus decided to parcel the contributions into four Parts (although there is admittedly a great deal of cross-over amongst these for the reasons explored earlier in the chapter), each of which revolves around key themes to have emerged from our initial call for papers.

In Part I, *Mobile Identities*, our contributors explore the imagination of three quite unique travellers who illustrate the mobile nature of identity and imagination and the centrality of mobility to human identity. This Part commences through the contribution of Adams, Chapter 2, in which she describes her Caribbean heritage and, more specifically, her relationship with Jamaica, which is a place that has been imaginatively instilled in her by her mother throughout her life, but is also reinscribed through ongoing negotiations of her imagination through continued travels, both abroad and at home. In her reflections, Adams offers a very personal rendering of the Caribbean, through which she reveals to the reader a complex and compelling weave of memory, childhood stories and sense of place, all of which work to sustain an identity utterly inflected with the imaginative. With similar personal flair, Bell (Chapter 3) introduces a variant of Thrift's non-representational theory to frame her experiences of travel as a mother with multiple sclerosis. Her chapter is hauntingly poignant, detailing with a frank openness how the imagination can be drawn upon as a central tool for coping with diminishing physical mobility. Part I closes with Chapter 4 by Waitt and Macquarie, and their introduction to a similarly compelling moment of personal reflection, this time offered on behalf of Janet and her experiences of homemaking. Like Bell, Waitt and Macquarie stretch out their analysis with the uptake of a performative and embodied approach, through which they explore imagination and travel through Janet's walks around the Illawarra Escarpment in southeastern Australia. All three contributions test the porosity between physical and imaginative travel, and do so by drawing the reader into very personal narrations of self.

As its title implies, Part II, *Tales of the Imagination*, explores a variety of literary accounts depicting travel and imagination. It commences with a contribution by Bennett-Hunter (Chapter 5), who introduces us to the imaginary journeys of French writers Xavier de Maistre and Joris-Karl Huysmans. Bennett-Hunter uses their work as catalysts for a broader philosophical exploration of travel and imagination, through which we are granted the very real sense that it is the imagination, rather than the more often cited 'reason', that defines what it is to be human. Following this philosophical tour de force, Hall, in Chapter 6, offers up a specific and fine-grained exploration of the historical significance of the railroad in the African American imagination. This he does via an exploration of the poetry of Sterling A. Brown, highlighting, in particular, its gendered nature and its continual influence upon artistic expression. Once again following the insights of a specific author, Heynders and van Nuenen discuss the work of Dutch writer Cees Nooteboom in Chapter 7. Theirs is a demonstration of the futility of trying to break apart imagination and reality in travel which, they argue, cannot be separated; instead, they point to the fusion of fiction and reality in all travel writing, even when the veracity of the real is being proclaimed or assumed. The real is amplified in the telling and the amplification is the domain of the imagination. Part II closes with the volume's strongest articulation of the social imaginary, drawing as it does from the work of Charles Taylor's *Modern Social Imaginaries* (2004). Here, Watson (Chapter 8) explores post-Second World War travel writing, carefully piecing together a repository of moods and characteristics that linger still in sustaining what Watson refers to as the Spanish Imaginary.

Part III, *Visual, Media, Representation*, explores a diverse range of portrayals of travel and imagination that extend beyond those contained within Parts I and II. Calchi-Novati (Chapter 9), for example, compels the reader towards an articulation of Antarctica crafted through the work of German filmmaker Werner Herzog. In so doing, Calchi-Novati aptly demonstrates the power of imagination in actualizing, and potentially transcending, a performative threshold in travel. In Chapter 10, Robinson shifts our focus through her explorations of the phenomenon of travelling toy mascots. There, she demonstrates how such mascots act as conduits for activating the imagination of their human travelling companions, and allow for a reimaging of tourism experiences for both the traveller and those observing their experiences and imaginings. Following this, Williams (Chapter 11) uses the trope of the matter transmitter in science fiction to transport us into new worlds, parallel universes and alternative realities in what are undeniable journeys of the imagination. The matter transmitter highlights the power of representations to transcend the 'here and now' and allow us to go somewhere else in our minds; a somewhere that can vary widely in how close it resembles one's 'reality' depending on the imaginations of creator and observer.

We change tack in Part IV, *Unsettling Imaginations*, to explore the darker side of travel and imagination, showing that the travels in our mind are not always comfortable, desirable or pleasant experiences. This readjustment begins with Chapter 12, in which Cooke and Frieze take us to Auschwitz and Auschwitz-Birkenau through the videotestimonials of eight Holocaust survivors. They simultaneously return us theoretically to the embodied and affective thinking introduced in Part I of the volume, and remind us of the ways in which imaginative travel is bodily made manifest. In their chapter, they pose important questions around imagination as the engine of the fusion of past and present. Likewise, they test our thinking about the impossibility of the past ever being more than memory and imaginative (re-)construction, but also the failure/limits of the imagination in various ways under certain travel conditions. The chapter also evocatively explores the emotions and embodied nature of remembered experience and return to places of traumatic experience. In a part that is implicitly characterized by notions of 'return', Pearce (Chapter 13) explores an alternative view of the Caribbean to that presented by Adams in Chapter 2. Using Andrea Chung's décollage art, which depicts the tensions between the idyllic tourism imagery of the Caribbean and its disconcerting colonial and slave history, Adams invites us on a multilayered investigation of travel and the imagination that insists on the political ideological work of fantasy and travel imaginaries and the deep implications of de-coupling travel imaginaries from social, cultural, economic and political circumstances. Finally, we close this part with Staiff (Chapter 14), who takes us on a series of journeys to Venice, beginning with the cinematic and moving through to several physical encounters. He details the prominence of Venice within his imagination and how the city has continued to be reimagined through an entwinement with ongoing lived experiences.

In the concluding chapter of the volume, Lean and Waterton reiterate the intentions of the book, inviting an inter- and multi-disciplinary cohort of scholars to build a cannon of work exploring travel and imagination. We offer some ideas for how this may take place, but give a cautionary warning that this theme should not be taken lightly. It is slippery, complex and difficult to pin down and needs to be carefully acknowledged as such.

Finally, we close this Introduction with a note about reading. We were struck, as we read our way through these contributions, by the way our imaginations were activated in the reading of the chapters; how we were imaginatively 'constructing' Spain, Venice, New York, the Holocaust, the Caribbean, Antarctica, matter transportation, racial and gender differences, disability, spirituality, life and death, along with the lives and experiences of our authors, their participants and their fictive creations, as we became entangled in the accounts. After all, we travel too, in the reading (cf. Marin 1993). These journeys resonated with all three of us, in sometimes similar, and yet at other times very different, ways owing to our own unique subjectivities, life experiences, travels and theoretical backgrounds. In some cases we were emotionally struck by accounts within the volume, both 'real' and 'fictional'. This highlights a level of exploration of travel and imagination that exists well beyond the text and images that lie in front of the reader. The reader's own imaginative journey is an integral part of the conceptualization of this theme and we invite the reader to pay attention to this as they navigate the volume's pages. Reading the volume is itself an active exploration of travel and imagination.

References

Anderson, B. 1983. *Imagined Communities: Reflections on the origin and spread of nationalism*. London: Verso.

Bærenholdt, J.O., Haldrup, M., Larsen, J. and Urry, J. 2004. *Performing Tourist Places*. Aldershot: Ashgate.

Coleman, S. and Crang, M. (eds) 2002. *Tourism: Between place and performance*. New York: Berghahn.

Cosgrove, D.E. 2006. *Geographical Imagination and the Authority of Images*. Heidelberg: Franz Steiner.

Cosgrove, D.E. 2008. *Geography and Vision: Seeing, imagining and representing the world*. London: I.B. Tauris.

Cresswell, T. 2002. Introduction: Theorizing place, in *Mobilizing Place, Placing Mobility: The politics of representation in a globalized world*, edited by T. Cresswell and G. Verstraete. Amsterdam: Rodopi, 11–32.

Crouch, D., Jackson, R. and Thompson, F. (eds) 2005. *The Media and the Tourist Imagination*. Abingdon: Routledge.

Daniels, S. 1992. Place and the geographical imagination. *Geography*, 77(4), 310–322.

Daniels, S. 2011. Geographical imagination. *Transactions of the Institute of British Geographers*, 36(2), 182–7.

Daniels, S., DeLyser, D., Entrikin, J.N. and Richardson, D. (eds) 2011. *Envisioning Landscapes, Making Worlds: Geography and the humanities*. Abingdon: Routledge.

Dann, G.M.S. (ed.) 2002. *The Tourist as a Metaphor of the Social World*. Wallingford: CABI Publishing.

de Botton, A. 2002. *The Art of Travel*. London: Hamish Hamilton.

Eco, U. (ed.) 2004. *On Beauty: A history of a Western idea*. London: Secker and Warburg.

Eliot, T.S. 1969. *The Complete Poems and Plays of T.S. Eliot*. London: Book Club Associates/Faber & Faber.

Franklin, A. 2007. The problem with tourism theory, in *The Critical Turn in Tourism Studies: Innovative research methodologies*, edited by I. Ateljevic, A. Pritchard and N. Morgan. Oxford: Elsevier, 131–48.

Franklin, A. and Crang, M. 2001. The trouble with tourism and travel theory. *Tourist Studies*, 1(1), 5–22.

Gravari-Barbas, M. and Graburn, N. (eds) 2012. Tourist imaginaries. *Via@*, 1(1)–5.

Gregory, D. 1994. *Geographical Imaginations*. Oxford: Blackwell.

Kaplan, C. 1996. *Questions of Travel: Postmodern discourses of displacement*. Durham, NC: Duke University Press.

Lean, G.L. 2012a. Transformative travel: A mobiliities perspective. *Tourist Studies*, 12(2), 151–72.

Lean, G. 2012b. The lingering moment, in *The Cultural Moment in Tourism*, edited by L.-J. Smith, E. Waterton and S. Watson. Abingdon: Routledge, 274–91.

Leed, E.J. 1991. *The Mind of the Traveller: From Gilgamesh to global tourism*. New York: Basic Books.

Light, D. 2009. Performing Transylvania: Tourism, fantasy and play in a liminal place. *Tourist Studies*, 9(3), 240–258.

Lowenthal, D. 1961. Geography, experience, and imagination: Towards a geographical epistemology. *Annals of the Association of American Geographers*, 51(3), 241–60.

MacCannell, D. 2011. *The Ethics of Sightseeing*. Berkeley: University of California Press.

McGinn, C. 2004. *Mindsight: Image, dream, meaning*. Cambridge, MA: Harvard University Press.

Marin, L. 1993. Frontiers of Utopia: Past and present. *Critical Inquiry*, 19(3), 397–420.

Minca, C. and Oakes, T. (eds) 2006. *Travels in Paradox: Remapping tourism*. Lanham: Rowman & Littlefield Publishers.

Osborne, P.D. 2000. *Travelling Light: Photography, travel and visual culture*. Manchester: Manchester University Press.

Picard, D. and Robinson, M. (eds) 2012. *Emotion in Motion: Tourism, affect and transformation*. Farnham: Ashgate.

Reijnders, S. 2011a. *Places of the Imagination: Media, tourism, culture*. Farnham: Ashgate.

Reijnders, S. 2011b. Stalking the count: Dracula, fandom and tourism. *Annals of Tourism Research*, 38(1), 231–48.

Roberson, S.L. (ed.) 2002. *Defining Travel: Diverse visions*. Jackson: University Press of Mississippi.

Robinson, M. and Jamal, T. 2009. Conclusions: Tourism studies – Past omissions, emergent challenges, in *The Sage Handbook of Tourism Studies*, edited by T. Jamal and M. Robinson. London: SAGE, 693–701.

Rojek, C. and Urry, J. (eds) 1997. *Touring Cultures: Transformations of travel and theory*. London: Routledge.

Ruoff, J. (ed.) 2006. *Virtual Voyages: Cinema and travel*. Durham, NC: Duke University Press.

Salazar, N.B. 2010. *Envisioning Eden: Mobilizing imaginaries in tourism and beyond*. New York: Berghahn.

Salazar, N.B. 2012. Tourism imaginaries: A conceptual approach. *Annals of Tourism Research*, 39(2), 863–82.

Schwartz, J.M. and Ryan, J.R. (eds) 2003. *Picturing Place: Photography and the geographical imagination*. London: I.B. Tauris.

Skinner, J. and Theodossopoulos, D. (eds) 2011. *Great Expectations: Imagination and anticipation in tourism*. New York: Berghahn Books.

Smith, L., Waterton, E. and Watson, S. (eds) 2012. *The Cultural Moment in Tourism*. Abingdon: Routledge.

Taylor, C. 2004. *Modern Social Imaginaries*. Durham, NC: Duke University Press.

Urry, J. and Larsen, J. 2011. *The Tourist Gaze 3.0*. London: SAGE.

PART I
Mobile Identities

Chapter 2

Embodied Travel: In Search of the Caribbean Self in Tropical Places and Spaces

Jennifer D. Adams

Introduction

Whenever I plan a trip to a new place, I always have a picture in mind of what this place will be like; what it may look like to walk down the streets, the structures I may see, the people I might pass, the voices I might hear and how I would feel being there. Before I take the actual trip I spend time in anticipatory travel (Sheller and Urry 2006); travelling in my imagination, conceived of what I have read or seen, other places I have visited, and experiences I have had to create a story of what it will be like to be in this new or different place. In my travels to tropical places this is even more evident because my imaginations also include stories about my mother's tropical upbringing.

My mother was born and raised in Jamaica, in the Caribbean. One of the Greater Antillean islands, it has a varied geography ranging from tropical broadleaf forests, temperate mountains and dry savannahs. She hails from a mountainous region – one that has thick tropical forests and rich soil for agriculture. While growing up, I always heard stories about my mother's Jamaica. She described the hours she would spend in the forest, her favourite place, picking fresh fruit, roasting river crawfish and root vegetables in gourds and getting lost in [sugar] cane fields. My mother painted a picture of a verdant childhood with endless supplies of fresh fruits and vegetables. Although she also recounted hardships and unspeakable challenges, her common narrative was one of freedom and abundance. As a child, I listened to her stories, either told directly to me or through overheard discussions with her cousins and siblings. I imagined Jamaica through her eyes as she led me through the forests and parks of the northeastern United States. The mountains and greenery evoked her embodied sense of place. I imagine that to her these deciduous trees with acorns and berries become broadleaf trees with cashews and fruits. It is through flora that my mother makes connections with place, and growing plants and gardening enabled my mother to re-create a sense of home in Brooklyn, New York. It was through this green lens that my mother showed me her Caribbean, a lens that I always take with me on my travels to real and imagined tropical places.

The Caribbean has been a region on the move from the colonial period through to the present times. The mobilization of plants, people, capital and material resources was central to the historical plantation complex (Sheller 2004) and networks of commerce that cross the air and sea, including images of tourism characterize the region today (Sheller 2004). Likewise, Caribbean identity and sense of place does not stand still. Mimi Sheller (2004: 15) argues that Caribbean writers maintain this sense of mobility in their writing, as 'to become truly Caribbean you must first go elsewhere; migration, exile, and return have become grounds for forging a pan-Caribbean identity'. As such, my travels have been a search for Self in the varied and global tropical contexts in which I visit. In this chapter I use an auto/biographical and auto/ethnographical approach (Roth 2005) to examine my experiences, as a daughter of the Caribbean, travelling through tropical places via novels, visits to museum halls and exhibits and through lived experiences in tropical landscapes. I will discuss how my movements through such places have been an ongoing exercise in the exploration of my identity as a person of Caribbean decent. According to Mimi Sheller tourism developed 'as a mode of moving through tropical landscapes and of experiencing bodily what was already known imaginatively' (Sheller 2001: 14). For me, the imagination that accompanies my travels is a means of making stories of my mother and Caribbean elders 'real' and a way of 'anchoring' my imagined Caribbean in physical tropical places. Imagination serves as the catalyst that pulls my body into a place to refit it with a refined sense of place and identity.

Place, Experience and Imagination

People's relationship to place is not only influenced by their lived experiences in places, but also memories and stories told by others about places. This is the place that is carried within as memories, emotions and values. John Malpas (1999: 34) describes this internal interconnection and nesting of places: 'places are juxtaposed and intersect with one another; places also contain places so that one can move inwards to find other places nested within a place as well as move outwards to a more encompassing locale'. This parallels Arturo Escobar (2001: 143) when he writes, 'place, body, and environment integrate with each other; that places gather things, thoughts, and memories in particular configurations; and that place, more an event than a thing, is characterized by openness rather than by a unitary self-identity'. Using the term 'event' to describe place speaks to its temporality and fluidity. In addition, Escobar's description gives life to place in that it has the ability to 'gather' those things that bodies carry within. These notions of place as being both internally constituted, outwardly interactive and temporal helps us to think about imagination and how that recursively shapes travel. Those imaginations of place become a part of what the body carries within and become outwardly expressed in the creation of place experiences.

I was born and raised in Brooklyn, New York. While it is quite far from the Caribbean as a geographic region, it is not far from the Caribbean that is embodied and enacted wherever Caribbean people find themselves. Antonio Benitez-Rojo (2006: 4) describes the Caribbean as a repeating island or meta-archipelago that 'has the virtue of having neither a boundary nor center'. Thus, in the centre of Brooklyn one can find oneself in a Caribbean milieu. However, for some of us who were born in the Diaspora and maintain a Caribbean identity, this Brooklyn Caribbean *is* the Caribbean. It is the food, music, colours and language that contribute to this identification with the region. The 'tropical paradise' we imagine, while may include media-fed images of pink-sand beaches and beautiful sunsets, also includes images from the stories told to us by our Caribbean born and bred ancestors and peers, as well as images gleaned through music, art and participation in cultural events. These images are those of mountains and streams, mangroves, fields of sugar cane and groves of citrus trees. They are also stories of Carnival, liming, beach outings and family gatherings. These stories also include issues of class, homophobia, gender inequalities, pigmentocracy,[1] poverty and other struggles that come with living in a colonial or postcolonial developing context. These are the experiences and stories that make up my imagined Caribbean – a Caribbean that I search for when I travel to tropical places.

Dropping Anchor in the Hybrid Space

Palm trees, sunshine and white sands are all images that come to mind when one thinks of vacationing on tropical islands. Godfrey Baldacchino (cited in Hay 2006: 21) describes this phenomenon: 'islands have occupied such a powerful place in modern Western imagination that they lend themselves to sophisticated fantasy and mythology'. Isolated, untouched, secluded are words that are often used to describe tropical islands and the experiences visitors are expected to have in them in tourism media (Sheller 2001). One ethnographer who visited Tahiti on vacation expressed her disappointment at not seeing a 'white tropical sandy beach' but rather a city that was 'dirty, expensive, busy, and a bit rude; no beachfront boulevard dotted with cafes' (Markula 1997: 203). She remarked that it looked like Paris; to her this urban vision was incongruent with what she imagined her vacation in the tropics to be. It is this myth of the exotic, unspoiled and close to nature that is used to sell the tropics (d'Hauteserre 2005). Tropical islands are seen as somehow being 'protected' from the things we wish to escape on vacation because they are positioned as outside of the conventions of the consistent movement of people, information and resources that mark progress and contemporary life. Elizabeth Deloughrey (2004: 300–301) notes:

> Island tourism has taken this isolation axiom to hyperbolic levels – in this
> paradigm, the tourist departs from his or her modern, temperate continent
> (or British archipelago), travels to the tropics in comfort and ease, arrives at a

1   The determination of wealth and status based on skin colour where light-skinned people have the highest social status, followed by the brown-skinned and with the dark-skinned people occupying the lowest rungs of the social strata (Lynn 2008).

'remote' island conveniently inhabited by 'natives' who are somehow isolated
from the same forces of modernity and globalisation that mark the tourist.

The Caribbean 'is constantly reassembled as a primeval, untouched site of luxuriant
profusion' (Sheller 2004: 17). This is reflected in the novel *A Small Place*, where
author Jamaica Kincaid (1988: 4) problematizes the tourist experience upon seeing
the beauty and lush vegetation of Antigua from the perspective of what Appadurai
(1998) would refer to as a 'bounded' native:

> For you are thinking of the hard and cold and dark and long days you spent
> working in North America (or, worse, Europe), earning some money so that
> you could stay in this place (Antigua) where the sun always shines and where
> the climate is deliciously hot and dry for the four to ten days you are going to
> stay there.

European travel literature helped to create this vision of the Caribbean as a Garden of
Eden, a 'tropical paradise in which the land, plants, resources, bodies, and cultures of
its inhabitants are open to be invaded, bought, moved, used, viewed, and consumed
in various ways' (Sheller 2004: 14). A region painted in terms of abundance is always
in service, everything is there for the taking including the irony of a tourist driving
on poorly maintained roads while thinking, 'Oh what a marvelous change these
bad roads are from the splendid highways I am used to in North America' (Kincaid
1988: 5). Kincaid (1988: 13) describes the sensual indulgences of the tourist in
this bounty, both in their imaginations and actual experiences: 'You see yourself
eating some delicious locally grown food. You see yourself, you see yourself ...',
the repetition in this phrase emphasizes both the seen and the imagined, the tourist
becomes a voyeur of her own experiences in this exotic tropical place.

    I also see myself in Kincaid's narrative in that space of conflict between being a
tourist and being a native. Like a tourist, I visit the tropics with my own images of
paradise and a certain degree of privilege of being able to escape my own 'banality
and boredom' (Kincaid 1998: 18). I also carry within my mother's stories of the
fruitfulness of the land and travel with the expectation of consuming bounties of
fresh fruit and fried fish, although I know that fruits are seasonal, agriculture is
limited and that the coral reefs and mangroves are disappearing. As a 'semi-native'
I have a certain degree of fluency in pan-Caribbean culture (understanding Creole
English, familiarity with foods and certain customs) and more specifically
Jamaican culture, but I am not native[2] by birth. I also have a sense of myself as
a racialized woman with a critical awareness of moving through different places
with brown skin; aware of my own internalized experiences with racism (Brock

2 Although the word native has been problematized because it implies a certain
degree of confinement to place and is often applied to people who reside outside of Western
norms and culture (Appadurai 1988), to me native also assumes a certain fluency – an ease
of movement through and familiarity with a place and its associated culture.

2005). Therefore, I can gaze through the windows of a taxi with the privilege of a tourist, while not being surprised when I encounter a crowded and dirty city, much like the city where I live, in a tropical landscape. It is in this hybridized space that I travel where I am both a tourist and a member of a subjugated group at once. Some recognize me as being not from *here* yet ascribed by others as not to be in the privileged space of a tourist (assumed to be from *there*). In this hybrid space I become a voyeur of my own experience with a dragging anchor seeking an identity 'catch' that will hold me in place. Through this space I pull my familial and cultural schema through a bodily experience of place, which then reshapes my imagined identity and connection to the Caribbean.

Escobar (2001: 146–7) argues that the view of contemporary people as 'migrants of identity' 'entails the loss of place as metaphor for culture' since identity is often described as a search and in terms of vicissitudes of time, place and space. While I understand that Escobar is concerned with the erasure of place in anthropological and geographical thought, I can counter that with my own experiences of being a migrant of identity – one who travels to different places to create or confirm identity (Desforges 2000). This does not negate place as a site of culture, but rather recognizes that culture occurs at the intersection of place and peoples' bodies. In this embodied space, this being-in-the-world/travelling-through-the-world, my body encounters and makes sense of experiences with and in places while finding my own place in the world (Low 2003). As I move through different places, the cultures that I encounter become mirrors that reflect different aspects of my own identity, sometimes illuminating the blemishes that I do not wish to see. Since being Caribbean has always been a key facet of my identity, I have found that my travels, especially those in tropical spaces, have always been a negotiation of my longing for and belonging to being in and of the Caribbean.

A recent trip to a small low-lying Eastern Caribbean island revealed this 'dragged anchor' syndrome as I was more conscious of travelling in the hybrid space. I went as a part of an interdisciplinary team from my university to teach and research alongside students in a Geographic Information System (GIS) field school setting. It was my first visit to this island and I wanted to enter this experience without presuppositions of a pan-Caribbean culture. It was a space of work, and being trained in critical educational research, I wanted to be more self-reflective about being in this hybrid space. This was not an island with high levels of tourism so the conscious awareness would allow me to view myself in this context without the noise of 'touristy' spaces; the real and imagined 'Margaritaville' reflected in tropical tourist towns (Bowen 1997). I wanted to assume an identity where my Caribbean-ness was not in the forefront, but rather my identity as a faculty member from a New York-based institution. I also wanted to try to experience not having suppositions about Caribbean culture, that we are all one and the same. We spent the first two days becoming familiar with the geography of the island. We visited different historic, cultural and natural sites of importance to the people who live there. We saw prehistoric pteroglyphs, contemporary hunting caves and salt ponds. As we drove through the dry tropical landscape with many low-lying thorny shrubs,

I reflected on a conversation I had with a man sitting next to me on the plane from New York. He was a developer with the plan of opening a luxury resort on the island.

'It will be a tropical paradise. Visitors will drive along the roads and come to this green oasis'.

He showed me a picture of what he called a 'typical' road on the island. It was white and rocky, the very same limestone roads we drove on during our island orientation. He then showed me artist depictions of the resort. Palm trees, broadleaf trees, and orchids – some of the flora more common in wetter tropical environments and what people probably expect to see in the Caribbean – a 'primeval, untouched site of luxuriant profusion' (Shelley 2004: 17). He showed me digital illustrations of the rooms:

'The rooms that do not have an ocean view will have reflecting pools'.

'It looks pretty dry there. Will water be an issue?'

'I plan on putting in a desalinization plant for the resort'.

I did not know what else to say at that point. I wanted to get on my soapbox about environmental concerns so I gently asked about LEED[3] certification. He danced around the point. I still had about three more hours to sit next to this man and did not want an awkward flight experience. However, I thought about our conversation in light of re-reading Kincaid's novel and scholarly articles about travel and the Caribbean. I immediately pictured the tourist in Kincaid's novel riding on the limestone roads to the oasis hotel while not thinking about consistent water shortage on the island, 'since you are on holiday ... the thought must never cross your mind' (1988: 4). I also felt offended because people who looked like me and lived there were not included in his image (aside from being in servitude, which I am sure translates in his mind to 'I'm providing jobs'). For an instant I left the hybrid space and viewed this project with the eyes of a native. It reminded me of a stanza from Olive Senior's poem, *Meditation on Yellow* (1994: 14):

> At some hotel
> overlooking the sea
> you can take tea
> at three in the afternoon
> served by me
> skin burnt black as toast
> (for which management apologizes)

The black or brown skin is an undesired view in the tropics unless it covers the person serving tea, making the beds, cooking and serving the food or calling themselves inventive names like 'Dr Quality' and ensuring your safety and fun on jet skis and hang-gliders at the beach.

---

3   LEED (Leadership in Energy and Environmental Design) is an internationally recognized programme that provides a framework for green energy design and construction in buildings and communities (http://www.usgbc.org/leed).

Since the roads were bumpy I was bounced back to the present and my desire to maintain an identity that did not connect with the landscape or people. We passed feral donkeys grazing on the side of the road and I thought about my mother's stories of riding donkeys in her childhood. I saw some mango trees and papaya trees and looked for fruit, while recounting both my mother's stories of climbing fruit trees and mine of eating fruit straight from my grandmother's tree in her yard in Jamaica. My supposed neutral identity was slipping away as I started to make small connections with the landscape, however, I was still reluctant to enact my Caribbean identity. For me, this would mean speaking English Creole, openly acknowledging my Caribbean roots and making explicit connections between my experiences there and my own identity and lived experiences. My resistance came from both wanting to be viewed as an outside researcher and not wanting to assume a certain entrée into the local culture because of my Caribbean-ness. Unlike other trips to Caribbean islands, where I almost immediately assert my identity as of the Caribbean (usually citing the Jamaican ancestry of my mother), on this trip, my Caribbean identity emerged.

I engaged in a research project learning about current gardening practices on the island. I immediately thought about my mother's garden and the connections of her gardening to creating a sense of place. Again, I resisted these seemingly automatic connections because I did not want to be in that hybrid space. I wanted to be in the space where, while not a tourist at leisure, I would be a visitor with a purpose on the island. I wanted to be perceived, as my white colleagues were, as someone there from the States to teach and do research. However, as identity seems stronger than will, the interactions with the gardens and gardeners did not allow my Caribbean identity to remain silent. As people told stories of their gardens, I listened as my accent became more pronounced and my familiarity with the plants became obvious. I became more rooted and aware that my Caribbean-ness is who I am and how I connect with different landscapes where I travel. Furthermore, on *this* island (as opposed to, let us say, a Finnish island) and being involved with *this* project (as opposed to testing well water) where it was my job to collect narratives about peoples' relationship with plants, the landscape and identity coalesced in ways for me that allowed me to see the gardens through my mother's lens. I looked for familiar plants, listened to the stories told by people about gardening in a familiar accent and dialect and learned of the similarities between their stories and those told by my mother. While land tenure laws and practices on this island were unfamiliar to me, the ways that people connected to the land and their love of gardening and plants evoked my sense of place and connected me to my Caribbean-ness. I could no longer look through the lens as only a visitor.

Portmanteau Biota and Repeating Landscapes

The lens that I use to view the world, especially when I travel, is the same lens that is my sense of place. I look for aspects of the landscape (and urbanscapes) that are familiar and new, surprising and some would say exotic things – things that are different from what I know and understand. When people travel, they not only carry their physical baggage, but they also carry their own cultural schemas that include their imaginations of place (Sheller 2004). These schema and imaginations inform the interactions people have and experiences they seek out during their journeys.

Landscapes are included in the schema and imaginations. People have notions of landscapes that are informed by their sense of place and ongoing interactions with different places (Wylie 2007). Although people often seek out unspoiled landscapes – pristine beaches, virgin forests – to get back in touch with nature, many of these landscapes, even if they appear 'natural', are human influenced constructions (Nassauer 1995). Portmanteau biota are the plants and animals that travelled with Europeans to and from their island colonies, radically altering the landscape (Deloughrey 2004). This included the humans (both voluntary and enslaved), as well as the plants, animals, vermin and disease; some of the biota were deliberately transported while others where unfortunate stowaways that wreaked havoc on endemic flora and fauna as well as indigenous peoples. However, the biota came, they changed the landscape rendering it a visual context for the relationship between colonization and the natural environment (Sheller 2004). In fact, much of Jamaica's signature flora and economically important plants are exotic (Alexander 2009). The portmanteau biota created repeating islands of tropical landscapes around the globe, in particular with those near the equator that were often deemed 'remote, exotic, and isolated by their continental visitors' (Deloughrey 2009: 2, see also Hay 2006).

Sailing has been a recent mode of travel for me as both a sport and way of visiting new places. One of my first sailing trips was to French Polynesia, where the portmanteau biota afforded me a connection to the land that my sailing companions did not have. From my knowledge of natural history, I knew that the breadfruit originated in this area of the world and was brought to the Caribbean by Captain Bligh to feed the slaves. It was at first rejected as another imposition and symbol of oppression. After emancipation when the freed slaves had more agency over the land and personal choices, the breadfruit became a beloved fruit and staple of signature dishes of several Caribbean islands (Sokolov 1993). When I went to Polynesia, I looked for the breadfruit as I wanted to taste the fruit in its place of origin. I was excited to learn that the sailboat had a grill to roast and share the breadfruit with my sailing companions. None of them have ever tasted breadfruit – it was exotic – and my knowledge of it made me feel that I had a connection to the land that they did not have because of the particular constellation of identity I carry in my imagined Caribbean.

Imagined Trips through Museum Halls

In preparation for my trip I frequented the Margaret Mead Hall of Pacific Peoples in the American Museum of Natural History, New York. The floor has a subtle blue hue that reflects the sky and water of the tropics. There is music gently piped through the hall; as you move through the hall and view the artefacts from the different Pacific Island cultures, you also hear the singing, chanting, drumming and dancing that defines the region. Although this is a large room within a larger building with hundreds of artefacts, most of them enclosed in glass cases, when I wander through this hall I wander through the Pacific. I feel the ocean lapping against my feet and familiar tropical breezes against my face. The artefacts – some old and some relatively contemporary – tell a story about the people and their relationship to the environment.

I worked at this museum as an educator for a number of years and I used to 'escape' to this hall when I wanted a break from my office. I left my world – overly air-conditioned office, dusty cabinets and pet snake – and through a 'secret' door (one that is obscured to the general public by a large display) I entered an imagined world of Pacific culture through the eyes of museum curators. Museums are places for imagination; they are places that allow people to learn and think in new ways and develop a larger world-view (Bedford 2004). While some may problematize the display and narrative of 'primitive people' in natural history museums, as a museum educator, it was also an opportunity to address the museum halls as historical artefacts themselves and to use dialogic methods to critically engage people with cultural artefacts. This allowed people to imagine world cultures in different ways, and to reflect on their own cultures and world-views.

I used this hall to counter the narrative of primitivism and hegemony of Western Modern Science (Semali and Kincheloe 1999) and demonstrate the relationship between environment and culture. I looked at the objects and thought about the scientific knowledge that Pacific peoples had to be able to make and use the various artefacts displayed. For fishing tools, they needed to know about animal behaviour. For the canoe making, they had to have some ideas about the laws of physics. I think of these examples within the disciplinary silos of Western Modern Science (I am a science educator and this is my training), but also recognized that the knowledge was holistic and probably could not be adequately described in terms from my Western perspective. However, through these objects and my travels though these halls, I developed my imaginations of the Pacific. I also had particular notions of Polynesian culture from watching hula dancers and learning about the Hawaiian *Malama I Ka 'Aina Sustainability* – to care for the land that we care for, an ethic of environmental care that situates the humans in servitude to the land (Chinn 2006). I learned about this from my colleague Pauline Chinn when I was thinking about the culturally meaningful ways people connect with environments and my own sense of place, as a Caribbean person, along with my connection to different places. So, when I went to Polynesia I looked for those things in the landscape that were familiar and to add physical context to my imaginations.

Here I return to Markula and her travels in Tahiti. She described herself as looking for culture she describes as 'authentic' but found this search to be disappointing and used it as an opportunity to reflect on her 'Westernness' and tourism. She reflects on her trip and the bias of Western culture towards a 'binary, hierarchical understanding of the world' (1997: 202). She described her search for a different or 'exotic' culture in terms of Wallerstein's (1979, cited in Markula 1997) core–periphery division where the core is more advanced or civilized and the periphery is the Other – primitive, exotic, different. This leads me to think about my own Westernness and how it influences what I look for in my travels. I never considered myself Western – being a woman of Afro-Caribbean decent in the United States I have always felt at the margins of the cultural 'West'. However, I am highly educated and have the resources to travel so, again, I land in a hybrid space. On my trip to Polynesia, I looked for the different and exotic. Like others, I was not immune to Gauguin's images of relaxed Polynesian women with tiare flowers tucked behind their ears, imagery of ancient volcanic mountains and colourful lagoons surrounded by *motu* or hula dancers with swaying hips (women) and the powerful warrior moves of the men. However, I would also look for the familiar, especially Captain Bligh's breadfruit. I wanted to see and experience this beloved food in the landscape of its origin.

One of the fun aspects of bareboat sailing is being able to visit local markets and buy provisions for our onboard meals. This allows me to see unique local products as well as those products that, although beloved, are symbols of how the legacy of colonialism still exists in the flow of goods and products around the globe. I visited the produce markets to look for tropical fruits, but especially for the breadfruit or *ulu*. I found a woman with several large ripe breadfruits laid out on a mat.

'How much for the breadfruit?'

In my best French, I ask the woman with several large breadfruits on a mat. She looked at me knowing that I was a traveller since I came from the marina close to the market.

'Do you know what to do with the breadfruit?'

Surprised by her question because this is probably one of the few times that I have been 'called out' as a stranger in a land of brown skin.

'We have a grill on the boat and I want to roast it'.

Now she returned the expression of surprise along with a smile. She asked me when I expected to roast it and she squeezed several of the fruits and handed her best selection to me.

'This one should be ready in a day or two. Where are you from?'

I assume that she was curious about my knowledge of cooking the breadfruit. I also wondered about my complexion and how I was being constructed as the Other in this land that was both familiar and strange to me. I often wonder about this when I travel to places beyond the Caribbean because my skin affords me the privilege of blending in;[4] assumed to be in the space of an immigrant

4   While blending in may be a privilege to me because it allows me to imagine myself as native or immigrant, rendering myself invisible in touristic contexts, to the actual natives or immigrants, their skin maintains their invisibility in society, or worse, their objectification and consumption by tourists (Tolia-Kelly 2006).

(in Europe) or connected by ancestry (in the Caribbean and sometimes the Pacific). Traveling by sailboat, however, puts me in the space of a tourist because of my mode of travel and association with my fellow sailors who are white (Gogia 2006).

I told her Jamaica and asked her if I could take breadfruit back with me to the States. She told me to ask for *ulu ama*, roasted breadfruit, in the market in Papeete, the capital of Tahiti. I did and went back to Brooklyn with several packets of roasted breadfruit that my mother froze and then thawed months later for Christmas breakfast.

Conclusion

According to Mimi Sheller (2004: 21), 'When bodies move they carry with them markers of gender, race, class, ethnicity and nationality. When people move (whether as migrants, workers or tourists) they also carry with them physical baggage'. I will add that people also carry within their imaginations, memories and associated emotions that intersect both with the outward markers and physical baggage they bear and with the places they encounter. As I describe in this chapter, my travels have been a practice of enacted imagination coupled with identity. Prior to my travels in Tahiti, I never roasted a breadfruit on an open flame (or stove for that matter), I only knew about roasting breadfruit from my mother's accounts. The act of roasting a breadfruit allowed me to perform a previously imagined Caribbean identity, and the act of preparing food in an 'authentic' way connected me to my mother's Jamaica and to my identity as a daughter of the Caribbean.

When I return from travels to the tropics, I carry my own portmanteau biota as gifts for my mother. For me these souvenirs allow me to do two things: return home with memories of my trips and, more importantly, assert my Caribbean identity through the transport of foods as a 'catalyst for reforming relationships with a territory of culture that is owned, valued, and inclusive' (Tolia-Kelly 2006: 346). I collect the seeds of different fruits that I eat and might even ask people who have gardens for some seeds. I brought an avocado-pear seed from Tahiti, it was a large fruit, larger than any avocado-pear I have ever seen or eaten. My mother planted it in a pot and it unfortunately fell prey to an eastern grey squirrel. On my trip to the low-lying dry island, I returned with a variety of seeds, including a spinach vine that my mother described and loved in Jamaica. These seeds are physical remembrances of my travels to the tropics. They become a part of the landscape of my mother's summer gardens in Brooklyn and help to reinforce her connections to the land and identity. I also collect other things like stones, seashells and photographs and some of the more typical tourist objects like T-shirts and bottles of rum. However most importantly, I collect memories through bodily encounters that confirm my Caribbean identity and anchor my imaginations with an expanded physical sense of place.

Acknowledgement

I would like to gratefully acknowledge Olive Senior for the use of an excerpt from her poem *Meditation on Yellow* in this chapter.

References

Alexander, C. 2009 (September). Captain Bligh's cursed breadfruit. *Smithsonian*, 40(6), 56–88.

Appadurai, A. 1988. Putting hierarchy in its place. *Cultural Anthropology*, 3(1), 36–49.

Bedford, L. 2004. Working the subjunctive mood: Imagination and museums. *Curator*, 47(1), 5–7.

Benitez-Rojos, A. 2006. *The Repeating Island: The Caribbean and the postmodern perspective*, 2nd edition. Durham, NC: Duke University Press.

Bowen, D. 1997. Lookin' for Margaritaville: Place and imagination in Jimmy Buffett's songs. *Journal of Cultural Geography*, 16(2), 99–108.

Brock, R. 2005. *Sista Talk: The personal and the pedagogical*. New York: Peter Lang.

Chinn, P. 2006. Preparing science teachers for culturally diverse students: Developing cultural immersion, cultural translators and communities of practice. *Cultural Studies of Science Education*, 1(2), 367–402.

Deloughrey, E. 2004. Island ecologies and Caribbean literatures. *Tijdschrift voor Economische en Sociale Geografie*, 95(3), 298–310.

Deloughrey, E. 2009. *Routes and Roots: Navigating Caribbean and Pacific island literature*. Hawaii: University of Hawaii Press.

Desforges, L. 2000. Traveling the world: Identity travel and biography. *Annals of Tourism Research*, 27(4), 926–45.

d'Hauteserre, A.M. 2005. Maintaining the Myth: Tahiti and its islands, in *Seductions of Place*, edited by A. Lew and C. Cartier. New York: Routledge, 193–208.

Escobar, A. 2001. Culture sits in places: Reflections on globalism and subaltern strategies of localization. *Political Geography*, 20(2), 139–74.

Gogia, N. 2006. Unpacking corporeal mobilities: The global voyages of labour and leisure. *Environment and Planning A*, 38(2), 359–75.

Hay, P. 2006. A phenomenology of islands. *Island Studies Journal*, 1(1), 19–42.

Kincaid, J. 1988. *A Small Place*. New York: Farrar, Straus and Giroux.

Low, S. 2003. Embodied space(s): Anthropological theories of body, space and culture. *Space and Culture*, 6(9), 9–18.

Lynn, R. 2008. Pigmentocracy: Racial hierarchies in the Caribbean and Latin America. *The Occidental Quarterly*, 8(2), 25–44.

Malpas, J.E. 1999. *Place and Experience: A philosophical topography*. New York: Cambridge University Press.

Markula, P. 1997. As a tourist in Tahiti: An analysis of personal experience. *Journal of Contemporary Ethnography*, 26(2), 202–24.

Nassauer, J. 1995. Culture and changing landscape structure. *Landscape Ecology*, 10(4), 229–37.

Roth, W.-M. 2005. Auto/biography and auto/ethnography: Finding the generalized other in the self, in *Auto/biography and Auto/ethnography: Praxis of research method*, edited by W-M Roth. Rotterdam: Sense Publishers, 3–16.

Semali, L. and Kincheloe, J. 1999. Introduction: What is indigenous knowledge and why should we study it?, in *What is Indigenous Knowledge? Voices from the academy*, edited by L. Semali and J. Kincheloe. New York: Falmer Press, 3–58.

Senior, O. 1994. *Gardening in the Tropics*. Toronto: McClelland and Stewart.

Sheller, M. 2001. Natural hedonism: The invention of Caribbean Islands as tropical playgrounds. Paper to the 25th Conference, Society for Caribbean Studies, University of Nottingham, UK, 2–4 July.

Sheller, M. 2004. Demobilizing and remobilizing Caribbean paradise, in *Tourism Mobilities: Places to play, places in play*, edited by M. Sheller and J. Urry. London and New York: Routledge, 13–21.

Sheller, M. and Urry, J. 2006. The new mobilities paradigm. *Environment and Planning A*, 38(2), 207–26.

Sokolov, R. 1993. A fruit freely chosen. *Natural History*, 102(9), 76–80.

Tolia-Kelly, D. 2006. Mobility/stability: British Asian cultures of 'landscape and Englishness'. *Environment and Planning A*, 38(2), 341–58.

Wylie, J. 2007. *Landscape*. New York: Routledge.

Chapter 3
The Jealous Imagination:
Travels *in* my Mind and *out* of my Body

Harriet Bell

Introduction

Over the past 15 years, work on non-representational theory (NRT) has done much
to elevate interest in practices of the everyday as a site of investigation (Thrift
1996, 1997, 1999, 2000a, 2000b, 2004, 2008, Thrift and Dewsbury 2000, Crouch
2002, Latham 2003, Lorimer 2005, 2008, Bissell 2009, 2010, Anderson and
Harrison 2010). With this focus on the everyday comes an assault on structuralist
ontologies, pointing to the importance of habitual performances and actions
instead of concentrating upon patterns of representation or meaning. NRT has
also argued for radical revisions to methodological paradigms, acknowledging the
fluidity of things, the importance of the pre-cognitive and play and the strength
of the muddly and unexpected. Though authors engaging with NRT have pursued
disparate routes, a particular concern has emerged with the body and affect and
'how to locate affect (and emotions) as embodied phenomena' (Lorimer 2008:
552).

For this chapter I want to look in particular at how movement for travel – both
'real' and imagined – might be understood in the context of this literature and
how this relates to my own experience of travel with limited mobility. I argue that
whilst a focus on the embodied and pre-cognitive somatic response is important
(Thrift 2008: 7) my own experience of using imagination in travel suggests that
there is perhaps a more complex relationship between body, movement, intention
and the imagination in everyday practice (Crouch 2002). What I try to show here
is that there is scope for understanding the imagination in travel as simultaneously
embodied, robustly cognitive and practical as well as emotive and fantastical, and
how imagination can be used as a strategy for coping with changing mobility.

I am fairly recently disabled and with this loss of mobility I have become
much more conscious of my body and its movement, the frustrations of its limits
and how I respond; its affects (Toombs 1992, 1995, Bissell 2009). Following Alan
Latham's exploration of the methodological implications of NRT and the potential
of diary-making as both performative and constitutive of the research process
(2003), I explore through diary-work my own experience of travel and variously
em-bodied and un-bodied responses to its planning and realization. Centring
upon a diary kept self-consciously for a single trip to Edinburgh, I show how,

for me, imagination can be both in-bodied and un-bodied, but invariably plays a central role in how my body experiences place and how I plan for that. In doing so, I am not laying claim to new conceptions of the body in terms of disability studies, which have been explored elsewhere (Dorn and Laws 1994, Butler and Parr 1999), nor to the embodied, 'lived' experience of disability so eloquently set out by Toombs (1995). Wilson summarizes the literature on embodied cognition and strategies to 'reduce the cognitive workload by making use of the environment itself in strategic ways' (2002: 628). In the context of disability, the imagination, in particular, has been claimed as inherently embodied and bound by specific experience (Mackenzie and Scully 2007: 342–4). What I want to explore here, however, is more the fluid relationship between the body, performance and the imagination in travel as I have experienced it.

In drawing upon the thinking of NRT, and the focus upon the everyday and affective, I want to propose imagination in travel as something that can be both fantastical but, equally, embodied and performative; solid, *in*-bodied, repetitive and mundane (Edensor 2007). In other words, I propose the imagination in travel as concerned with more than aspiration, fantasy or consumption and equally as embodied and practicable; one of the 'everyday skills that get us by' (Thrift 2008: 81).

Being More-than: Non-representational Theory and the Embodied

It is not the purpose of this chapter to provide a comprehensive review of non-representational theory, its burgeoning literature and its diverse trajectories which have been well-covered elsewhere (see Thrift 1996, 1997, 2000a, 2000b, 2008, Thrift and Dewsbury 2000, Lorimer 2005, Anderson and Harris 2010, Pratchett 2010, Cresswell 2012). It is worth, however, sketching out some of its key preoccupations as they relate to this chapter. Driven by a dissatisfaction with 'dead geographies' (Thrift and Dewsbury 2000), NRT prefers the performed practices of the everyday, seeing 'the production of meaning in action' rather than through 'pre-established systems and structures' (Cresswell 2012: 97). Drawing upon Merleau-Ponty (1962) and phenomenology, part of this is a focus upon the body and the affective, and the idea 'it would be possible to argue that human life is based on and in movement' (Thrift 2008: 5). Whilst 'movement' is construed as more than transfer from place-to-place, NRT proposes a focus upon the pre-cognitive and a simultaneous diminution of the role of cognitive intent (or decision to move). Thrift, in particular (1997, 2008), explores how 'the body operates in such a way that intentions or decisions are made before the conscious self is even aware of them' (2008: 7). For someone whose body regularly fails to respond in predictable or intended ways – where irregular movement associated with spasticity can seem a- or even anti- cognitive – this presents something of a conundrum.

Another characteristic of Thrift's (2008: 7) work in particular is to eschew the historical and the autobiographical, claiming in particular that the autobiographical can lead to a 'spurious sense of oneness' (2008: 8), although it is not entirely clear why this delimitation is a necessary consequence. I hope, however, that through the performance of diary-making, my autobiographical case study offers a means of examining the fluid interactions between imagined and realized performances of travel, and of in-bodied and un-bodied states, that can offer a means of facilitating and experiencing travel beyond the conventional real life/fantasy divide; and that through doing so I show that the rigours of NRT can be usefully extended into both the realm of the autobiographical and the 'individual, reflective subjectivity' (Bissell 2010).

Imagining Edinburgh

Contributing to this volume offered the opportunity to focus on a single instance of a requirement for, or invitation to, travel. I wanted to use a case that was sufficiently far from home to necessitate an intensity of planning that could be recorded in diary form. On 12 May 2012, an exhibition opened at the Inverleith House Gallery in Edinburgh of paintings by my late friend William McKeown. Willie died suddenly in 2011; I had been unable to attend his funeral and very much wanted to be able to make the gallery opening. But I live in the southeast of England and, as a result of having multiple sclerosis (MS), have very restricted mobility. I had been to Edinburgh before and could rely to some extent upon my memories of the place. But I also needed to imagine my way through the journey, to establish whether or not it could be undertaken in my less able state.

In planning my trip to Scotland I actively used imagination as part of a composite, or 'montage' (Latham 2003), of approaches that included memory, visualization, scribbled notes and doodles, as well as more conventional recourse to maps, websites and first-hand accounts. Imagining the experience and sensation of being in places – and of moving through them – has become part of my coping strategy for dealing with my loss of mobility over the last five years. MS affects individuals in different ways with very different degrees of severity, but most of us have had, or have, problems with vision, speech and mobility. I am now heavily dependent upon a stick and wheelchair. Walking is almost always acutely uncomfortable, if not painful. When I *am* walking my progress will be target-based, identifying and then moving from one potential – if unorthodox – resting point to another. So, a bin, a ledge, or the side of a planter will all become features of the walk that I both anticipate and make. This target-based walking is fundamental not just to how I manage on a daily basis but also to how I imagine travelling.

Imagining Travel: In and Out of Body

My use of 'imagination' in travel draws on two distinct, but not necessarily contradictory conceptualizations; the *practical*, in-bodied imagination and the *free* un-bodied imagination. So on the one hand, the imagination takes an embodied, even in-bodied form, where I imagine – and prefigure in some sort of spectral physical form – how different parts of my body will respond to physical stimuli presented by the changing environment of any journey; in other words, I imagine how I will 'feel'. Using this imagined experience of the journey, I then form strategies to assess how I will manage; whether the journey is something that I can contemplate. But I will also imagine an un-bodied version of myself making roughly the same trip. This journey will be out-of-bodied; fanciful and emotive. These fanciful imagined journeys will usually include flight and weightless walking. The flight has a distinctive character similar to the flying I sometimes manage in dreams, a sort of stuttering and swooping progress that is conducted only a short distance above the ground. The journey itself will often be punctuated by a concentration upon buildings, landscape or landmarks that I hope – or would like – to see.

There is an obvious divide between using imagination as part of the (performative) in-bodied, public journeys I make in my now-disabled state, of 'mentally simulating external events' (Wilson 2002: 633), and the private, flight-ful, unbodied trips I make that exist solely in my imagination. To myself I define this divide as between my *practical*, in-bodied travel imagination intended for the realization of the journey in a public place, and a *free* un-bodied travel imagination, which is entirely mine. The first use of imagination for travel is helpful and even essential; the other is where I can celebrate a journey without being encumbered by my bodied *self*. It is where I return to being the traveller as greedy consumer; albeit in a fantastical place. There is another aspect to these private, imagined trips. To a degree they are consolatory and I guard them jealously. Most of us are able to travel without *needing* imagination. But as my own mobility has deteriorated, so these *free* journeys have become more significant. Relying upon my imagination I travel extensively and, more than that, I really enjoy the *free* visits that I know I am now unlikely to make.

Imagining Walking: The Practical Application of Research

Although neither the imagined environment that I may project, nor my physical condition are/were in any way consistent with what happens in 'real life' I have found that if I cannot imagine my way through a trip in both the *practical* and *free* forms, then I know that I cannot make it. It is almost as though the imagining becomes part of the trip itself, both planned and actual. In this way I suggest that the internal and subjective voice of the imagination transcends the soma/psyche divide posited by NRT. In the case of the Edinburgh trip I *could* imagine it, and as a result of this imagining I structured and then adapted my travel plans. I discuss the course of planning this journey and its realization by reference to diary entries, email exchanges, websites used and some rough sketching I did.

My own use of imagination for managing my mobility developed from the writing of de Certeau (1984), and more recent geographers like Fenton (2005) and Phillips (2005) and their challenging of the orthodoxies of understanding walking and place.

I made a number of walkabouts with participants during my PhD research (Bell 2011), looking at views, touching things, or noting smells or sensations as we went. As with Latham's montage of research methods (2003) the walks supplemented not just filmed and recorded interviews but my own drawings and work with archives of architectural drawings and photography. Once home, I used visual recall, maps and imagination to picture those parts of the estates that I visited, but also those parts that I had not. I then developed a tactic where I would recreate these walks in my memory, often including a physical sense of the experience of discomfort that now came with increasing disability. And then I gradually began to move on beyond memory to imagine other walks that I had not, and increasingly could not, make.

Dear Diary

Latham (2003: 2004) has talked quite candidly about the genesis of his research methods in relation to diary work with participants and his growing awareness of the need to recognize this diary-making as performance, so allowing participants 'a gap between their everyday self and their diary-writing self'. My methodology for putting this single case study together was to make – perform – a diary of what I was thinking but at the times when I became aware of either thinking about, or embodying thinking about the Edinburgh trip. This diary work was erratic in terms of where I did it and was often scrappy, messy (Thrift 2008: 18) and incomplete. At times I found it quite difficult to attempt some kind of recording of what imaginative trips I was taking; it felt strangely intrusive. Reporting on the experience of your own imagined world is difficult. How much detail should I give? How to avoid the pitfalls of the bore that recounts every detail of their dreams? What I have attempted to set out here is the interaction between the images and sensations conjured up in my imagination and my response to this as something more than a simple recording of what went on. Of course it is an artificial construct, but I hope it sets out some of the complexity of how, for my travelling life, the *practical* and *free* imaginations interact.

Diary entries reproduced below are discursive, loosely edited extracts from my writing that refer to websites, emails and conversations used in planning the visit. They plot the progress towards the choices I made on whether and how to travel, and the role of imagination in making these decisions. To an extent they are constitutive of this particular piece of work (Latham 2003), and in part mark the performance of the decision-making process, and its vacillation between public and private domains. The diary entries were actually written on loose pieces of paper that I later collated, and often had other notes such as phone numbers or doodles on them (Figure 3.1). Some days I didn't feel like making them. Extracts are reproduced in their full, waffly glory, including grammatical oddities, but with some extra comments set in square brackets. The last section combines a diary record of the day of travel and the gallery opening and this distinction between planned and recorded events is marked out using italics.

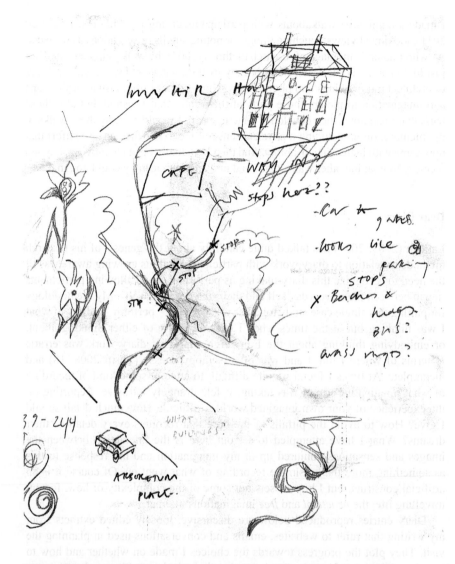

Figure 3.1 Reproduction of diary page with scales distorted according to imagined embodied response

Source: Harriet Bell.

15th April

Taking a walk in the gardens of Inverleith House. It's a *practical* walk. I have gone onto the house website and downloaded a map of the gardens. I have imagined myself into some nice clothes, plus walking stick. No wheelchair. I'm parked just outside the gate, as suggested in the site's access statement, even though I'm currently thinking of travelling without my car. It's a sunny evening; slightly autumnal. I am moving along between rests on benches (Lutyens-style wooden ones) and low, stone walls. The path is orangey gold gravel [I go so slowly that I almost always notice materials]. There is giant foliage around, but in places it has the cut-out look to it of plants in children's book illustrations. [I suspect that this mixing of realism with the illustrative is prompted by the graphics of the map of the gardens, although I adopt a much more 1960s/early 1970s aesthetic for my imagining]. I am looking at the shape of the walks and reckoning on the likely distance between potential benches. I can feel the heaviness in my legs increasing as I gauge the distance. As I start to lose all feeling below the knee I know that this is a place where there has got to be a stop. And at this point I draw up, into the sky and am looking down on the gardens, taking a view that is not quite bird's eye but that is at about two to three storeys off the ground. I make an assessment of whether a bench, or tree stump is likely to be found at this point and decide that it is. And then I'm off again, this time heading off into *free* imagined botanic gardens, speeding along the paths [I'm a very obedient *free* traveller and tend to observe ambulant protocols]. My favourite gardens here include water and bulrushes, mixed with beds crammed with traditional English perennials, which are always in flower and smell fantastic. This is encouraging. This mixing of in-bodied, *practical* and *free* imagination implies that I am confident in this part of the trip being possible.

20th April

Been scribbling. Trying out the number of stops I might need to get through the park. Abstracting results into quite a pretty pattern of dot-to-dot connections between assumed rests. Then abstracting this further by applying it into *practical* imagination [by creating the rhythm of stop-and-start walking on a route based on these shapes]. Am scooting along, hovering just a few inches above the ground, moving from one targeted stop to the next. My legs are dangling – more inert than they currently are in practice. I seem to have abandoned the in-bodiedness for this part of the *practical* imagining. The plants are quite high on either side of the path but I make good progress, even though the building of Inverleith House doesn't feature. I know I can definitely make this part of the trip.

Looking at hotels online again, using discount travel websites. One advises that some event is going to be on in Edinburgh that weekend so rooms are more expensive than I am expecting. I make a whirlwind *free* tour round the city, thinking about areas that are accessible, but also appealing. No idea where some of these places are and make some fantasy districts up that are far more urban and East coast North American in character than Edinburgh. One even reminiscent of Marrakech. But I'm having a lovely time swooshing around, looking for cafes. Come back to some *practical* imagining. Know that Edinburgh traffic is currently difficult because of tram construction works. Picture self in taxis in stationary traffic in various invented, mostly suburban locations around the city, and also waiting for taxis, or stuck in remote industrial areas without access to one. Legs start to feel heavy and there's no way that I can walk to another place to get one. Start to feel agitated from this short *practical* trip. Rationally, I know that I can always phone for a taxi but I don't want to be left feeling vulnerable in this way. Decide to contact family I have in Edinburgh to see whether they could face putting me up.

21st April

Email back says that I'm welcome. This makes things much more possible. I was not making progress with my imagined hotel visits. The lack of availability had forced my imaginings out of central Edinburgh into places which either didn't exist or where I would be dependent upon bus or taxis. I'm usually quite confident about using buses but didn't seem able to imagine it in this instance. Not sure whether this is my imagination failing rather than it being indicative of the journey being problematic.

24th April

Need to check on whether flights still available at checked prices. Guess may have missed the boat on the good prices. Check slightly obsessively through the day – there seem to be some ok fares still available and they're competitive with the train. Suddenly picture self on sleeper train. Check on rail site for fares. Plane still holds up well. Imagine taking the sleeper and needing the loo in the night. Somehow morph this into vaguely remembering sleeper train journeys made with school through Switzerland and Russia. On one journey a suitcase fell on somebody's head. Fuse memory and imagination from this to take the sleeper train on a *free* journey. Place self in bunk without necessity of sharing cabin. Can feel the cold cotton of the sheets and the scratchiness of the blankets on my legs. This is odd as I can't feel much on my legs these days. My feet are already too hot but I can hear station noises coming in from the open window. I can smell hot chocolate. Why? I'm not really sleeping much on this *free* journey. This suggests to me that it's a bad idea. Too fantastical. The train's out.

26th April

Booked flight and access assistance with own wheelchair. Remember travelling from Luton airport this way before. Didn't like the airport wheelchairs. If I take mine it will be easier and, I think, less humiliating [why?]. Can drive close to short stay parking. Picture myself wrestling wheelchair out of car and tottering across to terminal. [I imagine this in terms of intermittent walking, pushing and self-propelling in the wheelchair]. Strangely I am very weighted in this imagined journey; rooted to the ground. My imagining has become in-bodied, I am very physically aware of how my legs will be feeling; their desperate heaviness and how I hunch over the handles of the chair, using it to prop myself. In this scenario I know that people don't realize the chair's mine, even when I get into it. I'm already envisioning a scene in which I'm glaring at thoughtless people who dart suddenly in front of me as I approach the doors. I'm cross with them; even imagine faces and forms for them. Most are middle-aged professionals. They are particularly unobservant I've noticed. So desperately tired and heavy, doing this.

But once I'm inside the terminal I relinquish responsibility for my *self* and my chair and I'm off floating again. Very vague idea of distance. Look at airport website to try to get a more accurate sense of distance inside the terminal, although am notoriously bad at judging them from measurements. Still not got much more sense of it other than that it's further than I think. But in a way this doesn't matter. I know that I'm going to hand myself over to be pushed by somebody else and now I am flitting around, *free* visiting shops that I won't visit, and may not even be there, seeing lights flash past like driving on a motorway and feeling a bit important.

30th April

Been thinking. Most of this trip is going to be over the weekend. M [eight-year-old daughter] might want to come to Edinburgh. In fact, she might not be happy if I go without her. I imagine a scene with her reproachful at missing out and me trying to explain why I'm not taking her. Feebly. I imagine trying to tell school why I've taken her out – there's not enough time to apply formally in advance. If I'm honest, I'm thinking that it would be nice to have her with me. Flying solo is daunting, though I know I can do it. Am now developing this idea into a happy, *free* scene. We are giggling together at the airport, waiting to get on the plane – laughing at my frustration with other passengers who try to push past me. [This is a recurrent theme in everyday life; my bad temper in the face of the lack of consideration of others.] She is now pushing my wheelchair around the Botanic Gardens. No idea how we got here. I seem to have jumped from a happy bit of *free* imagination into a mash-up of various botanic gardens I've been to over the years and this is not the garden of Inverleith House. But it's a nice trip. The day is slightly overcast but dry and the plants are the intense green of a hot day when rain is imminent. I can see down into the pond as though I've lifted up, out of the chair. And then it's gone.

1st May

Booked M flight as well. Am thinking about how we can get from here, in the house, to the plane. Worrying. Rang up easyJet and sorted out my own wheelchair travelling. Apparently my chair may be checked in and I will be transferred in one of the airport wheelchairs. Imagine having separation anxiety over the chair and think of those anonymous things that they lend you at the airport. Also imagine poor M trotting at speed to keep up with cracking pace of wheelchair pusher as experienced last time. All too anxious.

Still trying to picture how the two of us are going to get into the terminal. This is functioning as a clear barrier in my imagination – I don't seem to be able to progress my *practical* journey past the terminal entrance. I Google-search for maps of the airport and parking tariffs. Various parking options come up on screen – ranging from long distance off-site parking and catching a bus to someone meeting us and bringing the car back. About £40 difference. Always is more expensive managing disability, but I'm not sure that my lease contract on the car allows others to park it for me. And then I see myself lurching round the car park on foot, M in tow, trying to locate the pick-up point. No good.

At the moment I'm just floating around above the car parks. Wondering whether drop-off means just as much walking/pushing chair as the park and bus-it option. Trying to project out from overhead map. The bits I can remember or imagine better from these prompts I'm coming down to ground for. But I'm also imagining pushing a trolley with luggage, which is odd, as I can't.

3rd May

Still stuck imagining myself in the car park at Luton airport, but alternating this with looking at city guides for Edinburgh. Seem to be thinking from one bit of car-park surface to another, but concertinaing the airport terminal so that it's one big whoosh of getting pushed towards passport control. Before I know it I'm out onto the tarmac next to the plane and M is also taking flight, tagging along. For the bits of the airport that I know I won't have to walk I'm reducing the size of that part of building, and the distances covered accordingly. But although I'm reducing its size, I'm also imagining myself rooted in the wheelchair as part of this. No flying; right down at ground level. [Perhaps this is because I 'know' what it feels like and how little control I have over this part of the journey.] I am imagining the sensation of rushing along and a vague impression of light and shapes and people without having time to assimilate those images.

11th May

Up too late. Need to be out of house by 4 [a.m.] tomorrow to allow enough time to get checked in [extra early as required by the airline]. Imagine myself waking from heavy sleep to find insufficient time to get there. Have had to dump the associated vignettes of car abandoned on side of road and me running for the plane with daughter in tow. Can't run. This is making me more anxious. I don't have a fall-back option. If we're late we miss the plane. I don't want to imagine missing the plane but I do. I imagine us walking up to the gate [note; walking] and it being closed against us. Stern faces shaking their heads in bleached out colours against an all-too-bright sun outside. 'No, no. You are late. Too LATE!' We are turned away. I am depressed that I have missed the plane. It shows that I am not able to manage. Even though I seem to have imagined myself as a walking incompetent, rather than otherwise.

12th May

Up, washed, dressed. Drive to Luton airport through 50mph controls on motorway. No hideous traffic and I deliver us to the correct car park and find the disabled parking spaces. Glare at other cars to check for their disabled driver Blue Badges. Unload my wheelchair and our small bags and push it, still folded, across the road to the opposite bus stop. It's dark and it's cold out here. We sit on a bench and wait for the bus. When it arrives everyone else charges on through the middle door and I have to lumber forwards and bang on the door of the driver to get his attention. He is surprised when he finds out that it is my own wheelchair I am asking about. I adopt a martyred expression. The bus is too full to get me into the chair and onto the bus, so he gets another passenger to move after I tell him that I will fall over if asked to stand. I am embarrassed, but a couple of other passengers look after the chair and find M a seat.

We arrive at the terminal and there is only a short walk to the entrance. Still quite dark; still cold. People rushing past us. I feel unsteady. M pushes me in the chair some of the way, we find the check-in and I sit, heavy in the chair in the queue. We are moved from the queue to an empty desk, checked in and sent to the special assistance desk at the front of the airport. There are a few people in wheelchairs waiting to be carted off to various gates. We eye each other.

The experience of getting through the airport is rather like being a large parcel. We shoot past queues, are very thoroughly and solicitously searched, and at various points are parked in designated locations with other wheelchair-ers, ready for the next round of assistance. We have about 20 minutes at one base so I send M to buy doughnuts from the concession immediately opposite, where I can see her. Eventually we're pushed out to the tarmac and have to wait while the fuel feed is detached. First up the steps. I had not thought about how hard the climb is. Wonder if I'll get stuck, once I'm halfway and picture a stampede of other passengers, but finally manage it. Plane journey mostly spent trying to sort M's ears which are hurting. Last off the plane. Chair emerges from somewhere and we are reunited. I am pushed out and parked where we expect to be met. After a few text messages we are.

Spend rest of morning imagining Inverleith House. Seem to be thinking of it in terms of an enfilade of rooms, quite dark, with small pictures on the ground floor walls, interspersed with antique furniture. The building expands and contracts variously, according to how confident I feel about getting through. I don't seem to have any in-bodied sense of myself. Perhaps because I'm nervous. But I have a very strong sense of the architecture; much of it a montage of the many smaller country houses and villas I visited in my previous life as a historic buildings case officer. [This professional background is how, through a close friend and a rather circuitous route, I came to know Willie.] I rehearse a few conversations with people who might be there, one of which involves explaining why I am walking with a stick. [This happens quite often when I haven't seen people for a while, but I'm not sure why I'm being so self-absorbed.] Talk to family about getting there.

Family member who has accepted invitation to come too kindly insists on driving us. I had imagined taking a taxi and arranging to be collected. This allows me not to have to imagine the collection by taxi. It's a relief.

The gallery opening goes well. The space is much lighter; more expansive than I had imagined and the garden access more precipitous. The work looks terrific. I am glad to have made the journeys and glad to have brought M. I get to Inverleith House from the car with a stick and a wild burst of adrenalin propels me up the (unexpected) hill with only two stops. But once inside the gallery the profound leg heaviness I had anticipated returns. I simultaneously want to look at the work, grieve for my friend and sit – if not lie – down. I hadn't anticipated how sad I would feel and how this weight of grief would fuse with a visceral regret at leaving my wheelchair. There is no distinction between what I think and how my body feels.

Conclusion

Through this chapter I have tried to propose an understanding of the imagination in travel as set both with*in* and with*out* the body. Drawing upon the thinking of non-representational theory I set out to show how my own (mundane) travel practices rely upon the imagination in both acutely in-bodied and un-bodied forms. I draw a divide between what I call the *practical* and *free* travel practices of imagination, using the term 'practice' deliberately, as the two forms of imagination are shown here as recurrent over time (Thrift 2008: 7). Through exploring these *practical* and *free* imaginative practices I have shown how I use my imagination both as part of planning for travel, and as a compensatory tool for a personal loss of mobility. My imagination functions both as something inherently somatic, and as something of the psyche – liberating, allowing me to roam where my body is no longer able, or refuses to be brought. In this way I wonder about Thrift's apparent rejection of the body as defined and separate from cognition, and his insistence upon the pre-cognitive 'where intentions or decisions are made before the conscious self is even aware of them' (2008: 6–7). I have tried to show through this inherently personal chapter that my practices and performance of the travel activity depend upon a two-fold framing of imagination where my conscious self refers to and draws upon imaginative practices in both bodied and un-bodied forms. There is a fluidity between the in-bodied and un-bodied, the intentional, automatic and the fantastical. But there is also a very definite place for the embodied cognitive that comes through *practical* imagination. Although emerging from my own experience of travel as a disabled person, I hope that this exploration will go some way towards opening up discussion of imagination in travel as something more than greedy, transient and elusive, but instead as an important *practical* component of the experience of planning *for* travel and *of* place.

In memory of William McKeown 1962–2011

Acknowledgements

Thanks to the editors and Polly Hawkes and Margo Huxley who all commented on earlier drafts of this chapter.

References

Anderson, B. and Harrison, P. 2010. *Taking Place: Non-representational theories and geography*. Farnham: Ashgate.

Bell, H. 2011. Listing, 'significance' and practised persuasion at Spa Green housing estate. London. *Social and Cultural Geography*, 12(3), 212–23.

Bissell, D. 2009. Visualising everyday geographies: Practices of vision through travel-time. *Transactions of the Institute of British Geographers*, 34(1), 42–60.

Bissell, D. 2010. Passenger mobilities: Affective atmospheres and the sociality of public transport. *Environment and Planning. D, Society and Space*, 28(2), 270–289.

Butler, R. and Parr, H. 1999. *Mind and Body Spaces: Geographies of illness, impairment and disability*. London: Routledge.

de Certeau, M. 1984. *The Practice of Everyday Life*, trans. S. Randall. Berkeley: University of California Press.

Cresswell, T. 2012. Review essay: Nonrepresentational theory and me: Notes of an interested sceptic. *Environment and Planning D: Society and Space*, 30(1), 96–105.

Crouch, D. 2002. Surrounded by place: Embodied encounters, in *Tourism: Between place and performance*, edited by S. Coleman and M. Crang. New York: Berghahn Books, 207–18.

Dorn, M. and Laws, G. 1994. Social theory, body politics, and medical geography: Extending Kearns's invitation. *The Professional Geographer*, 46(1), 106–10.

Edensor, T. 2007. Mundane mobilities, performances and spaces of tourism. *Social and Cultural Geography*, 8(2), 199–215.

Fenton, J. 2005. Space, chance, time: Walking backwards through the hours on the left and right banks of Paris. *Cultural Geographies*, 12(4), 412–28.

Latham, A. 2003. Research, performance, and doing human geography: Some reflections on the diary-photograph, diary-interview method. *Environment and Planning A*, 35(11), 1993–2017.

Lorimer, H. 2005. Cultural geography: The busyness of being 'more-than-representational'. *Progress in Human Geography*, 29(1), 83–94.

Lorimer, H. 2008. Cultural geography: Non-representational conditions and concerns. *Progress in Human Geography*, 32(4), 551–59.

Mackenzie, C. and Scully, J.L. 2007. Moral imagination, disability and embodiment. *Journal of Applied Philosophy*, 24(4), 335–51.

Merleau-Ponty, M. 1962. *Phenomenology of Perception*, trans. C. Smith. New York: Humanities Press.

Phillips, A. 2005. Walking and looking. *Cultural Geographies*, 12(4), 507–13.

Pratchett, M. 2010. *A Rough Guide to Non-Representational Theory*. [Online]. Available at: http://merlepatchett.wordpress.com/2010/11/12/a-rough-guide-to-non-representational-theory/ [last accessed 24 April 2013].

Thrift, N. 1996. *Spatial Formations*. London: Sage.

Thrift, N. 1997. The still point: Resistance, expressiveness, embodiment and dance, in *Geographies of Resistance*, edited by S. Pile and M. Keith. London: Routledge, 124–51.

Thrift, N. 1999. Steps to an ecology of place, in *Human Geography Today*, edited by D. Massey, J. Allen and P. Sarre. Cambridge: Polity Press, 295–323.

Thrift, N. 2000a. Performing cultures in the new economy. *Annals of the Association of American Geographers*, 90(4), 674–92.

Thrift, N. 2000b. Afterwords. *Environment and Planning D: Society and Space*, 18(3), 213–55.

Thrift, N. 2004. Summoning life, in *Envisioning Human Geographies*, edited by P.J. Cloke, M. Goodwin and P. Crang. London: Arnold, 81–103.

Thrift, N. 2008. *Non-representational Theory: Space, politics, affect*. London: Routledge.

Thrift, N. and Dewsbury, J.-D. 2000. Dead geographies – and how to make them live. *Environment and Planning D: Society and Space*, 18(4), 411–32.

Toombs, S.K. 1992. *The Meaning of Illness: A phenomenological account of the different perspectives of physician and patient*. Dordrecht: Kluwer Academic Publishers.

Toombs, S.K. 1995. The lived experience of disability. *Human Studies*, 18(1), 9–23.

Wilson, M. 2002. Six views of embodied cognition. *Psychonomic Bulletin & Review*, 9(4), 625–36.

Chapter 4
Travel-as-Homemaking

Gordon Waitt and Patricia Macquarie

In recent years tourism studies has become enlivened by incorporating the influential 'performance turn'. Approaching the study of tourism from the perspective of entire bodies and different bodies has challenged conceptualization of subjectivity, senses and space in tourism studies not as separate realms but as co-constituted. An embodied approach in tourism encompasses a variety of issues and topics including challenging heteronormativity (Johnston 2001), problematizing Urry's (1990) tourist gaze (Jordan and Aitchison 2008, Urry and Larsen 2011), paying attention to the sensual body (Saldanha 2002, Waitt and Duffy 2010) as well as extending research agendas by focusing on the role of emotions and affect (Johnston 2007). The shift from representational to embodied approaches acknowledges that people do so much more when they travel than only read guidebooks, advertisements, go on sightseeing tours and take photographs. Places are never sensed and made sense of by sight alone.

In this chapter we present some findings of a research project that addresses an embodied approach to travel and imagination. This chapter is about evocations of home in leisure travel narratives; and how home is differently imagined and re-imagined in relation to return travel. Drawing on feminist, post-structural, geographical theory on 'the body', our basic argument is that imagination is always embodied and spatial and becomes a means to shape and reshape ourselves and places. We focus on the themes of imaginaries, travel and homemaking, enabling us to address three concerns. First, our concern is with the more routine forms of travel that have tended to be overlooked in a field of study normally more focused on the extraordinary rather than the everyday. As Towner (1995: 339–42) pointed out, tourism studies tends to be 'concerned with the more remarkable travel events in people's lives'. Overlooked are the seemingly more mundane everyday activities that are part of 'remarkable' travel events, such as waiting in airports and sitting in hotel lobbies, as well as the 'remarkable' travel events found in everyday activities, as in our case study, walking through a nearby rainforest. Second, our concern is with domesticating mobility. As noted by Franklin and Crang (2001: 11): 'So often mobility has meant travel and excitement, and freedom from the domestic, a flight from a feminized realm.' Domesticating mobility requires remaining alert to how elsewheres may be also part of the home realm. Third, our concern is with a field of tourism studies that is becoming sensually more diverse through emphasizing the body and taking on board the sensuous, embodied and performative dimensions of travel.

The empirical data for this chapter are drawn from a larger project investigating the importance of the Illawarra Escarpment in the lives of people living in Wollongong, New South Wales, Australia. The project used diaries, walk-alongs, home-visits and a form of ethnographic narrative analysis to offer insights about the relationship between the imaginary, travel and homemaking. The Illawarra Escarpment is comprised of a line of cliffs of Hawkesbury Sandstone that runs for over 100 kilometers almost parallel with the coastline from Stanwell Park in the north, to Nowra in the south (see Figure 4.1). For people living in metropolitan Wollongong, the Escarpment is a highly visible, iconic feature, rising almost vertically to a height of 400 metres. The Escarpment is also the western boundary of the metropolitan area. Historically, urban encroachment onto the Escarpment was limited by a combination of distance from metropolitan centres, restricted access, geological instability, as well as large coal mining leases. More recently, the declaration of biodiversity conservation zoning measures to 'protect' the Escarpment as habitat has limited urban development. The escarpment is part of Dharawal country that includes the Wadi Wadi, Korawal, Elouera, Jerrungarugh and Tharawal clans. Aboriginal knowledge of escarpment places is forged by the stories and songs of the *Alcheringa*. The Aboriginal cultural significance of escarpment places is neither obviously marked to the non-Aboriginal eye nor incorporated into management plans. Some non-Aboriginal residents may be familiar with how the *Alcheringa* provides insights to the law and spirit of the country. However, only a person with kinship ties to country can gain full knowledge of the cultural significance and protocols prescribing normative behaviour of escarpment places (Berndt and Berndt 1988).

The chapter unfolds as follows. We begin by providing a conceptual framework to explore the intersection between the imaginary, travel and homemaking. Drawing on a feminist, post-structural ontology, bodies and spaces are mutually constitutive in our conceptualization of the imaginary. The concept of the imaginary which we are employing is therefore not one in which 'invented' worlds are contrasted to 'real' worlds. Imagined worlds are not conceptualized as inner, perceived, mental images that are projected onto a neutral, physical world. There is no neutral, objective world to which we can gain access. What exists in the world for us requires 'the body'. In this chapter, to know something by imagination is to exist in a particular embodied relationship to one's context or social space. This, in turn, has important implications for one's ability to act, as well as one's capacity to be acted upon. Next, we outline a justification for why Wollongong, and the northern Illawarra in particular, provides an interesting case study, and one relevant to investigating tourism as the extraordinary everyday. We then outline our methods. Finally, we explore how one participant, Janet, came to imagine the Illawarra Escarpment as simultaneously home and elsewhere. This tension between imagining the Illawarra Escarpment as home and elsewhere we argue is the outcome of embodied relationships of everyday walks and returning from travelling beyond the Illawarra.

Figure 4.1 The Illawarra Escarpment looking north towards Stanwell Park from McCauley's Beach, Thirroul

Source: Gordon Waitt.

Travel, Imagination and Homemaking

Feminist geographers emphasize the spatiality of subjectivity, and how travel can evoke a sense of belonging and alienation, enabling possibilities for the transformation of self. Rather than regarding identities as fixed definable characteristics of say a tourism industry, feminist geographers increasingly stress the relational, lived, spatially-mediated and embodied attributes of subjectivities and space. We argue that all forms of travel involve a spatial (re-)configuration of an embodied self, from everyday walks to overseas sojourns. A feminist understanding of subjectivity as spatially mediated turns tourism studies towards an understanding of the self as performative, sensuous, relational, embodied and geo-historically specific.

This shift to embodiment draws on affective ontologies that address how immaterial forces are assembled and distributed across, between and on human and non-human bodies, collective and individual. Thrift (2004: 85) referred to affect as the sense of 'the push of the world' that threads together the moments of everyday life. We offer one articulation of an affective ontology to conceptualize the way the body senses this 'push' to help think about the intersection between the imaginary, travel and homemaking. While affect is always present, we are interested in how the body senses affect through its everyday interactions with the world. An affective ontology offers a way to rethink how imagining relates to travel.

Pertinent here is Probyn's (2003) theorization of embodied, spatial and performative subjectivities. This helps us to unpack the affective and emotional dimensions of imagination, travel and homemaking. Probyn draws much from Deleuze's (1988) account of affect. For Deleuze, affect is not reducible to just personal feelings, or what a particular body can do, but rather what augments, or shrinks, capacities a body might have for relations with other bodies. As Deleuze elaborates (1988: 123), 'a body affects other bodies, or is affected by other bodies; it is this capacity for affecting and being affected that also defines a body in its individuality'. The important point for our argument is that fleeting and temporary moments of heightened affective intensity go beyond experiences as individual emotion and enable an exploration of the creativity and possibilities of relations between bodies and things embedded within particular discourses. An insistence on the embodied and affective relations does not mean jettisoning the representational and cultural context. Here, the concept of habit is relevant. Following Deleuze (1988: 60), *habit* is conceived as the '*a priori* conditions under which all ideas are formulated and behaviour displayed', that is 'remembered' by the body. The acquisition of habits allows a person to move their body into action without explicit thought. Following Ingold (2000), while habit may gradually reduce the potential of the body to do things otherwise, habit and repetition do not reduce awareness. Instead, Ingold (2000) argues that habit makes an increased awareness possible. Just as repeated actions and experience become embodied and automatic at a level below conscious, we also become conscious of differences automatically without any conscious intention or special watchfulness. For Ingold (1999), responsiveness intensifies with the fluency of action. The habitual sensuous information below conscious awareness that is inscribed into the body becomes a resource for the fast reflex action of automatic responses. Considered in this light, bodily habits can be extended on the basis of an embodied existence. Hence, the view while walking through a remnant rainforest like that of the Illawarra may tap into essentialistic Romantic discourses to constitute the thresholds of an environmental identity, 'home', 'elsewhere' and/or 'nature'. At the same time, by regularly walking through the rainforest a realm of new possibilities exists to obtain a different understanding of self and the world through the heightened intensities of being there. This visceral experience would tend to unsettle any culturally mediated representations of the rainforest and bushwalkers.

A feminist perspective of imaginary and travel therefore attends to 'the body' that is alert to situated knowledges, intensities of experiences, embodied histories, experiential practices and performativities. The imaginary we aspire to is therefore not that prescribed by representations but has a phenomenal orientation. Imagining the world is a mode of being in relation to it. As Merleau-Ponty ([1945] 1962: 42) argued, the body's spatiality is not a 'spatiality of position', but a 'spatiality to situation', in the sense that it is always 'directed towards a certain existing or possible task'. However, this must not obscure the social and the cultural. A feminist perspective of imaginary often overlaps with phenomenology, but makes explicit theoretical connections with broader social systems of politics and power. Through our everyday activities we are initiated into social imaginaries which make possible shared practices and responses. As Butler (1993) and Gatens (1996) argue persuasively, bodily imaginaries render certain modes of embodiment more intelligible and legitimate than others, which are suppressed or marginalized. Likewise, Perera (2009) discusses how a national imaginary is nourished and legitimated through a particular bodily imaginary (clothing, activities, gestures) and spatial imaginary (borders, capitals and territories). From a feminist, post-phenomenological perspective, it is essential to recognize that imaginaries are forged, sustained and challenged through embodied subjectivities that implicate corporeal forms, personal histories and social and cultural contexts. The process of forming and changing imaginary significations is therefore a creative and personal one. Imaginaries we are offered have to make not just cognitive sense to us but also affective sense. Imaginaries must change our modes of experiencing our worlds in ways that we can recognize as desirable and livable. Imagining home, then, is more than simply retrieving memories of homes past; it is about the affective and emotional experience of places that can become felt and called home. Hence, imagining home is a way of understanding our relation to the world as ongoing tension between self and the world. Drawing on Merleau-Ponty, Grosz (2005: 128) argues that imagining is a:

> way of understanding our relation to the world, not as one of merger or oneness or of control and mastery, but a relation of belonging to and of not quite fitting, a never-easy kinship, a given tension that makes our relations to the world hungry, avid, desiring.

Thus, home is never fully achieved, never full arrived at, even when we are in a place we call home.

The Extraordinary Everyday: The Illawarra, New South Wales, Australia

The research discussed in this chapter investigates return travel in the context of the northern suburbs of Wollongong, New South Wales Australia, in the late 2000s. The northern coastal suburbs of Wollongong, framed by the Illawarra Escarpment, make an interesting case study that illustrates what Franklin and Crang (2001: 8) termed 'the extraordinary everyday'; that is blurring of the distinction between the everyday and holiday through the circulation of inventories for appreciation and taste from the tourism industry. For the northern Illawarra, this blurring is not new. As Metesula and Waitt (2012) illustrate, touring the Illawarra has been rendered or reconfigured as an interesting destination for visitors since 1910. In the early eighteenth century, the tourism industry targeted primarily Sydneysiders, encouraging them to travel the 51 miles by, initially, train, and later car, to appreciate the possibilities for camping, hiking, picnicking or bathing.

European Romantic ideologies are central to configuring the Illawarra as a 'nature' tourism destination. As Menhennet (1981) argued, Romanticism is infamously tricky to define. Very simply, the Romantic Movement in Europe dates from the 1750s, and was an artistic, literary and intellectual movement that constituted 'wilderness' and 'the rural' as the antithesis of the city and industrialization. This imagining of nature has both aesthetic and moral components. The aesthetic components refer to the ways that Romanticism provided theories of landscape aesthetic that valued nature as 'beautiful' and 'sublime' and the rural as 'picturesque'. The moral component alludes to how wilderness and the rural are stereotyped as offering rejuvenation, self-discovery, creativity, a simple/pure existence and slower pace of life. As Horne (2005) and Hudson (2000) discuss, central to the nineteenth-century tourism activities in Australia, that helped stabilize understandings of class and gender, were experiences of the sublime, beauty and picturesque. Frawley (1999) outlines how the aesthetic and moral components of wilderness and popularity of bushwalking practices were central to the emergence of Australian environmental politics in the 1970s.

In the Illawarra, one of the first tourist guides was published in 1910 by the Wollongong Citizens Association. This guide constituted and circulated the essentialized tendencies of the coastal 'idyll' in response to the rapid rise of industrialization in Sydney.

> 'This is ILLAWARRA', a land fashioned for Fairies, to dwell upon; a spot smiled upon by Nature, in one of its generous moods ... Illawarra is beyond the power of painting – 'Unless to us Mortals, it were given, To dip his brush, in dyes of Heaven'. (Foreword, *The Illawarra tourist guide: Wollongong Citizens Association*, Hamey Studios, c1920s writer and artist David Christie Murray)

Drawing upon Romantic ideologies, the scenery of the Illawarra became understood as offering restorative and regenerative possibilities despite the longstanding presence of coal mining. In the 1920s and 1930s, although the growth of the coal industry and diversification into steel and copper industries occurred, guidebooks continued to draw on familiar Romantic narratives to fashion the northern Illawarra as an escape from the frenzied pace of city living to an earthly paradise. For example, one guidebook published by the Commissioner for Railways, New South Wales, *By Train in Daylight through the Beautiful Illawarra*, refers to an 'enchanting journey', 'tantalizing spots', 'virgin forest and ocean expanse'; and tells of the 'kaleidoscope sequence of unsurpassed views' and 'scalloped seashores and placid inlets, towering mountains and sloping meadows'. The figure of the tourist invoked by the Commissioner for Railways also illustrates the gendered assumptions of touring practices and travellers discussed by Pratt (1992); the figure of the masculine traveller, gazing upon the Illawarra turned into feminized object of pleasure. Similarly, *Wilson's Rail, Road and Sea Guide to the South Coast and*

Southern Highlands New South Wales (1929: 51) helped circulate understanding of views from hiking trails built in the Illawarra as a 'must see' picturesque destination:

> The Mountain climb to the world-renowned Sublime Point (1,330 feet high) up the steep ladder of steps rewards the tourist with a Panoramic view of the landscape and seascape unsurpassed in any part of the world.

Drawing on a European Romantic ideology, set against a backdrop of wilderness, hiking in the Illawarra was cast as freedom from the city and work, and legitimized as means to a healthier body and mind. Likewise, motor touring guidebooks of the Illawarra helped to popularize the view from Sublime Point as a tourist attraction. The *Picturesque Illawarra: The garden of New South Wales* (Hennessy 1930: 3) explained that:

> The Prince's Highway and other roads enter the district by several mountain passes which wind through the beautiful Australian native bush, and so it is that the motorist, before descending one of these passes, is confronted by a panorama of outstanding beauty, a blended picture of seaside, bush and mountain scenery. In particular, the views from Sublime Point and Bulli Pass Lookouts have been lavished with expressions of admiration by Australian and Over-seas visitors.

However, Wollongong City Council did not actively promote tourism in the early 1900s. Instead, for aldermen the regional economic future was tied to the coal and steel industries. Indeed, by the 1950s, Wollongong had become imagined as the Sheffield of the South, displacing the earlier geographical imaginations of the Illawarra as the Brighton of Australia. Only since the 1980s, when the steel industry collapsed, leaving the Illawarra labour market in pieces, has Wollongong City Council actively pursued tourism. Wollongong City Council initially promoted the Illawarra as the 'Leisure Coast' to counter images of smokestacks, unemployment and toxins. Consequently, since the 1980s there has been an ensuing proliferation of tourist attractions. In addition to the re-circulating archaeologies of tourism that frames the beach and the escarpment as picturesque, entertainment is now also derived from driving the Grand Pacific Drive, visiting the Sea Cliff Bridge, hang-gliding from Bald Hill and learning about the coal mining past, seasonal migration of whales, or the one time visit of D.H. Lawrence to Thirroul.

Methods

This chapter draws on our ethnographic analysis of the diaries, walk-alongs and follow-up conversations with Janet, who had recently resigned from a managerial position to look after her first child. Janet is from an Anglo-Australian, middle-class background in country Victoria. At the time of the project, Janet is aged in her thirties and her child celebrated a first birthday. Janet held tertiary education qualifications and has lived with her husband in the Illawarra for two years. Together they purchased a house in the northern suburbs of the Illawarra. Her data was drawn from 18 participants in a project conducted in 2010 on the intertwining nexus of self–world relations with the Illawarra Escarpment. Participants kept reflexive diaries about their encounters, activities and experiences over a two month period. Janet's data was selected for this chapter because at one level accounts of travel from women with babies are largely absent in the literature. At another level she wrote most of her diary entries after returning from walks through the Illawarra Escarpment or from travelling beyond the Illawarra. Her diary was comprised of 14 dated entries written about herself and her everyday world having returned to her house on the escarpment from elsewhere. Each entry is a discontinuous narrative or series of stories; reflections on events in retrospect. Each entry therefore provides reflective insights into how travel made, or re-made, different dimensions of her located subjectivities in and through the Illawarra Escarpment. A sense of situated environmental subjectivity was provided through her reflections on imaginings of what was do-able or thinkable about the Illawarra Escarpment. In addition we documented her environmental subjectivity and embodied experiences through participant observation of body language when one of us joined her on her regular rainforest walk and visited her home for follow-up conversations. Working with Janet in situ allowed us to develop a deeper insight into the affective knowledge recorded in her diary. A form of analysis, termed by Gubrium and Holstein (2009: 22) 'narrative ethnography', was employed to interpret the stories not as 'factual-truthful accounts' nor for linguistic content, but as phenomenological interactions constitutive of socio-cultural worlds. This involves close scrutiny to not only where things were said, but listening to how things were said (tone, rhythm, emphasis) through the experience of remembering and retelling. These methods enabled the body to become the focus of analysis.

The Embodied Relationships of Everyday Walks

Within the context of the city, the conditions and possibilities of walking have previously drawn much attention in order to better understand the performative attributes of identities and lifeworlds (see Tester 1994, Solnit 2000). Walking, when conceptualized as constructed in and through the everyday and embodied dynamics of home life, shifts the focus of tourism studies from the 'special times' of annual events or holidays to the 'special times' of everyday rhythms. The everyday rhythms of Janet's daily routines as a mother form a 'backdrop to life against which the usual and the unusual unfold' (Edensor 2010: 14). Her 'backdrop' is the invariant, though slowly changing, bodily rhythms, and caring routines for her baby: his meals, sleeps, plays and baths. Also the routine maintenance work of looking after her household and family: the cleaning, washing, shopping and cooking. Against this backdrop, regular rainforest walking felt good as a break from the physical work of caring for house and family:

> It was lovely to leave the clearing up [after visitors for Gabriel's first birthday lunch] and house activity and go for a walk. (30 September, diary)

In the context of Janet's domestic routines, rainforest walking sets up counter rhythms that are valued as facilitating bodily connections outside the realm of social reproduction and domestic labour. The rainforest walk through the escarpment is valued as an easily accessible elsewhere to rhythms that comprise the domestic. Janet's words substantiate Lorimer and Lund's (2008: 195) argument that 'elsewhere can simply mean landscapes that are not workaday'. In Janet's words, unlike the rhythms that sustain her family house, she has no responsibility for maintaining the rhythms of the escarpment:

> It is like being given a gift that one can just relax and enjoy. I like the knowledge that it all happens whether I am there or not. It is not dependent on you. Also, if you walk an area often you feel as if you own it, you notice changes. But you don't have to maintain or be responsible for it – it all happens without you. (December, walk-along)

For Janet walks are valued as a 'gift'. Janet enjoyed and valued walking through the escarpment as an opportunity to 'go' somewhere elsewhere yet feel at home. The practice of walking in and through the rainforest has the capacity for her to reassemble her sense of self. Regular rainforest walking offers possibilities for her body to relax. Walking through the rainforest resonates a capacity of belonging. The intensities of 'fitting' to the familiar rhythms of the escarpment are so strong that she has a sense of ownership. As Waitt et al. (2009) argued, walking is a process of territorialization, a boundary making practice through which people feel a sense of belonging or detachment. By assigning value to what belongs, or not, walking is an inherently political process. Walking sustains, or ruptures, these boundaries through how representations are imagined, felt and observed.

Social imaginaries of the Illawarra escarpment emerge as part of the process of how walking through the escarpment relates to Janet's life as simultaneously home and elsewhere. Images, symbols and representations help construct normative understanding of practices and belongings. As Wylie (2007: 130–131) says:

> Discourses are sets of beliefs, knowledges and practices that both enable and constrain what can be said and done with respect to any given subject. Thus a particular culture of landscape … is a discourse which sets a limit on what constitutes acceptable forms of walking, and within that limit, enables the expression and elaboration of new and innovative cultural forms of walking.

Discourses or ideologies 'enable or constrain' – in other words 'what augmented or diminished capacities a body might have for relations with other bodies' (Wylie 2007: 5). Janet arrives with an embodied history of walking experiences in and through forests and mountain places fashioned by different environmental ideologies.

Janet illustrates the importance and endurance of elements of the diverse and temporally and spatially situated social imaginaries of a romantic nature. Crucially, Romantic discourses are felt as impulses during her rainforest walks, rather than as pre-scripted. When asked what she would miss if no longer able to regularly walk escarpment paths, Janet replied:

> [I] would miss the serenity, the movement of the trees, the immediacy, connecting with what is real. I find it calming, reassuring. (December, follow-up conversation)

Janet's words confirm the argument of Lorimer and Lund (2008: 194–5), who write that 'most obviously, mountain landscapes are therapeutic, places where people go to put their self more in tune with what are commonly perceived as the timeless rhythms, elements, volumes and surfaces of wild, romantic nature'. However, there is more going on than the evocation of cultural resonance with romantic nature. For Janet, the bodily affect of habitual walking and connecting with the familiar forest rhythms corresponds to the passage from one experiential state to another that she described as calming and reassuring. Janet articulates the character of subjectivities and space as relational through her connectedness with things. The relational interactions made possible by walking are what Janet spoke of as 'real'. Tuning into other rhythms by visiting the rainforest and walking the footpaths can be understood as a form of relief from her workaday world that increased her capacity to carry out her domestic responsibilities.

Janet illustrates how the Romantic web of values both enables and constrains a particular social imaginary of the escarpment. Romantic nature emerges through walking practices. Belongings and non-belongings are inscribed through embodied histories and affects erupt in moments of encounter. Normative elements include narratives about what behaviours are permissible, who belongs where and how Janet perceives the moral status of other bodies (human and non-human). Understanding the escarpment through the embodiment of Romanticism, walking with her dogs to appreciate the aesthetic qualities of forest views becomes normative behaviour.

> As I was about to start on our slow hill climb up to the power line lookout, I looked up to the top of the escarpment. The topography, rock formations, cliffs and vegetation all combine to create a totally unique and inspiring view. I feel very lucky to be able to live so close to this view. I also looked along the track we were going to walk up and saw from a distance the stand of tree ferns we often admire when we walk past. From further away they made a wavy blanket of soft fern leaves and look stunning, all stepping down the steep hillside. (16 September, diary)

The Illawarra Escarpment is reflexively produced and experienced in ways that confirm Janet's repertoire of embodied values and performative habits coded by a version of a Romantic ideology. Walking for Janet becomes enjoyable in part through providing access to certain views of the horizon and encounters with tree ferns that she admires. Located in the eye of Janet, she describes escarpment views as 'unique' and 'inspiring'. Moreover, following the argument of Wylie (2006), views have the affective capacity for self-reflection, thereby providing possibilities for alternative perspectives. The reflective capabilities and capacities of the visual experience are provided by the medium of depth that recedes from the viewer. As Lorimer and Lund (2008: 194) argue: 'There is a distant horizon-hovering openness … that enables people to raise to consciousness an aspirant version of their self'. Rather than simply prescribing meanings over the Illawarra Escarpment, views become the means for heightened self-reflexivity, offering possibilities to connect in different ways with the rocks, plants and animals of the escarpment. In walking there is creativity, rather than privileging historical definitions of Romanticism that fix meaning.

Mindful of Janet's embodied histories and environmental discourses, she illustrates the diverse affective-physicality of encountering different human and non-human bodies.

> We encountered …
> Fantastic whip birds
> A catbird – the first one I'd heard for the Spring
> Pam and her cattle dog
> A trail bike rider – most unfortunate as I hate them as much as leeches!
> (15 September, diary)

> We encountered …
> no other humans – yippee!
> lots of bird calls
> some rustling in the bushes as the forest critters scurried away.
> (16 September, diary)

Anticipating the absence of humans and encounters with birdlife, Janet's sense of connectedness to the escarpment is enhanced by a respectful stance of wonder towards hearing bird-calls, or catching the fleeting movement of a lizard. In contrast to the thrill of listening to birds, Janet records her anger towards the acts and sounds of trail-bike riders because of how they generally 'destroy' the rainforest.

At the same time as Janet orients herself through the escarpment by seeking views she appreciates as scenic, the plants and animals orient her understanding of this place thus unsettling cultural resonances of the escarpment. For example, Janet comments on the role of leeches in her decision to walk, or not, particular rainforest footpaths. The pleasures of rainforest walking are diminished by her anxiety about the presences of leeches that heightens awareness of the porosity of the boundaries of human and non-human bodies. Janet suggests the rainforest becomes familiar through how a person becomes attuned to the iterative and incremental feel, look, smell and sounds of the constellation of trajectories that comprise the rainforest as a meaningful whole, yet always has unexpected moments with constant comings and goings and oscillations between past and present, here and elsewhere. For example, Janet becomes enthralled in observing seasonal change. In Janet's words 'you notice changes'.

> We had a great walk in the rainforest today. It was wet underfoot, but not soaking wet. The birds were very active, especially the whip birds. I also noticed a lot more spring flowers since our last walk. I think I spotted a few tiny orchids, but with two border collies pulling me along, I didn't get much time to stop and look. (4 November, diary)

Spring flowers or the call of particular birds become a source of pleasure. The work of Ingold (2000) on habit is helpful here to better understand how our conscious attention is only arrested by things that stand out of the ordinary.

At the same time, the embodied rhythms of walking facilitate a connection with trees that enable Janet to welcome trees into her backyard and unsettle the way views are coded within Romanticism. Indeed, trees in Janet's backyard become more valued than ocean views.

> At home in the rainforest … I feel like we live in the rainforest and we have lots of large trees around our house. The sea and sky provide a lovely blue backdrop for the green canopy. It's not how most people see our view. They think the trees block our view of the water but I don't agree. I think the trees are the view. (18 September, diary)

As Head and Muir (2005: 92) argue, people are 'most likely to welcome trees into their backyard and lives … when they are entwined, sometimes literally, with the rhythms of daily or family life'. As in the case of Janet, through the regular bodily rhythms of walking, large rainforest trees come to belong in her backyard. The continuity between the domestic and the escarpment is blurred through the continuity, connectivity and commonality provided by embodied connection to rainforest trees. Janet is aware that her personal sense of aesthetics with regards to views may differ from other people. Through Janet's regular rainforest walks, large rainforest trees belong in her backyard and are one way to maintain her imaginary of the northern Illawarra as home.

The Embodied Relationships of Travelling Beyond the Illawarra

In this section we argue that travel to unfamiliar places is a process that may throw the familiar imagination of places into relief, by heightening our embodied evaluations. Journeying beyond the northern suburbs of Wollongong is a process that helped Janet make, and remake, points of connection between herself, family and the Illawarra Escarpment as home. For example, Janet assessed the affective experience of the Illawarra Escarpment arriving back from a weekend trip to the Blue Mountains, New South Wales.

> We haven't walked in the rainforest for a few days. We were away on the weekend, visiting the Blue Mountains. It was a spectacular place, lots of cliffs, gorges and valleys, trees and tree ferns. We visited quite a few places and did some great walks. The trip home was quite long and it is always such a relief to turn onto Bulli Pass and see Wollongong spread out below. We check the surf at Sandon Point first, then open our windows to get some sea air into the car. I love that the escarpment provides such a distinct homecoming. It really provides a dramatic break from the climate, roads and landscape up the top, to the sea air made cooler by the rainforest, and the narrow, winding roads. And while it's not as expansive or large as the Blue Mountains, it is still an impressive geographic feature that gives a distinct identity to the region and towns. I like the combination of the escarpment and the ocean. (26 September, diary)

Janet's description of the Illawarra Escarpment as homecoming illustrates the spatiality of subjectivity. Reflecting on arriving at the top of the Bulli Pass provided insight to her affective knowledge that helps to imagine the Illawarra Escarpment not only as a physical, social and cultural boundary of home but also an embodied one. Janet's body is affectively tuned not only to the pleasures of the sea and mountain views but also to the winding roads, smell and feel of cooler sea air. The spatiality of subjectivity is again illustrated by the sense of relief arriving at the top of Bulli Pass and witnessing the Illawarra Escarpment. We suggest how Janet's body judges the affective forces of the Illawarra escarpment as relief illustrates how such intensities work as moments of reassurance of self in the world.

Similarly, Janet's diary entries suggest the active role of the body as judge when travelling elsewhere and the way this alerted her to how the situational histories and experiences of living with the Illawarra Escarpment become embodied:

> I have been thinking about the environment we are bringing Gabriel up in, and the escarpment is a major part of that for me and him. It's partly the environmental benefits the escarpment creates such as clean air, habitat for birds and animals, water quality etc. But it's also the imprint it will have on him mentally and as a person. It is so precious being able to walk with Gabriel in the rainforest where he sees trees and birds and takes in the calmness of his surrounds. It will also be part of what he considers home. Quentin and I have a friend who has grown up and lived all her life in the Wollongong region. She loves it here and has no intention to live anywhere else. She said to us that when she travels she feels a bit open or exposed without the escarpment running along the west. I love the fact that this topography gets so ingrained into you and I think it's great that

66   *Travel and Imagination*

Gabriel will have that too. Mind you, I don't think you need to grow up and live
here your whole life to develop that notion. (6 November, diary)

The escarpment has an active presence in mutually constituting self and the world –
in Janet's words, the 'topography gets so ingrained into you'. It is this very visceral
way of learning and imagining that she wishes her son to experience, appreciate
and embody. Through the affective repertoire of the body, Janet acknowledges
when people travel embodied histories and experiences of familiar settings may
become more significant. Travel becomes a mechanism to make people aware of
these familiar juxtapositions. Janet illustrates how the Illawarra Escarpment offers
possibilities of becoming and belonging through fixing assurances and certainties.

The way our bodies are integral to making sense of places is again illustrated
by Janet's travel to the Blue Mountains, New South Wales. For instance Janet
wrote:

The Blue Mountains didn't have a great deal of water, and it took a slight
mental adjustment on my part to stand and look at a view and not see water.
(26 September, diary)

Visiting the Blue Mountains enabled Janet to reflect on the Illawarra Escarpment,
offering possibilities to confirm, or challenge, normative understandings. More
generally, Janet illustrates how travelling may unsettle the familiar and expected
cultural resonances. Travel may trigger a process of reflecting on the meaning and
relationship with familiar places. As Janet notes:

It's funny how things in your everyday life become so normal, then looking at
some other view or place makes you think again about what you see everyday.
(26 September, diary)

'Reflecting on' is a process of making comparisons, gauging, measuring one object
or situation against another, qualifying an experience by comparison with another.
Clark (2001) helpfully refers to this process as 'off-line thinking', as opposed to
'on-line thinking', which is that kind of thinking that occurs when the body is
fully engaged in action. Clark (2001: 145) defines off-line thinking, or reflecting
on, as 'our ability to engage in second-order discourse, to think about (and
evaluate) our own thoughts'. It is not always a necessarily completely conscious
or intentional process although it often is. Rather than fixed in the imagination,
Janet points to how places are made and remade through the process of 'reflecting
on' the experiential practices and performances of travel that bears traces of earlier
experiences of there and elsewhere.

In her diary, Janet provides two further examples that underscore the importance
of travel to the dynamics of place-making. The first example illustrates how travel
practices and performativities become an embodied resource available on recall

for producing meaning and making sense by contrasting, comparing, collating and recomposing, measuring and evaluating.

> We had a lovely holiday in the Cook Islands. We had two weeks of holiday time, enjoying the beach, local culture and beautiful scenery ... It was a great contrast to Thirroul/northern Wollongong, with ocean surf beaches. In particular, what really struck me when we got home was how linear the escarpment is. We had just spent two weeks on a small island – the whole island is 31 km around – where the view inland was impressive. It was quite a contrast coming home and looking north up to Stanwell Park and beyond, at just how long the escarpment is. The green headlands marking distance along the coast was quite striking after our holiday away. (4 November, diary)

From the perspective of travel and place, Janet's imaginaries of the Illawarra Escarpment as home are nourished and enlivened by her experience of a family holiday to a beach resort in the Cook Islands. Janet's corporeal connections to the Illawarra as home are reinforced through a process of reflection, contrasting and comparing. Janet acknowledges how travel offers possibilities for the material juxtaposition of familiar sites to suddenly appear very different. For example, on returning from the Cook Islands she noted 'how linear the escarpment is' and 'how long the escarpment is'. These material qualities of the Illawarra Escarpment may offer either a sense of entrapment or reassurance, or a mix of these. For Janet the Illawarra Escarpment became more significant having been elsewhere, describing the views as 'impressive' and 'striking'. Reflecting on the Illawarra Escarpment, having just returned from the Cook Islands, Janet reconstituted her embodied knowledge of the escarpment as special.

The second illustrates how travel and artwork dovetail to provide opportunities for comparisons, for the familiar to appear very different, and to produce feelings of 'privilege' and 'rightness'. Returning from visiting this exhibition she wrote:

> We went to the NSW [New South Wales] Art Gallery on the weekend and saw the exhibition of Sidney Nolan paintings. His paintings of the Victorian landscape were impressive, from the flat wheat fields of Mount Arapiles, to the dusty eucalypt forests of the Ned Kelly paintings, to the impressive Riverbend series. While not all the same, he really captured the feeling of the landscapes. Pretty flat, sandy, red-coloured, open woodland. To come home to our home in the rainforest in Thirroul was a great contrast and made me think again about the escarpment. It is so very green, lots of different colours of green ... The Sidney Nolan pictures showed a familiar landscape and reminded me of places I've previously lived in and visited. They contrasted starkly to the escarpment and gave me some new lenses to look at it again. It's a beautiful and unique place, I feel privileged to live amongst it and, at the very least, have it as the backdrop to my everyday life. (24 November, diary)

Janet exemplifies what Crouch (2010: 5) termed 'flirting with space', that is 'the more explorative, uncertain and tentative ways in which our surroundings become engaged in living'. Janet illustrates how travel, and artwork, offered possibilities to reflect on presence of the Illawarra Escarpment in everyday life. In her words, the artwork provided her with 'new lenses with which to look at it [the escarpment] again'. For Janet, encounters with Sidney Nolan's paintings changed in register the meaning of the 'different colours of green', becoming more significant in her ability to imagine the Illawarra Escarpment as home. As Crouch (2010: 14) argues, 'we set our lives in moments where we can "go"' elsewhere. Travel has the capacity to disrupt or reassure our imagined belonging. The capacity to imagine is a fluid, unfolding sensuous process, rather than fixed by representation, that involves shuttling between erecting and dismantling, aligning and comparing, past and present, here and elsewhere. For Janet, the lively process of shuffling and reassembling from visiting Sidney Nolan's artwork rendered the Illawarra Escarpment as home.

Arrivals, Departures and Imaginings

Through considering travel as an affective ontology, the imaginary process of homemaking may be grasped as unfolding over a life-course, rather than fixed or bounded by representations. Sensuous experiences of mobility provide insights as to why Janet can imagine the Illawarra Escarpment as home. We have argued that the role of the Illawarra Escarpment in the process of homemaking is relational, malleable, reflexively produced, experiential and performative. Janet's household roles and responsibilities do not rupture longstanding notions of home aligned with gender roles. Janet is the primary-carer for the baby and does most of the domestic work: the cooking, cleaning and washing. The domestic responsibilities of staying at home with her baby become more manageable because of the relief provided by return walks through the escarpment rainforest coded by a version of a Romantic ideology and understood as an elsewhere from the domestic realm. Possibilities to re-assemble understanding of the self are offered through the familiarity of rhythm and continuity with the rainforest. Regularly walking through the rainforest helps sustain Janet's domestic everyday because of temporary moments of heightened intensity felt as relief and belonging. For Janet, through moving, feeling and thinking with plants, animals and rocks, the Illawarra Escarpment was felt to be a nurturing context that extended her capacity to be a mother. The materiality of the Illawarra Escarpment was articulated as an important way to extend her son's sensuous experience of the world by learning to feel 'at home' there. Furthermore, Janet's ability to sense and call the Illawarra Escarpment home emerges as an outcome of a process of comparison opened up by artwork and travelling elsewhere. Returning from elsewhere opens up possibilities for unsettling the familiar through seeing new permutations for assembling and reassembling the materials that make the Illawarra Escarpment work as a coherent whole. Janet registered change in the shape, length and colour of the Escarpment. In a process that implicitly included her body, the meaning of the Illawarra Escarpment was reconfigured as home.

A feminist affective ontology enables thinking beyond ideas of the imaginary as binaries of the 'real' and the 'envisioned'. We have argued that home and travel are not oppositional ideas. Instead, home is an inherent part of travel and vice versa. Imaging home is characterized by an ongoing process of circular movement – between action and reflection, absence and presence, the embodied experiences of past and present, here and elsewhere. Home becomes felt through the body by travel producing moments to 'go' elsewhere, for example from responsibility to escape, stress to calm, anxiety to relief and vice versa. Going elsewhere may trigger a process of re-assembling the heterogeneous materials that make coherent sense as home. Travel and imagining home becomes a dynamic process that produces senses of belonging and/or marginalization.

References

Berndt, R.M. and Berndt, C. 1988. *The Speaking Land*. Ringwood: Penguin.

Butler, J. 1993. *Bodies That Matter: On the discursive limits of sex*. New York: Routledge.

Clark, A. 2001. *Mindware: An introduction to the philosophy of cognitive science*. New York: Oxford University Press.

Crouch, D. 2010. Flirting with space: Thinking landscape relationally. *Cultural Geographies*, 17(1), 5–18.

Deleuze, G. 1998. *Bergsonism*. New York: Zone Books.

Edensor, T. 2010. Introduction: Thinking about rhythm and space, in *Geographies of Rhythm: Nature, place, mobilites and bodies*, edited by T. Edensor. Farnham, 1–20.

Franklin, A. and Crang, M. 2001. The trouble with tourism and travel theory? *Tourist Studies*, 1(1), 5–22.

Frawley, K. 1999. A 'green' vision: The evolution of Australian environmentalism, in *Cultural Geographies*, edited by K. Anderson and F. Gayle. South Melbourne: Addison Wesley, 265–93.

Gatens, M. 1996. *Imaginary Bodies: Ethics, power and corporeality*. New York: Routledge.

Grosz, E. 2005. *Time Travels: Feminism, nature, power*. Crows Nest: Allen & Unwin.

Gubrium, J. and Holstein, J. 2009. *Analysing Narrative Reality*. London: SAGE.

Head, L. and Muir, P. 2005. Living with trees – perspective from the suburbs, in *Proceedings of the 6th National Conference of the Australian Forest History Society*, edited by M. Calver, H. Bigler-Cole, G. Bolton, J. Dargavel, A. Gaynor, P. Horwitz, J. Mills and G. Wardell-Johnson. Rotterdam: Millpress, 84–95.

Horne, J. 2005. *The Pursuit of Wonder: How Australia's landscape was explored, nature discovered and tourism unleashed.* Victoria: Miegunyah Press.

Hudson, B.J. 2000. The experience of waterfalls. *Australian Geographical Studies,* 38(1), 71–84.

Ingold, T. 1999. 'Tools for the hand, language for the face': An appreciation of Leroi-Gourhan's gesture and speech. *Studies in History and Philosophy of Biological and Biomedical Sciences,* 30(4), 411–53.

Ingold, T. 2000. *The Perception of the Environment: Essays in livelihood, dwelling, and skill.* London: Routledge.

Johnston, L. 2001. (Other) bodies and tourism studies. *Annals of Tourism Research,* 28(1), 180–201.

Johnston, L. 2007. Mobilising pride/shame: lesbians, tourism and parades. *Social & Cultural Geography,* 8(1), 29–46.

Jordan, F. and Aitchison, C. 2008. The sexualization of the tourist gaze: Solo female tourists' experiences of gendered power, surveillance and embodiment, *Leisure Studies,* 27(4), 329–49.

Lorimer, H. and Lund, K. 2008. A collectable topography: Walking, remembering and recording mountains, in *Ways of Walking: Ethnography and practice on foot,* edited by T. Ingold and J. Lee. London: Ashgate, 185–200.

Menhennet, A. 1981. *The Romantic Movement.* London: Croom Helm.

Merleau-Ponty, M. [1945] 1962. *Phenomenology of Perception,* trans. C. Smith. New York: Routledge.

Metesula, C. and Waitt, G. 2012. *Tourism and Australian Beach Cultures.* Bristol: Channel View Publications.

Perera, S. 2009. *Australia and the Insular Imagination: Beaches, border, and boats.* New York: Palgrave Macmillan.

Pratt, M.L. 1992. *Imperial Eyes: Travel writing and transculturation.* New York: Routledge.

Probyn, E. 2003. The spatial imperative of Subjectivity, in *Handbook of Cultural Geography,* edited by K. Anderson, M. Domosh, S. Pile and N. Thrift. London: SAGE, 290–299.

Saldanha, A. 2002. Music tourism and factions of bodies in Goa. *Tourist Studies,* 2(1), 43–62.

Solnit, R. 2000. *Wanderlust: A history of walking.* New York: Viking.

Tester, K. (ed.) 1994. *The Flâneur.* London: Routledge.

Thrift, N. 2004. Summoning life, in *Envisioning Human Geographies,* edited by P. Cloke, P. Crang and M. Goodwin. London: Arnold, 81–103.

Towner, J. 1995. What is tourism's history? *Tourism Management,* 16(5), 339–43.

Urry, J. 1990. *The Tourist Gaze,* 1st edition. London: SAGE.

Urry, J. and Larsen, J. 2011. *The Tourist Gaze,* 3rd edition. London: SAGE.

Waitt, G. and Duffy, M. 2010. Listening and tourism studies. *Annals of Tourism Research,* 37(2), 457–77.

Waitt, G., Gil, N. and Head, L. 2009. Walking practice and suburban nature-talk. *Social & Cultural Geography,* 10(1), 41–60.

Wylie, J. 2006. Depths and folds: On landscape and the gazing subject. *Environment and Planning D: Society and Space*, 24(4), 519–35.
Wylie, J. 2007. *Landscape*. London and New York: Routledge.

Guidebooks

Hennessy, M.P. 1930. *The Picturesque Illawarra: The garden of New South Wales By train in daylight through the Beautiful Illawarra*. Circa 1930. Published by the Commissioner for Railways, New South Wales (no pagination).
The Illawarra Tourist Guide: Wollongong Citizens Association. Circa 1920s. Wollongong: Epworth Press.
Wilson's Rail, Road and Sea Guide to the South Coast and Southern Highlands, New South Wales. 1929. Sydney: Wilson's Publishing Company.

PART II
Tales of the Imagination

Chapter 5
The Imagination in the Travel Literature of Xavier de Maistre and its Philosophical Significance

Guy Bennett-Hunter

> I could be bounded in a nutshell, and count myself a king of infinite space.
> — *Hamlet*, II, ii

In this chapter, I present some philosophical reflections on the theme of the imagination. The main inspiration for these reflections comes from two writers, both of whom are mentioned in Alain de Botton's (2003) *The Art of Travel*: Joris-Karl Huysmans and Xavier de Maistre.[1] De Botton uses both of these writers in his book as 'guides', people whose work prompts his own ruminations, Huysmans in the first chapter and de Maistre in the last. Speculatively, I infer from this structure that de Botton has identified a similarity in the two writers' attitudes to the relationship between travel and the imagination such that he regards it as appropriate to begin with one and to end with the other. There is a sense, I think, in which the wheel is meant to come full circle in de Botton's book. Both Huysmans and de Maistre seem to be of the opinion that the nature of the imagination is such that it makes travel possible anywhere, notably and counter-intuitively in the place where travel typically both begins and ends: in the traveller's own home. As I shall shortly suggest in more detail, Huysmans and de Maistre seem to agree that travelling in the imagination alone is preferable in certain ways to the real thing. Whether or not I am right in my speculative attribution of this observation to de Botton, I want, in this chapter, to extend it. I want to suggest that, although Huysmans and de Maistre do indeed draw similar conclusions about travel, they do so for very different reasons. I argue that Huysmans and de Maistre have radically opposing views of the nature of the relationship between the world of the imagination and the real world and therefore of the relationship between travel and the imagination. Using this contrast as a point of departure, I examine the role of the imagination in de Maistre's travel literature and draw out its philosophical

---

1 Indeed, less famous than his brother Joseph, Xavier de Maistre's literary reputation has been given a recent boost by his mention in de Botton's book. This material has also been reprinted in the foreword to a new English translation of de Maistre's travel literature published by Hesperus Press.

significance, articulating some philosophical insights that de Maistre provides
about the nature of the imagination per se and its role in human life.

Huysmans *et* de Maistre: A Superficial Similarity

I start, then, with the superficial similarity between Huysmans and de Maistre.
Des Esseintes, the anti-hero of Huysmans's (2003) decadent masterpiece, *Against
Nature*, is an aesthete, a connoisseur of experience in all its forms. And this
reflects the fact that, in Huysmans's novel, we are presented with a person whose
imagination is especially sensitive to the impressions of his senses, in whatever
way these impressions are generated. During the course of experiments indulging
his sense of smell, des Esseintes savours perfumes, which artificially recreate
familiar fragrances. As he rubs a pellet of styrax between his fingers, for example,
his room is filled with 'an odour at once repugnant and delightful, blending the
delicious scent of the jonquil with the filthy stench of gutta-percha and coal tar'
(Huysmans 2003: 110). These sensory impressions stimulate his imagination to
the point where, 'as if by magic, the horizon was filled with factories, whose
fearsome chimneys belched fire and flame like so many bowls of punch. A breath
of industry, a whiff of chemical products now floated on the breeze he raised by
fanning the air' (Huysmans 2003: 110). Never one to settle for half measures, des
Esseintes indulges these olfactory indulgences to excess. Huysmans informs us
that he 'frantically scattered exotic perfumes around him, emptied his vaporizers,
quickened all his concentrated essences and gave free rein to all his balms' (2003:
111). This sensory overload affects des Esseintes physically but, as is more often
the case, it is his imagination that overcomes him. The mingled scents give him a
headache, 'as if a drill were boring into his temples', and make him feel faint as
he realizes that he will have to forego these pleasures for the sake of his physical
health (Huysmans 2003: 111, 114–15). He retreats to his study and opens the
window in order to recover from the effects of this cocktail of aromas in the fresh
air. But it is just as des Esseintes is beginning to relax that his imagination gets the
better of him:

> He threw the window wide open, delighted to take a bath of fresh air; but
> suddenly it struck him that the breeze was bringing with it a whiff of bergamot
> oil, mingled with a smell of jasmine, cassia and rose-water. He gave a gasp of
> horror, and began to wonder whether he might be in the grip of one of those evil
> spirits they used to exorcise in the Middle Ages. (Huysmans 2003: 115)

As these seemingly imaginary scents mingle, 'assailing his jaded nostrils', they
begin to unsettle him, 'throwing him into such a state of prostration that he fell
fainting, almost dying, across the window-sill' (Huysmans 2003: 115).

As this olfactory escapade shows, the key thing to note about the imagination
of des Esseintes is that it has a more potent effect on him than does reality. He is

sensitive to real sensory impressions only in so far as they are filtered through his imagination; and he is, in general, far more sensitive to purely imaginary sensations. This separation between the two worlds (the world of the imagination and the real world) is what drives des Esseintes's obsession with the counterfeit. In an earlier sequence of the novel, he tires of his incredible collection of fake plants and flowers and capriciously decides instead to take the reverse approach and build a collection of natural flowers that look like fakes (Huysmans 2003: 83). This project is only possible because his experience of the flowers is filtered through his imagination such that it appears to him 'as if cloth, paper, porcelain and metal had been lent by man to Nature to enable her to create these monstrosities' (Huysmans 2003: 87). Des Esseintes prefers the imaginative world, in which these plants 'seemed to have been cut out of oilskin or sticking-plaster; some all white like the Albane, which looked as if it had been fashioned out of the pleura of an ox or the diaphanous bladder of a pig' (Huysmans 2003: 84), to the real world in which these are simply unusual plants.

This division between the two worlds applies no less to des Esseintes's abortive attempt at travel, Huysmans's description of which compounds and reinforces that division. Des Esseintes's decision to set off on a long journey to London, his only attempt to venture outside his house, is made to contrast with his physically unenterprising, yet impressively imaginative, adventures with his perfume bottles. Inspired by his readings of Dickens and Poe, this expedition is described as an attempt to 'turn ... dream into reality ... travelling to England in the flesh as well as in the spirit', 'a longing to ... afford some relief to a mind ... drunk with fantasy' (Huysmans 2003: 118). But his attempt to execute and to realize the plan turns out simply to echo and repeat the old imaginary expeditions. During the time he spends en route to Paris and in taverns while waiting for his train, his imagination transfigures his French surroundings into English ones and transforms his fellow drinkers and diners into Londoners. His imagination allows him genuinely to feel that 'he could claim to be a naturalized citizen of London' (Huysmans 2003: 126). Reluctant to move from his seat in a tavern near the Gare Saint-Lazare, he is reported as having thought to himself: 'what was the good of moving, when a fellow could travel so magnificently sitting in a chair? Wasn't he already in London, whose smells, weather, citizens, food and even cutlery, were all about him? What could he find over there, save fresh disappointments ...?' (Huysmans 2003: 128). His final, considered attitude towards travel in the real world is expressed in a statement of preference instead for the world of the imagination, which, for him, is far more powerful:

> When you come to think of it, I've seen and felt all that I wanted to see and feel. I've been steeped in English life ever since I left home, and it would be madness to risk spoiling such unforgettable experiences by a clumsy change of locality. As it is, I must have been suffering from some mental aberration ... to have rejected the visions of my obedient imagination and to have believed like any ninny that it was necessary, interesting and useful to travel abroad. (Huysmans 2003: 129)

Having aborted his trip and returned to his home in Fontenay, des Esseintes is described by Huysmans as 'feeling all the physical weariness and moral fatigue of a man who has come home after a long and perilous journey' (Huysmans 2003: 129).

In relation to the specific practice of travel, then, the similarity between Huysmans's anti-hero and Xavier de Maistre might seem obvious. De Maistre's travel literature is a tongue-in-cheek account of his pioneering new mode of travel, known as 'room travel'.[2] Under house arrest for six weeks in 1790, de Maistre undertook a journey around his bedroom. He repeated the journey eight years later, this time travelling at night and venturing as far as the window ledge. Accounts of these journeys, which are collected in *A Journey around my Room*, constitute a daringly original departure from familiar travel literature, before and since de Maistre's time. As we read de Maistre extolling the advantages of room travel over its more conventional alternative, we might think we can detect echoes of Huysmans's (2003: 128) vivid portrait of a man who 'could travel so magnificently sitting in a chair'. De Maistre lists the many people for whom room travel will be a welcome invention: the poor, the sick, the cowardly (who will be safe from robbers and natural disasters) and the indolent. Envisaging thousands of people to whom room travel opens up for the first time the possibility of travel, de Maistre exhorts them all, in humorous paradox, to follow him: 'Let all the lazy arise en masse! ... [B]e so good as to accompany me on my journey ... yielding merrily to our imagination, we will follow it wherever it pleases to lead us' (de Maistre 2004: 4). Indeed, one of de Maistre's (2004: 14) first noteworthy encounters on his journey is with his armchair,

> in which I had leant back so that its two front legs were raised two inches above
> the ground; and by leaning to the right and the left, and thereby advancing
> slowly forward, I had imperceptibly come up to the wall. – This is the way I
> travel when I'm not in any hurry.

The superficial similarity between Huysmans's des Esseintes and de Maistre is that they both appear to view travel in the imagination as being superior or preferable to the real thing. But it becomes clear that they in fact have radically opposing views of the nature of the relationship between the world of the imagination and the practice of travel, carried on in the real world.

Opposing Views: The Relationship between the Two Worlds

Huysmans's protagonist, as we have seen, aborts his only attempt to venture outside his home on the grounds that he has already been to London in his imagination

---

2   With the term 'travel literature', I refer to his *A Journey around my Room* and
A Nocturnal Expedition around my Room, collected in de Maistre (2004).

while, in reality, he only got as far as Paris. To effect a 'clumsy change of locality', des Esseintes reflects, would simply 'spoil ... such unforgettable experiences' (Huysmans 2003: 129). For des Esseintes, his senses impress him in so far as they are filtered through his faculty of imagination. But he seems to be implicitly reasoning from the fact that the imagination is involved in any significant act of perception to the idea that it is sufficient unto itself. It is as though he reasons implicitly (and fallaciously) that, since imagination is a necessary condition for the kind of experiences which he values, it is therefore a sufficient condition; he seems to believe, in other words, that reality is dispensable. De Maistre, I suggest, shares des Esseintes's premise (that the imagination is involved in the kinds of acts of perception with which both are concerned) but does not draw the fallacious conclusion that it is therefore possible to dispense with reality. Whereas des Esseintes draws a sharp divide between the world of the imagination and the world of reality, de Maistre takes pains to blur the distinction, considering reality as fully accessible to him, in all its richness, only in so far as he imaginatively engages with it. Although he may appear to agree with des Esseintes that travel in an armchair is preferable to the conventional mode, this is not because he views room travel as being any different from the conventional mode of travel but, on the contrary, because he sees that, aside from differences in practical convenience, there is no difference in principle between these two modes. Whether the terrain is workaday or exotic, cramped or sprawling, it is the traveller's imagination which endows it with significance and which thereby connects and binds the traveller with the regions traversed. That de Maistre is travelling in relative confinement, and in a relatively familiar environment, simply serves more strongly to emphasize his premise: that the essence of travel, the point of engaging in it, is the imaginative state of mind which it cultivates in the traveller, binding him or her to the terrain. And, if this is so, there is no good reason why travel may not be valuably engaged in within the confines of a single, familiar room, however idiosyncratic such an expedition might at first sound and however ironically the description of such a journey might at first be read.

In the remainder of this chapter, I want to illustrate how this conception of the role of the imagination, as de Maistre conceives it, comes across in his travel literature and point out its more generally philosophical significance.

The Imagination in de Maistre's Travel Literature

It is clear that de Maistre regards his journey as an effort of the imagination. He compares it to that of Milton's Satan traversing Chaos in *Paradise Lost*, describing that ambitious expedition as 'one of the great efforts of the imagination, and one of the finest journeys ever undertaken, – next to the journey around my room' (de Maistre 2004: 54). When released from his 42-day confinement to his room, he composes a kind of ode to the '[e]nchanting land of the imagination' which he now has to leave, describing his newly rediscovered freedom in negative terms as a feeling of being 'shackled in chains once more!' (de Maistre 2004: 66). As de Maistre comes to realize, 'real' freedom is slavery compared to the imaginative freedom he has experienced during the course of his journey.

The imaginative nature of de Maistre's journey is partly determined by his openness, like that of any conventional traveller, to new and unplanned experiences. As a result of this imaginative attitude, de Maistre can have the same spontaneous experiences, in the same unusually greater number, that make all travel worthwhile. During the practice of travel the imagination is what binds us to those parts of the world whose unfamiliarity makes for a new intensity of experience. And this is no less true of de Maistre's humble journey. The fact that he is travelling in the confined and familiar space of his room does not necessarily entail that his journey will be any shorter than it would otherwise be, nor that it will yield experiences that are more boringly predictable than those yielded by a conventional journey. For he is clear that the imagination can be employed even here. As he writes of his cramped terrain, 'I will be crossing it frequently lengthwise, or else diagonally, without any rule or method. I will even follow a zigzag path, and I will trace out every possible geometrical trajectory if need be' (de Maistre 2004: 7). The import of this imaginative effort is that a very large number of possible experiences are available even in familiar environments. And, if the travel is imaginatively engaged in, this large number of possible experiences will be available even in the most familiar and confined of environments. This imaginative sense of near-infinite possibility seems to come to de Maistre, in the context of one specific experience, early on in his journey:

> the first rays of sun come to disport themselves on my bed curtains. I can see
> them, on fine summer days ... the elm tree outside my window breaks up these
> rays in a thousand different ways ... then, a thousand cheerful ideas fill my
> mind. (de Maistre 2004: 8)

The imagination is most often applied by de Maistre to elucidate the meanings of the objects he experiences in his environment. Engaging with these specific objects, he explores their associations, which lead him to thoughts concerning their more universal human significance. One example is his bed; he asks, 'Is there any theatre which arouses the imagination more, or awakens more tender ideas, than this piece of furniture in which I sometimes lose myself?' (de Maistre 2004: 8). De Maistre imaginatively moves from the specific and personal significance of his own bed (which, he even tells us, is pink and white) to the specific role it plays in the lives of others, like his own:

> Isn't it in a bed that a mother, overwhelmed with euphoria at the birth of her son,
> forgets the pains she has suffered? It is here that fantastic pleasures, the fruit of
> the imagination and hope, come to arouse us. Finally, it is here, in our delightful
> beds, that we can forget, for one half of our life, the sorrows of the other half.
> (de Maistre 2004: 8)

This line of thought then leads into further reflections of more abstract and universal scope on the significance of 'The Bed' to human life and death in general and as a whole:

> A bed witnesses our birth and our death; it is the unvarying theatre in which the human race acts out, successively, its captivating dramas, laughable farces, and dreadful tragedies. It is a cradle bedecked with flowers; it is the throne of love; it is a sepulchre. (de Maistre 2004: 8)

De Maistre's imaginative engagement with the objects that surround him also, perhaps appropriately, extends to those pre-eminent bearers of significance, works of art. He engages in a similar way with an engraving on his wall, inspired by Goethe's *The Sorrows of Young Werther*, which shows Charlotte wiping Albert's pistols. Not only is de Maistre drawn, by his meditations, into the imaginative world of the engraving so that it becomes, for him, a reality, but he also draws a universal significance from the scene:

> How many times have I not been tempted to break the glass over this engraving, to pull that Albert away from his table, tear him limb from limb, and trample him underfoot! But there will always be too many Alberts in this world. (de Maistre 2004: 28)

The role of the imagination at this point on de Maistre's journey, as his account presents it, is to transport him. It makes present to him things that are otherwise inaccessible to direct experience, in this case the characters in Goethe's fictional story, their predicaments and their lives. On his Nocturnal Expedition, too, his imagination transports him as he looks at the starry sky from his window: 'I make my imagination travel as far beyond their sphere as my gaze travels to reach them from here', he writes, 'I am effortlessly conveyed to a distance which few travellers before me have reached' (de Maistre 2004: 94). But de Maistre is, of course, still in his room and it is his imagination that has allowed him to achieve the effect of travelling impossibly vast distances. Despite the contrast I suggested earlier between des Esseintes and de Maistre, the latter appears too, at times, to separate this imaginary world from the real world: 'I find ... in this imaginary world, the virtue, the goodness, the disinterest that I have never yet found combined in the real world in which I live' (de Maistre 2004: 51).

The Philosophical Significance of the Imagination in de Maistre's Travel Literature

I suggest, however, that, aside from its relatively limited tendency to transport him to purely imaginary realms, the imagination has a far more important role in de Maistre's travel literature and one that is of greater interest from a philosophical point of view. The imagination does not just transport de Maistre from the confines of his room but this transportation also serves to remind him of the near-infinite possibility open to him and the real reason why he is undertaking his journey at all: namely, his firm belief that the true benefits of travel are available, regardless of the size or familiarity of the regions traversed and visited. The imagination also, and importantly, is what transfigures the tiny corner of de Maistre's world to which he is confined during the course of his journey. Through the imagination, he is able to view his room, which he once took for granted, with fresh eyes; it is transfigured from a humdrum, workaday space into a wonderful world. His imagination binds him to his familiar corner of the world with a renewed intensity.

As he brings his imagination to bear on the objects he encounters on his journey, the memories and associations connected with them come to mind. As he looks at letters he has received from friends who have since died, he resurrects their authors in his imagination and the letters themselves assume a poignancy that they previously lacked:

> What an intense, melancholy pleasure it feels when my eyes run over the lines traced by someone who is no longer alive. Here is his handwriting, it was his heart that guided his hand, and this letter is all I have left of him! (de Maistre 2004: 47)

As he contemplates, too, the beautiful view from his room, he becomes aware that he has become habituated to it and has stopped truly experiencing it in the fullest, richest sense. As he writes, 'even the most beautiful vista soon wearies you when you see it too often; your eye gets used to it, and you don't appreciate it any more' (de Maistre 2004: 81). As de Botton (2003: 251) points out, de Maistre's aim is to use his imagination to reverse the process by which he has become habituated to his familiar surroundings. And it is this imaginative process, reversing the process of habituation, that intuitively seems to be the point of all travel. If we go to a place to which we are not habituated, then we will be bound to the world more strongly and with a new intensity. But, in de Botton's (2003: 246) view, the spring of de Maistre's work consists in 'a profound and suggestive insight that the pleasure we derive from journeys is perhaps dependent more on the mindset with which we travel than on the destination we travel to'. In fact, de Maistre's travel literature shows that it is not necessary to go anywhere at all, except around one's room. With the appropriate imaginative mindset, it is perfectly possible to look at the mundane and familiar with new eyes. It is possible, in other words, for the imagination to transfigure the everyday world. As de Botton (2003: 251) puts it, alluding to his own attempt to follow de Maistre's example, discovering the regions of his own home city afresh, our practical 'grid of interests' reduces the space we inhabit to its function. In de Botton's (2003: 250) case, a London bus becomes 'a box to move us as rapidly as possible across an area which might as well not exist, so unconnected is it to our primary goal'. De Botton explains the motivation for both de Maistre's restricted journey and his own imitative attempt as being the same as that of Alexander von Humboldt for conventional travel: 'I was spurred on by an uncertain longing to be transported from a boring daily life to a marvellous world' (von Humboldt, cited in de Botton 2003: 253).

The nature of this transfiguration of the world, which, in de Maistre's travel literature, is effected by the imagination, can be illuminated by consideration of Heidegger's remarks on the nature of art, which, for him, among other things, effects a comparable transfiguration. In his famous essay, 'On the origin of the work of art', Heidegger draws a distinction between objects in which the material from which they are made is 'used up' and those, in the case of art, in which the nature of the material, essential to the object's significance, is 'used'. A piece of equipment, like a hammer, disappears behind its usefulness; the grain of the wood is not essential to the hammer's function, so it is ignored. But in the work of art, the nature of the material is not similarly incidental but rather essential to the experience of the work itself. For example, the colour of a stroke of paint in a work of art shines forth in the work but, Heidegger (1978: 172) tells us, when 'we analyze it in rational terms by measuring its wavelengths, it is gone'. Utility (what de Botton calls our 'grid of interests') reduces the work to its component parts, preventing us from truly experiencing it and acknowledging significant details. Whereas the mason 'uses up' stone, the sculptor does not, except when his work 'miscarries' (Heidegger 1978: 173). The painter, too, does not 'use up' paint or pigment but 'uses' it, such that 'colour ... rather only now comes to shine forth' (Heidegger 1978: 173). Art, for Heidegger, concerns the interplay of 'world' and 'earth': 'world' meaning the familiar and revealed while 'earth' represents the opaque and unexplained ground on which the world is founded: the humble materials from which it is constructed, for example. In the work of art, in Heidegger's (1978: 174) language, 'earth juts through the world'; the world is transfigured by the imagination and made transparent to its mysterious ground and source, which is unusually and fleetingly brought to light. In my view, de Maistre has intuited the philosophical point made much later by Heidegger: that our everyday, ordinary or practical, as opposed to our artist's or traveller's, view on things reduces those things to mere function, occluding a richer and more interesting way of looking at the same things. As de Maistre (2004: 92) puts it, in relation to the view of the starry heavens from the window in the roof of his room:

> If the firmament were always veiled to us, if the spectacle it offers us depended on some entrepreneur, the best boxes in the rooftop theatre would be quite unaffordable, and the ladies of Turin would be fighting over my skylight.

For de Maistre, it is not necessary (indeed, for him, it is not possible) to go to foreign climes, parts of the world that are ordinarily 'veiled' to him, but to apply his imagination to the familiar confined space in which he lives. As with art, though (and de Maistre's corpus of travel literature surely qualifies as such), the point is made by Heidegger (*contra* des Esseintes) that we do not have to choose between the world of the imagination and the world of reality; the dichotomy is a false one.

De Maistre, too, is trying to show us that the 'two worlds', alternately and listlessly inhabited by Huysmans's anti-hero, are not mutually exclusive. For example, de Maistre imagines a portion of his journey conducted on horseback when, in the world of reality (as he readily admits), 'I'm sitting astraddle my window' (de Maistre 2004: 123). This somewhat absurd observation does not prevent him from justifying his use of a cushion for comfort (after a brief reluctance to do so) in terms of the system of equestrian etiquette operative in the real world, describing it as:

> something I would never had [sic] dared to do a few days before, for fear of being jeered at by the cavalry; but since, the day before, I had at the gates of Turin met a band of Cossacks who had arrived on similar cushions from the borders of the Palus Maeotis and the Caspian Sea, I decided that I could, without infringing the laws of horsemanship – for which I have the greatest respect – adopt the same custom. (de Maistre 2004: 120)

De Maistre's rejection of the Huysmansian division between imagination and reality means that his imagination not only, or primarily, transports him far beyond the walls of his dwelling, it also binds him to that terrain with all the intensity of the explorer's perilous expedition. Whereas travel, for des Esseintes, is rendered pointless by the division between imagination and reality, de Maistre's refusal to entertain that division makes real travel not only worthwhile but also possible without leaving his room – and in a way that it is not for des Esseintes. As he travels around that room, looking upon it and its contents with fresh eyes, de Maistre's imagination transfigures it into a marvellous world.

Imagination *versus* Reason: Transcending the Dichotomy

In this section, I want to make some further remarks on the philosophical significance of this transfiguration and refer to the contrast between the imagination and the rational mindset more familiar to philosophers. De Maistre's (2004: 95) humorously perfunctory attempt at a metaphysics, Chapter 16 of his *Nocturnal Expedition*, is worth quoting in full:

The System of the World

> I believe, then, that as space is finite, creation is also finite, and that God has created in his eternity an infinity of worlds in the immensity of space.

The first point to note about de Maistre's 'System' is that it is apparently self-contradictory: space is finite, yet somehow able to contain an infinity of worlds. Doesn't Hamlet's line, which forms the epigraph to this chapter, seem more appropriate with its reference to the kingdom of *infinite* space? I want to suggest that the tension can be attenuated by taking account of the main theme I have been drawing out: de Maistre's resistance to a separation between the imagination and reality. Once this dichotomy is rejected, I think, it is possible to make sense of his view that, while space is finite, it contains an infinity of worlds. It can be argued, in my view, that although the physical world is finite, the imagination is able to transfigure it into a place of increased possibility. The number of these possibilities, if not strictly infinite, is large enough to be described as 'near-infinite'; like Borges's (2000: 81) library, de Maistre's imaginative world is infinite for practical, if not for mathematical, purposes.

To see this more clearly, it may help to consider some remarks on perception and its objects made by the phenomenologist, Maurice Merleau-Ponty, which make clear the way in which the world of perception posits an infinity of possible perspectives on the objects which make it up. Merleau-Ponty begins by observing that objects are typically seen from different angles and appear to us from one or from a series of such angles. Referring to Leibniz, he makes the point that the object itself is not apprehended in any one of these appearances but seems rather to be graspable only in 'the geometrized projection of ... all possible perspectives, that is, the perspectiveless position from which all can be derived ... seen from nowhere' (Merleau-Ponty 1962: 77). Of course, all seeing is seeing from somewhere, seeing from a certain perspective. But, as Merleau-Ponty (1962: 79) illustrates, I attribute to a lamp not just the qualities visible from my own perspective 'but also those which the chimney, the walls, the table can "see"; but back [*sic*] of my lamp is nothing but the face which it "shows" to the chimney'. Thus modifying his opening Leibnizian intuition that the object in itself, in so far as such exists, is the object seen from nowhere, Merleau-Ponty (1962: 29) now suggests, on the contrary, that it is the object seen from everywhere: 'the completed object is translucent, being shot through from all sides by an infinite number of present scrutinies which intersect in its depths leaving nothing hidden'. This synthesis of perspectival horizons is, according to Merleau-Ponty (1962: 80), 'presumptive'. Even if I were to take my own perception of the object and add to it in my imagination the largest possible number of other perspectives, I would still only have 'a harmonious and indefinite set of views of the object, but not the object in its plenitude' (Merleau-Ponty 1962: 80). According to Merleau-Ponty's line of thought, objects themselves turn out to be imaginary as their 'substantiality' slips away:

> [I]f there is to be an absolute object, it will have to consist in an infinite number of
> different perspectives compressed into a strict co-existence, and to be presented
> as it were to a host of eyes all engaged in one concerted act of seeing. (Merleau-
> Ponty 1962: 81)

I suggest that de Maistre's insistence on jettisoning the division between the world of the imagination and the real world shows that he has intuited in advance the import of Merleau-Ponty's argument, advanced centuries later. Our 'presumptive' positing of a world of real objects is dependent on an imaginative synthesis of infinite spatial (and also temporal) horizons, as Merleau-Ponty sketches, while our everyday perspective is constituted by only a limited number of such possible horizons. De Maistre seems to be making the same point when he sets out his *System of the World*: his imaginative journey causes him to adopt different and unusual perspectives on the objects he encounters so that he becomes aware that his ordinary, everyday perspective consists in a limited number among an infinity of such perspectives. It is his recognition of this fact, and his imaginative realization of some especially striking alternative perspectives, that transfigures de Maistre's world; this imaginative process turns his familiar region of space from a small part of finite space, into 'an infinity of worlds'. And it is owing to his imaginative engagement with the terrain across which he travels that, as he states, 'I am bound by bonds of affection to everything that surrounds me' (de Maistre 2004: 109).

Conclusion: Imagination as a Distinctively Human Capacity

De Maistre's advocation of a self-consciously imaginative bond between himself (the subject) and his room (the world) is in tension with a purely rational perspective. His 'System of the World' is self-contradictory, given the assumption that the world of the imagination is totally distinct from the real world. But Merleau-Ponty's argument can be used to bolster de Maistre's rejection of the dichotomy with its counter-intuitive conclusion that our routine and taken-for-granted positing of a real world of objects, distinct from the imaginative world, goes beyond the limits of the evidence of actual experience and therefore has, at best, limited warrant (Merleau-Ponty 1962: 81). Just because the refusal of the dichotomy goes against some of our deepest assumptions, Merleau-Ponty intimates, it does not follow that it is therefore irrational, if the rational is understood as being intimately connected with the evidence accessible to direct experience in the world of perception. De Maistre distinguishes between the 'soul' and the 'beast'; between the imaginative, emotional side of human nature and the mechanical, rational side. As he looks at the night sky from his window with the fresh perspective cultivated by his journey, he imagines being king and passing a law that requires everyone to spend some time contemplating the night sky once every evening. De Maistre (2004: 92) presents a humorous dialogue between his soul, personified as the king, and Reason (who 'in my kingdom has only a limited right of remonstrance'), personified as a humble courtier who points out all the rational flaws and practical problems involved in realizing such a scheme. But, I suggest, Merleau-Ponty demonstrates that a de Maistrean line of thought should not advocate the flagrant contradiction of Reason but only the limiting of her 'right of remonstrance' in the face of the imagination.

De Maistre's journey is imaginative rather than rational and, despite its significant philosophical interest, it is, as such, more closely connected with the emotions than it is with philosophical argument. De Maistre's own emotions appear to be more responsive to his imagination than is the rational side of his nature. And I venture that we readers of de Maistre's travel literature may find that his texts speak to our own emotions rather than our rational capacity to engage with and to analyse arguments. De Maistre's conviction that his dead friend, whose letter he encounters on his travels, is not dead forever does not have its origin in a syllogism but rather in an emotional orientation towards the world, which is especially responsive to his imagination. But the imagination yields negative as well as positive emotions. As de Maistre contemplates an engraving of a shepherdess on his wall, he regards it as a peaceful and idyllic scene and he wishes that he could inhabit the world of the engraving and live there with her. But the tranquillity evaporates as his imagination turns to the 'demon of war' which he sees invading even this sanctuary, concluding that 'there is no rest on this melancholy earth' (de Maistre 2004: 33).

De Maistre's association of the imagination with the emotional, rather than the rational, aspect of human nature leads him to reverse, and therefore to counterbalance, the traditional, Aristotelian philosophical picture that our capacity to reason is what makes us distinctively human. What makes us distinctively human, for de Maistre, is our capacity to imagine. For, as I hope I have shown, it is the imagination that, on de Maistre's journeys around his room, binds him to his world with that new intensity which the imagination alone can furnish. De Maistre's insight, often neglected, that the imagination, as much as reason, is a central faculty which makes us distinctively human, is made most keenly apparent to him when he begins to experience the loss of that faculty. This has the alienating effect of divorcing him from the imaginative world and giving what is, for him, the false impression that that world is entirely separate from the world of reality. The words in which he describes that experience, which may serve as a warning to us fellow travellers, are appropriate ones with which to end:

> I was all at once deprived of imagination and enthusiasm, and delivered over to melancholy reality, without any right of appeal. Lamentable existence! One might as well be a dry tree in a forest, or an obelisk in the middle of a city square! (de Maistre 2004: 112)

References

Borges, J.L. 2000. The library of Babel, trans. J.E. Irby, in *Labyrinths: Selected stories and other writings*, edited by D.A. Yates and J.E. Irby. London: Penguin, 78–86.

de Botton, A. 2003. *The Art of Travel*. London: Penguin.

de Maistre, X. 2004. *A Journey around my room*, trans. A. Brown. London: Hesperus Classics.

Heidegger, M. 1978. The origin of the work of art, in *Basic Writings*, edited by D.F. Krell. London: Routledge, 143–206.

Huysmans, J.-K. 2003. *Against Nature (A Rebours)*, trans. R. Baldick. London: Penguin.

Merleau-Ponty, M. 1962. *Phenomenology of Perception*, trans. C. Smith. London: Routledge.

Shakespeare, W. 2005. *Hamlet*, edited by A. Thompson and N. Taylor. London: The Arden Shakespeare.

Chapter 6
The Prominence of the Railroad in the African American Imagination: Mobile Men, Gendered Mobility and the Poetry of Sterling A. Brown

Michael Ra-shon Hall

Introduction

The railroad, train and Pullman porter are prevalent figures in African American literature, film and music. Examples are numerous: the collage art of Romare Bearden in the graphic arts and the 1933 Hollywood film *Emperor Jones* starring Paul Robeson as a porter, the autobiographical writings of Zora Neale Hurston, both anthropologist and literary artist, and poet and columnist Langston Hughes. In this chapter on travel and imagination I examine how railroad imagery, mobile men and gendered mobility figure in the poetry of scholar and literary artist and critic Sterling A. Brown (1901–89) as a reflection of African Americans' cultural historical experiences of racial and gendered paradigmatic restrictions on modern mobility. By gendered mobility, I refer to a modern paradigm – dominant in the United States at least from the close of the Civil War in 1865 until the Second World War – in which men were not only far more mobile than women, but the very mobility of men was predicated on the domesticity of women. Brown's poetry dynamically and critically refracts this moment in African American cultural history, particularly because mobile men and African American vernacular culture influenced much of Brown's literary art.

The poems I treat include 'Long Gone' and 'Sister Lou' from Brown's first and most successful volume of poetry *Southern Road* (1932) and 'The Law for George' from Brown's rejected second volume of poetry *No Hiding Place* (1980) written in the years following the publication of *Southern Road*, but not published until 1980 (see Brown (1980) for these poems). Exploring images of mobile railroad men in Brown's poetry, specifically, and African American cultural history, arts and letters more broadly, I consider the experiences of porters as gleaned through the cultural history of the Brotherhood of Sleeping Car Porters and Maids (BSCP). The BSCP, founded in 1925 by A. Phillip Randolph, was the first successful black labor union in US history (Bates 2001).

I begin with a brief overview of the railroad, train and porter in African American cultural history, arts and letters. Then I explain the significance of the porter as a heroic figure in African American cultural history and imagination, noting the historical shadow masking women's experience of the railroad. Finally, I foreground the importance of the railroad and mobile men like the porter in the poetry of Brown and analyse the cultural history refracted in Brown's literary art, specifically addressing the racial and gendered paradigmatic restrictions on mobility reproduced in his vernacular-inflected musings. I conclude this chapter with a reflection on the continued influence of the train and railroad in African American artistic expression up until the present.

The Railroad in the African American Imagination: Literature, Visual Art and Music

Railroad imagery is prevalent in African American literature, visual art, film and music. The train features prominently in literary works by Faith Ringgold, Nikki Giovanni, James Baldwin, Richard Wright, Toni Morrison, Claude McKay, Ralph Ellison, Zora Neale Hurston, August Wilson and others, 'in which the train, train history, and legendary train figures such as Harriet Tubman or John Henry serve as literary symbols' (Zabel 2001: 4). Similarly, Hurston's autobiography *Dust Tracks on a Road* includes a blues-inspired folk song about the southern railroad which she encountered during her ethnographic travels in the US South ([1942] 1996: 149–50), and Hughes' autobiography *The Big Sea* includes a blues-inspired poem about the railroad which the poet wrote while in Washington, DC, circa 1924–25 (1963: 209).

Further, the train and railroad feature heavily in African American visual art with such examples as the collage art of Romare Bearden, most notably 'The Train' (1975) which references the cultural historical experience of the Underground Railroad. The Underground Railroad was a network of secret routes and safe houses, most associated with American Civil War hero Harriet Tubman, which guided many nineteenth-century enslaved persons out of the US South to the 'free' US North. A more recent example is the contemporary mixed media pieces of Radcliff Bailey with such examples as 'Self-portrait' (2005) and 'Untitled' (2011) from Bailey's 2011 solo exhibition *Memory as Medicine*. In both 'Self-portrait' and 'Untitled' Bailey uses railroad tracks to signify the railroad and train as symbols of freedom and continuity in African American cultural history and imagination.

Finally, railroad imagery is a definitive characteristic of early modern African American music with the train symbolizing 'escape, freedom, hope, loneliness, the tension between traditional and modern life, severed relationships, and wanderlust' (Kornweibel 2010: 271). As Theodore Kornweibel notes, 'Railroads generated new forms of culture, like track-lining and train-calling chants, while reshaping others, including work and protest songs and the blues' along with big band swing, jazz, rock 'n' roll and the spirituals (Kornweibel 2010: 271–2). Examples are numerous from spirituals inaugurated by enslaved persons like 'Low [Swing] Down the Chariot and Let me Ride' and 'The Gospel Train', to later transformations in the blues tradition like 'Freight Train Blues' recorded by Trixie Smith in the 1920s and Walter 'Buddy Boy' Hawkin's 'Woking on the Railroad' (Kornweibel 2010: 272–86).

African American artists have employed the railroad and train in literature, visual art and music more broadly as signifiers of freedom. Indeed, as vessels of modern mobility and embodiments of freedom for many African Americans living in the period 1915–70 and desiring to escape a US South characterized by white racial intimidation and violence, trains and railroads served as the very antithesis to the ownership, confinement to land and shackles to place that defined the experience of enslavement in the antebellum US South. These conceptions of freedom, however, are complicated by historical experiences of confinement including enslavement, Jim Crow segregation and racial discrimination and gendered restrictions on women's mobility. The struggle by porters for better conditions in their employment represents a striking example of the paradox of freedom and confinement in the experiences of African Americans. Further, the porter as a historical figure provides a bridge between the hospitality of antebellum southern plantation life and the service work to which African Americans were confined long after emancipation (Perata 1996: XIX). Because historical experiences of mobile railroad men, coupled with railroad imagery and vernacular expression, provide inspiration for many of Brown's poems, an understanding of porters' experiences and porters' significance in the African American (and broader American) imagination is useful to an examination of Brown's work.

The Pullman Porter in US Cultural History: The Porter in the American Imagination and a History of Struggle against Paradigmatic Restrictions on African American Mobility

George Pullman founded the Pullman Palace Car Company (PPCC) in the 1860s, employing former enslaved African American men (Santino 1989: 6) beginning in the 1870s and perpetuating 'the link between African Americans and slaves' (Bates 2001: 5) as a selling point. By the 1920s, the PPCC was 'the largest employer of black labor in the country' (Santino 1989: 8). Due to the PPCC's advertising and bit part roles for African American men in Hollywood films of the 1920s and 1930s, the porter became a staple of the mainstream American imagination from the late 1860s to 1940s. Through advertising and film, the porter became identified as a relatively jovial African American man readily available for service and always with a smile (Santino 1989: 1). Indeed, the porter became the living symbol most associated with the PPCC and, as Jack Santino indicates, '[t]o whites the porter represented service and luxury; to blacks, he represented status and mobility, both physical and social' (Santino 1989: 8).

**Figure 6.1 Interior view of Pullman car with porters waiting to serve
            passengers, 1920 or before**
Source: Robert Langmuir African American Photograph Collection, MARBL, Emory
University.

The solidarity demonstrated by porters can be attributed in part to the cultural
homogeneity of the group as a class of workers, a homogeneity centred on a shared
mobility and mobility-based identity. Though sharing a mobility-based identity
around which they organized to gain and protect civil rights, porters were confined
to servitude within the space of the Pullman car (a restricted mobility at least) as a
condition of their mobility as modern travellers/workers.

In many ways, the conditions under which porters, and other African Americans,
were mobile reveals the status of modern African American travellers often as a
dual, conflicting and paradoxical position of mobility and restriction, freedom and
confinement. Though African American men in particular enjoyed the physical
and economic mobility afforded by railroad company service jobs, struggles
against the Jim Crow segregation practices of many railroad companies reminded
African American men and women of societal restrictions they endured many
decades removed from enslavement. Sometimes reminders of the limits imposed
on African American mobility precipitated violent conflict. In one notable instance
in 1884, a train conductor and two other white men forcefully removed journalist,
sociologist, suffragist and newspaper editor Ida B. Wells from the ladies' coach
after Wells not only refused the conductor's order to enter the smoking car but
also 'sunk her teeth into the back of his hand' when the conductor first attempted

to eject her from the ladies' car (Kornweibel 2010: 240). The unique predicament of modern African American travellers, a veritable 'confinement in freedom', is one against which porters organized in order to move beyond a mobility attendant with restriction, a freedom saddled with discriminatory limits.

On 25 August, 1937, after several years of organizing, protest and negotiation, the PPCC finally acquiesced to the demands of the Brotherhood, signing a contract including a substantial 'reduction in the work month from 400 to 240 hours and an annual wage package that increased porters' salaries by a total of $1.25 million' (Bates 2001: 126). With the contract's signing, the Brotherhood became the first black labour union to sign a labour agreement with a major American corporation (Bates 2001: 126–7). Due to porters' success in early campaigns against segregated spaces and for civil rights, they garnered a heroic position in the minds of many African Americans. As such, porters provided inspiration for creative works by artists like Brown for whom mobile men and train travel offered a means through which to creatively explore paradigmatic restrictions on modern mobility.

Men and Trains in the Literary Imagination: Race, Gender and Paradigmatic Restrictions on Afro-modern Mobility in Brown's Poetry

Literature, film, music, visual art and scholarship have contributed much to understanding African American men's experience of US railroads, as well as attending to men's visibility in the many representations of railroads. However, little attention has been given to African American women who are largely absent from cultural histories and representations of the railroad experience, except as implied bodies in the broader cultural history signified by the prevalence of the train and railroad in visual art and media. Brown's poetry provides a literary lens through which to examine the role of gender and mobility to the absence of women in the cultural history of the American railroad. Moreover, because mobile men and vernacular expression inspired Brown's poetry, with verses often rendered in the folk idiom, his literary art reflects aspects of the paradigmatic restrictions on mobility which characterized the cultural history of African American travel between 1865 and the 1940s.

Travel and mobility are central to Brown's poetry, particularly his first collection *Southern Road* (1932). Not only does Brown replicate a gendered paradigm of mobility in this volume, but he also meditates on the significance of the railroad to the modern experience, particularly of African American men who frequently worked as porters on trains or as stevedores, shipmates, redcaps and chauffeurs. It is in part a result of the job opportunities afforded men in transportation service that a gendered paradigm of mobility becomes so pervasive. Such jobs were not initially available to African American women, many of whom worked as domestics in their own homes and in the homes of white families, in addition to work as nurses, teachers and in the garment industry.

Poems of particular interest in *Southern Road* (Brown 1932) include 'Long Gone', in which the speaker describes his love of mobility and of the train, and 'Sister Lou', in which Brown offers a transcendent portrayal of a woman's mobility by train. The themes of travel and mobility prominent in *Southern Road* continue in *No Hiding Place* (Brown 1980). In this volume, Brown offers a precarious image of black men's mobility (mobile women are all but absent from Brown's oeuvre) in 'The Law for George'. Taken together, these poems not only offer diverse perspectives on conditions of modern mobility, but specifically refract paradigmatic restrictions on women's (as well as men's) mobility.

The railroad and train are recurrent in Brown's poetry. In both 'Long Gone' and 'Sister Lou' the image of the train is quite overt as Brown depicts it. 'Long Gone', though not explicitly about a porter, presents the voice of a mobile, self-proclaimed 'railroad man' addressing his stationary lover and explaining to her the reasons why he must at times privilege his mobility over her companionship:

> I laks yo' kin' of lovin',
>   Ain't never caught you wrong,
> But it jes' ain' nachal
>   Fo' to stay here long
>
> It jes' ain' nachal
>   Fo' a railroad man,
> With a itch fo' travelin'
>   He cain't understan' ...
>
> I looks at de rails,
>   An' I looks at de ties,
> An' I hears an ole freight
>   Puffin' up de rise,
> (Brown 1980: 22)

In 'Long Gone' the male speaker of the poem expresses to his lover an anxious desire to travel and not remain static. He associates the impulse for mobility with the railroad and train and naturalizes his desire for travel, 'asserting the foreignness of stasis and domesticity [to him]' (Sanders 1999: 49) almost as a masculine claim to mobility. Here, as in the early literary works of Hurston, most notably the novel *Jonah's Gourd Vine* ([1934] 1990), gendered paradigmatic restrictions surface to complicate the train image as an image of freedom and continuity in the African American imagination. The train appears here, much as it does in *Jonah's Gourd Vine*, as a masculine image intimately tied to men's mobility and modern self fashioning. The speaker acknowledges that his naturalization is without a rational foundation; yet, he consigns his lover to stasis as the anchor and embodiment of home:

An' I knows de time's a-nearin'
  When I got to ride,
Though it's homelike and happy
  At yo' side.

You is done all you could do
  To make me stay;
'Tain't no fault of yours I'se leavin –
  I'se jes dataway.

I is got to see some people
  I ain't never seen,
Gotta highball thu some country
  Whah I never been.
(Brown 1980: 22)

**Figure 6.2 Pullman porter standing on rear platform of train car preparing
for departure, August 1896**

Source: Robert Langmuir African American Photograph Collection, MARBL, Emory
University.

Depicting his relationship to mobility as an undeniable, natural impulse superseding reason or compromise, the speaker explains his need to answer the call to travel without fail and leaves little room for negotiation or discussion with his lover. In many ways the speaker's attitude and pose towards his lover suggests she simply accept the terms he has outlined. There is no alternative. The train is calling, and he must ride. The poem concludes with a return to a naturalized, masculine claim to mobility, reiterating the theme established in the beginning stanzas of the poem:

> I don't know which way I'm travelin' –
>   Far or near,
> All I knows fo' certain is
>   I cain't stay here.
>
> Ain't no call at all, sweet woman,
>   Fo' to carry on –
> Jes' my name and jes' my habit
>   To be Long Gone ...
> (Brown 1980: 23)

Offering no information about his travel destinations or length of time away, the speaker reiterates a naturalized claim to mobility divorced from any consideration of his lover's desires, perhaps even for her own experiences of mobility. Indeed, he concludes his address by noting it is simply his 'habit/ To be Long Gone'.

In 'The Law for George', a poem explicitly referencing the name white passengers often called porters, Brown employs a third-person limited perspective to address a spectrum of African American male service workers. At its heart, 'The Law for George' is a warning to African American male service workers, especially those working in transportation service, about the dangers of socializing with white women outside of uniforms designating professional servitude. The third person speaker of the poem addresses five types of service workers, a porter, cook, redcap, houseman and chauffer, offering similar advice to all. Three of the five service workers are transportation workers, a feature which not only reflects the service work African Americans performed to allow modern travellers the luxury of service in transportation, but also reveals how African Americans were often limited to positions of service in their own early modern experiences of mobility, transportation and travel. As such, Brown's poem captures quite concretely important dimensions of early African American modern travel and transportation. In particular, the poem reflects the restrictions, limits and confinement paradoxically endured by African Americans despite the function vessels of transportation like the train performed as signs of freedom and continuity for African Americans. Put another way, travel insinuates itself in Brown's poems underscoring travel as a problem of mobility in African American travel and imagination. The speaker advises the porter first:

Take her tray
Into her Pullman compartment
She may be in morning all–shabby
Take her gin and gingerale
She may be in cool of the evening lingerie
That's all right
You got your white coat on, ain't you?
Okeh.
(Brown 1980: 172)

In his working environment and white uniform, the porter often occupied otherwise precarious positions, such as waiting on white women who thought nothing of undressing in front him (Perata 1996: XIX). A white woman would hardly have felt comfortable undressing in front of a white hotel bellboy (1996: XIX) and surely would not have felt as nonchalant in her interactions with the same porter in civilian life. Still, because the PPCC was concerned over the dubious lawsuits it received from passengers claiming to have been sexually harassed by porters it often hired female spotters whose job it was to attempt to seduce porters (Perata 1996: 78). Centring on figures of mobile men like the porter, Brown's poem reflects this aspect of US cultural history and reveals practices of social decorum and professional dress which provided the necessary distance (and thereby security) for African American men who worked in close proximity to white women.

After noting the revealing dress in which the porter might find his white female passenger as he provides professional service, the speaker assures the porter that he is secure from accusation as long as he dons his white uniform. Brown uses the white coat as a subversive literary device signifying the kind of veil behind which porters performed service in order to safeguard the integrity of their employment against accusation. Even more, the white coat references the limits placed on social interactions between black men and white women in broader US society as well as in the paradoxical microcosm represented by the train car. The speaker spends the second half of his address to the porter focusing on the dangers of social interaction without donning the protective white garb and outside the space of the Pullman car:

But don't ever ride
With her in a Pullman
Without that white coat on
Don't even buy
No ticket for a Pullman
She might just be thinking 'bout riding
You fool you
You want to make the lady paint?
(Brown 1980: 172)

Crossing barriers in social engagements was a serious offence for porters as evidenced in the accounts of service workers like James T. Steele (Pullman Buffet and Lounge Car Attendant, 1936–60):

> You had to be so careful when you catch a lot of single white women, because a lot of 'em are put on there to try to trap you, see? And you got to have damn good willpower not to get yourself messed up, 'cause [Pullman] would pay you $77.50 a month, and they pay $2,000 to get something on you. See? A lot of porters was caught, and you had to be careful. (Perata 1996: 78)

The speaker's insistence on keeping the white coat on and maintaining professional interaction with white women, then, reflects not simply a literary device in Brown's poem, but also the actual circumstances of African American men's employment particularly in transportation service jobs requiring interaction across racial lines. To be without the white coat, without a signifier of servitude, left one vulnerable to accusations of sexual harassment or worse. Indeed, even to be with the white coat did not entirely insulate African American men from conjecture and suspicion in their professional work; conjecture and suspicion predicated on stereotypes of black male sexual aggression and prowess circulating in the white American imagination. In addition to 'Long Gone' and 'The Law for George', mobile men offer inspiration for other poems by Brown including 'Odyssey of Big Boy' from *Southern Road*, a poem modelled on the experiences of itinerant performer Calvin 'Big Boy' Davis (Sanders 1999: 42), and *The Last Ride of Wild Bill* (Brown 1975). Mobile women, however, do not occupy such a prominent place in Brown's constellation.

In one of Brown's few (if not only) representations of mobile women, 'Sister Lou', he depicts a woman's relationship to the train and mobility via a transcendent (as opposed to corporeal) context. Brown's introduction of Sister Lou's mobility (or perhaps lack thereof) stands in marked contradistinction to his rendering of a railroad man's mobility in 'Long Gone'. While the train appears as a corporeal image in 'Long Gone', tied to men's mobility in the physical world, the train functions as a metaphysical image in 'Sister Lou', divorcing the physicality or corporeality of the train image from women's mobility:

> Honey
> When de man
> Calls out de las' train
> You're gonna ride,
> Tell him howdy.
>
> Gather up yo' basket
> An' yo' knittin' an' yo' things,
> An' go on up an' visit
> Wid friend' Jesus fo' a spell.

Show Marfa
How to make yo' greengrape jellies,
An' give po' Lazarus
A passel of them Golden Biscuits.
(Brown 1980: 54)

In contrast to Brown's presentation of a mobile man on the train, his depiction of a mobile woman comes not only post mortem, but attendant with all the accoutrements of domesticity (e.g. basket, knitting items, jellies and biscuits). As the speaker of the poem instructs, Sister Lou is to teach another woman 'Marfa' (Martha) how to make jellies in heaven. Furthermore, the speaker of the poem is not Sister Lou (first person), but a third-person limited speaker addressing Sister Lou. Unlike 'Long Gone' in which the mobile male speaker provides the dominate point-of-view for the poem's narrative, Sister Lou's perspective (her voice) is completely absent. The juxtaposition in representations of mobile male and female subjects should not be understated. Consciously or not, Brown's juxtaposition foregrounds the paradigm of mobility restricting women's travel. The poem even attempts to present a vision of Sister Lou transcending paradigmatic restrictions on mobility via death and the afterlife; though ultimately, the attempt is unsatisfactory.

Considering the train's employment in the African American imagination as a metaphor for the paradox of freedom and confinement in the African American experience, Brown's decision to have Sister Lou's post mortem train ride end in a transcendent realm (heaven) gestures to a tradition of African Americans striving to move beyond the paradox of freedom and confinement, struggles waged in the realm of the real and the realm of the imaginary. Still, Brown's description of Sister Lou's arrival in heaven relays a sense of confinement even in transcendence. In fact, the speaker's instructions to Sister Lou in the stanzas preceding the conclusion of the poem suggest a different kind of confinement through eternal rest and stasis:

Then sit down
An' pass de time of day while.

Give a good talkin' to
To yo' favorite 'postle Peter,
An' rub the po' head
Of mixed-up Judas,
An' joke awhile wid Jonah.

Then, when you gits de chance,
Always remeberin' yo' raisin',
Let 'em know youse tired
Jest a mite tired.

Jesus will find yo' bed fo' you
Won't no servant evah bother wid yo' room.
Jesus will lead you
To a room wid windows
Openin' on cherry trees an' plum trees
Bloomin' everlastin'.

An' dat will be yours
Fo' keeps.
(Brown 1980: 55)

In contrast to the sense of unbounded possibility Brown relates in 'Long Gone', 'Sister Lou' concludes with the sense of a final destination, a place where there is no need to seek adventures far beyond the picturesque view from the window of one's heavenly quarters. Though the juxtaposition in Brown's representations seems to suggest transcendence in the afterlife as one of the few contexts in which women's mobility by train is possible, his attempt to imagine a context for women's mobility is troubled by its own iteration of confinement and stasis. Here, as in 'Long Gone', the train as a sign of freedom is complicated by the reminder of paradigmatic (and indeed corporeal) restrictions on women's mobility. Though Brown presents the image of a woman's mobility by train in 'Sister Lou' he does so while placing corporeal limits to her travel by train. Rather than leaving the reader with a sense of contentment as Sister Lou embarks on a new adventure in eternal (unbounded) paradise, the poem's final depiction is of a tired old woman who has made her last journey and now rests eternally in perpetual stasis.

Conclusion

The railroad, train and porter hold a prominent place in the African American (and indeed American) imagination. The prevalence of these figures can be seen in literature, music, film and visual art and culture. In this chapter, I have explored travel and imagination in the poetry of Sterling Brown. Railroad imagery and mobile men like the porter figure centrally in Brown's often vernacular-inflected poetry, compositions which not only represent the paradox of freedom and confinement in the historical experiences of mobile African American male service workers but also mirror paradigmatic restrictions on women's mobility pervasive from 1865 until the 1940s. For Brown, poetry served as a medium through which the poet imparted his understanding, not only of the diversity of black life in the US South, but also of the railroad's significance to the African American modern experience. As such, his poems hold a dual importance as both literary abstraction and art, and historical documentation of lived experiences and folk idiomatic expression.

Travel in the African American imagination has been complicated by historical experiences of confinement and restriction. The complexity of travel in the

African American, and indeed broader American, imagination is nowhere more punctuated than in the literary, visual and musical works by African Americans which employ the paradoxical image of the train and railroad to signal both freedom and limitation. As I have shown in this chapter, despite the function of the train and railroad as signifiers of freedom and historical continuity, racial and gendered paradigmatic restrictions on mobility demanded African Americans reconcile the freedom train with its restrictive counterpart the Jim Crow train. The result has been a vibrant tradition of artistic expression centred on the train image and its paradoxical significations.

From the 1940s to the present, the train and railroad have continued to be compelling (if ambivalent) influences in the African American imaginary. This much is clear from such artistic works as Ann Petry's best-selling novel *The Street* (1946) featuring a struggling, mobile female protagonist Lutie, Robert Hayden's poem 'Runagate Runagate' (1985), a 1962 historical poem portraying the Underground Railroad, Albert Murray's novel *Train Whistle Guitar* (1974), Romare Bearden's collages like 'The Train' (1975, see Schwartzman 1990) also referencing the cultural historical experience of the Underground Railroad, August Wilson's play *Two Trains Running* (produced 1992), and Colson Whitehead's novel *John Henry Days* (2001), to the very recent work of visual and mixed media artist Radcliff Bailey exhibited in 2011. Two important shifts in the employment of train and railroad imagery can be seen in the works of Petry and Bailey with Petry offering one of the earliest ante mortem literary depictions of a female protagonist's mobility by train and Bailey shifting the use of train and railroad imagery in visual art to the use of railroad tracks (as opposed to the locomotive) as signifiers of historical continuity. Still, the use of folk heroes like John Henry as literary symbols continues in the very recent work of writers like Whitehead. Despite paradoxical significations owing to historical experiences of paradigmatic restrictions on mobility, the train and railroad continue to provide metaphorical and symbolic significance as vessels of history, memory, continuity and freedom in the African American imagination.

Acknowledgment

Excerpts from 'Long Gone', 'Sister Lou' and 'Law for George', from *The Collected Poems of Sterling A. Brown*, selected by Michael S. Harper. Copyright ©1980 Sterling A. Brown. Reprinted by permission of the Estate of Sterling A. Brown.

References

Bates, B.T. 2001. *Pullman Porters and the Rise of Protest Politics in Black America, 1925–1945*. Chapel Hill: University of North Carolina Press.
Brown, S.A. 1932. *Southern Road*. New York: Harcourt, Brace and Co.

102   *Travel and Imagination*

Brown, S.A. 1975. *The Last Ride of Wild Bill: And eleven narrative poems.*
  Detroit: Broadside Press.
Brown, S.A. 1980. *The Collected Poems of Sterling A. Brown.* New York: Harper
  & Row.
Hayden, R. 1985. *Collected Poems: Robert Hayden,* edited by F. Glaysher. New
  York: Liveright.
Hughes, L. 1963. *The Big Sea: An autobiography.* New York: Hill and Wang.
Hurston, Z.N. [1934] 1990. *Jonah's Gourd Vine.* New York: HarperPerennial.
Hurston, Z.N. [1942] 1996. *Dust Tracks on a Road.* New York: HarperPerennial.
Kornweibel, Jr., T. 2010. *Railroads in the African American Experience:
  A photographic journey.* Baltimore: Johns Hopkins University Press.
Murray, A. 1974. *Train Whistle Guitar.* New York: McGraw-Hill.
Perata, D.D. 1996. *Those Pullman Blues: An oral history of the African American
  railroad attendant.* New York: Twayne Publishers.
Petry, A. 1946. *The Street.* Boston: Houghton Mifflin.
Sanders, M.A. 1999. *Afro-modernist Aesthetics & the Poetry of Sterling A. Brown.*
  Athens: University of Georgia Press.
Santino, J. 1989. *Miles of Smiles, Years of Struggle: Stories of black Pullman
  porters.* Urbana: University of Illinois Press.
Schwartzman, M. 1990. *Romare Bearden: His life and art.* New York: Harry N.
  Abrams, Inc.
Whitehead, C. 2001. *John Henry Days.* New York: Doubleday.
Wilson, A. 1992. *Two Trains Running.* New York: Plume.
Zabel, D. 2001. 'Two Trains Running': The train as symbol in twentieth-century
  African American Literature. PhD diss., University of Connecticut.

Chapter 7

Tourist Imagination and Modernist Poetics: The Case of Cees Nooteboom

Odile Heynders and Tom van Nuenen

Introduction

Standing before the painting 'Girl interrupted at her music'[1] by Johannes Vermeer in The Frick Collection in New York, Dutch writer Cees Nooteboom suddenly realizes that the work of art triggers a 'nationalist feeling'; he is a traveller experiencing the phenomenon whereby the image he is looking at is more closely related to himself than to the American viewer next to him. Although he knows that nationalist sympathies have become suspicious and must be resisted, he feels that he shares something with the two painted figures – the girl in red and her friend/admirer. He shares their history, their city and he is familiar with the interior of their home: 'I live in such a house' (Nooteboom 2009: 13).[2] Striking are not only his observations on the intimacy in Vermeer's paintings, the way they depict one isolated moment in time – one *Augenblick* – or his comments on the refinement of the colours, but particularly his recognition of the two people in the picture as 'landgenoten' (fellow countrymen) and how they activate his imagination. He is the writer with the 'eyes of a painter',[3] the traveller intuitively reflecting on the political realm of nationalism, and he is the tourist visiting museums and cities as historical sites deliberately training himself to turn off the sounds and images of the contemporary and to imagine the historical reality. When reading Nooteboom's work, we are confronted by the concept of 'tourist imagination' as the mediation of images, and we are challenged to rethink it in the context of modernist ideas on observation, perception and cognition.

Countless globetrotters share their adventures with the world on a daily basis, in travel guides like *Lonely Planet*, on television networks such as the *Travel Channel*, or through 'round-the-world-websites' such as whereareyounow. com. The contributors to these travel projects are charged with the same task:

---

1   See http://67.99.191.20/media/view/Objects/273/3381?t:state:flow=8866b8c5-741 0-489f-9cd6-3d7d55a89524, retrieved 12 November 2012.

2   Original: 'Ik ken hun stad, en ik ken hun interieur: ik woon zelf in zo'n huis' (Nooteboom 2009: 13).

3   Characterization by German painter Max Neumann in the documentary *Hotel Nooteboom* by Heinz Peter Schwerfel (2007).

to meticulously describe their journey and experiences. Popular as it may be, travel writing may be one of the most daunting tasks an author can be faced with. It aims at depicting the strange, the exotic, the dangerous and the often inexplicable. Since travel primarily concerns a sense of difference, its experiences invite 'speculation, reverie, mind-voyaging and a variety of other acts of imagination' (Rojek 1997: 52). The interaction between reality and fiction is a key element of travel writing – even though it is often not presented as such. Most travel books and blogs focus on the traveller as an eyewitness and are founded on a sense of realism and proof, the experience of physical presence and the conviction of a possibly truthful retelling of one's experiences. But the witness is a fabrication: one sees what one is trained and expected to see, one sees what one knows from the consumption of films, books, television, newspapers and photography. The framework of what one can experience on a trip is for a large part already defined in the tourist's original culture (Craik 1997: 118).

It is in this context that the concepts of 'imaginative travel' and 'tourist imagination' become relevant. The former concept was put forward by John Urry (2002b: 256), giving it a rather strict definition, namely 'to be transported elsewhere through the images of places and peoples encountered on radio and especially the ubiquitous TV'. Imaginative travel is connected with virtual travel – travel through the Internet – which 'reconfigures humans as bits of information, as individuals come to exist beyond their bodies' (Urry 2002b: 266). Against such a backdrop of the virtual, Urry wonders why there is still a widely felt need for corporeal travel – physical proximity to peoples, places or events. He argues that seeing a certain place (face-the-place) or experiencing something 'live' (face-the-moment) still is considered important, because it is through co-presence or bodily proximity that social connections of commitment, intimacy and trust can be reinforced (Urry 2002b: 262).

The concept of 'tourist imagination' explores the imaginative and cognitive activity a tourist performs: 'an imaginative process which involves a certain comprehension of the world and enthuses a distinctive emotional engagement with it' (Crouch et al. 2006: 1). It is through imagination that tourists negotiate their own meaning and space, by shifting between different spheres and causing reality to be reorganized to fit expectations. Tourist imagination is contrasted with melodramatic imagination as the capability to see conflict and social failure. The former can only begin where the latter has ceased to operate 'because conflict seems antithetical to pleasure' (Crouch et al. 2006: 10).

In the following we will argue that, in the modernist literary tradition of Dutch author Cees Nooteboom, corporeal proximity to, or co-presence at, certain places is supplemented with what we call *imaginary proximity* as experiential historical resonance. We use this term to refer to the activity of the literary author adopting the role and embodiment of different mediatized travel figures, in order to appropriate the places he visits. In this sense, 'imaginative travel' means more than travelling through mediated imagery, since it incorporates a sense of reflection and serious play with images, involving perception, cognition, imagination and identification. Modernist literature explores the 'filter of awareness' in order to show various perspectives on, and nuances in, reality (Fokkema and Ibsch 1984: 125). A typical aspect of modernism is its distrust of the objective, material facts, and their subsequent transformation into a filtered reality. The awareness of one person in different moments correlates with a doubt of chronology (Fokkema and Ibsch 1984: 131).

This chapter is concerned with how the imaginary proximity of the literary author as traveller could be related to concepts used in tourism studies. We are interested in parallels in the disciplines of tourism and literary studies, regarding experiences of time and space, and with a special focus on the traveller in the double role of actor and spectator. The argument in this chapter unfolds as follows. In the first section, after a brief introduction to Nooteboom's work, we focus on the spectator and, in particular, on ways of seeing performed by the travel writer, and we elaborate on the concept of 'telescopic eye'; the subsequent section concentrates on the travel writer as a *playing* actor and discusses in more detail a presupposed link between tourist imagination and modernist poetics; the penultimate section offers some close readings of Nooteboom's travel writing on geographically, as well as culturally, interesting places. The last section presents a conclusion and a discussion.

The Travel Writer as Spectator: The Gaze

The writing career of Cees Nooteboom (born in The Hague in 1933) spans a period of over 50 years. His oeuvre includes novels, travel writings, poetry and essays on art. Having been awarded several international prizes,[4] Nooteboom can be considered one of the great contemporary European authors (and one of the perennial favourites for the Nobel Prize in Literature). While in the Netherlands he has long stood in the shadows of such authors as Harry Mulisch (1927–2010) and W.F. Hermans (1921–95), he is especially famous in Germany and France. Yet, academic writing on Nooteboom offers a somewhat one-sided reading, being centred mostly on the post-modern form and narrative devices, rather than focusing on the content of mobility in space and time. Nooteboom's first novel, *Philip and the Others* ([1955] 1988), was written after a youthful Grand Tour of Europe and, in fact, the author has never stopped travelling since. A visit to his official website makes this immediately clear, as it shows a map of the world covered with pointers indicating places the author has described either in his fiction or in his travel writing or in both.[5] In his debut, we already get a first taste of how the author injects fiction into the realist position of the traveller as an eyewitness. In his travel writings, Nooteboom analyses phenomenological data and uses his imagination to

---

4   Karlsmedaille für Europäische Medien [Germany], Prijs der Nederlandse letteren [Prize of Dutch Letters] 2009. Commandeur des Arts et des Lettres [France], Pegasus Prize for Literature [USA].

5   See www.ceesnooteboom.com, retrieved 29 October 2012.

underline and transform the particularities and historical dimensions of the places he visits. As he himself puts it:

> There is always a fictional element in travel writing, if only because you have to choose from a huge amount of material. It never is a report from a to b and subsequently to z. One lies in travel writing ... One recreates to enhance credibility. (Brokken 1984: 20)[6]

Nooteboom's use of imagination, his Cervantian *feigning the truth*, cannot be scrutinized without taking into account its strong visual emphasis. From tourism studies we know that the best way for the travel writer to frame the experience of mobility is through visual images. There are hardly more effective ways of capturing a moment than by pushing the button of a camera and rendering it permanent as a photograph. Shooting pictures serves as an 'objective' testimony of someone who has been somewhere (Sontag 2003: 26). One can simply take a photograph with a cell phone and share it immediately with friends (Bell and Lyall 2006: 136).[7] It should come as no surprise then that Rojek and Urry (1996: 7) insist that when analysing tourism, a focus should rest upon the examination of the human senses, the eye in particular. This importance of the visual is informed by critical philosophical views on gazing as presented by Michel Foucault, phenomenologists Jean-Paul Sartre and Maurice Merleau-Ponty, and psychoanalyst Jacques Lacan.[8] An in-depth study of the gaze within tourism studies was first presented in *The Tourist Gaze* in which Urry argued the fundamentally visual nature of tourist experiences. The gaze organizes the encounters of visitors with other places and the places of 'others' providing a sense of competence, pleasure and structure to those experiences (Urry 2002a: 145).[9] The gaze orders and regulates the relationships between the various sensory experiences. The question of course is, how the writer turns visual observations (image) into words (language), how he switches from gaze to phrase.

Before answering this question we first need to bring together a cluster of related concepts taken from tourism as well as literary studies: gaze, look

---

6   Brokken citing Nooteboom: 'In een reisbeschrijving zit altijd een fictief element, alleen al omdat je uit een enorme hoeveelheid materiaal moet kiezen. Het is nooit een verslag van a naar b en vervolgens naar z. Je liegt in reisbeschrijvingen ... Je herschept om de geloofwaardigheid te vergroten' (Brokken 1984: 20).

7   This sense of speed or immediacy when taking pictures is typical of contemporary tourists. It contrasts with the writer's *slowness*.

8   For a further analysis of Nooteboom in the context of Merleau-Ponty, see: http://ebookbrowse.com/eindversie-hong-kong-odile-heynders-doc-d43781994, retrieved 12 November 2012.

9   Urry adopts Foucault's notion of the gaze but subsequently focuses only on the one doing the gazing as opposed to the disciplining effect of those being gazed upon (whether they are actually being watched or not) and the way this structures responses, behaviours or attitudes.

(or glance), point of view (or focalization) and (perspective of) narration. Mieke Bal's *Travelling Concepts in the Humanities* (2002) is helpful here. According to Bal, the gaze, in a common sense, is the look that the subject casts on other people and things, examples being when Nooteboom gives a plain description of a route or a hotel room. In a *critical* use, the gaze is flexible and subjective, offering a more complex perspective. This gaze is a visual order in which the gazing subject is caught (Bal 2002: 35–6). Obviously, the second gaze is what we are dealing with in most of Nooteboom's texts: when he (often from the position of an I-narrator) is looking at something, it is immediately clear that what we are reading about is really not the thing that is being seen, but the author's susceptibility in regard to it. It is not the object, but the experience (as *Erlebnis*) of looking, seeing and watching that is described, as is illustrated in:

> But this was Munich. He had not come here to recall all this, but to look. Yet as he sat there quietly with his glass of Volcano wine he seemed to be caught up in the eye of the storm of memories. How strange it was. Time itself, that weightless thing, could only go in one direction. (Nooteboom 2007: 60)

Sitting in a German city the narrator wonders about history and his ties to time and memory. What he sees is not immediately present there, what he sees is what he makes up. And he does this consciously: 'Some cities live up to their responsibilities. They supply the traveller with the image he has of them, even if it is a false one' (Nooteboom 2007: 49). This is a perfect and paradoxical description of the tourist imagination that is unbounded and restricted at the same time (Crouch et al. 2006: 5). The modernist knows that reality only exists in the potential of recreation of the facts (Fokkema and Ibsch 1984: 132).

Gaze in the common sense has to do with 'point of view' as a technical-visual term. Gaze in the critical sense can be connected to point of view as focalization, or *envisioning*: creating an image. Mieke Bal (2002: 38) has coined the dynamic concept of 'the gaze-as-focalizer', implying that both visuality and narrativity are articulations of envisioning (opening perspectives). As Bal (2002: 39) explains:

> what becomes visible is the movement of the look ... the look encounters the limitations imposed by the gaze ... The tension between the focalizer's movement and these limitations is the true object of analysis.

Nooteboom as a literary travel writer happens to be an expert at gazing, focalizing and recreating. In an interview he declared that he had made seeing his 'specialty' (Cartens 2006: 169). The author allows imagined objects and subjects to seep through the things he observes, underlining and wiping out their boundaries at the same time, blurring images of past and present, reality and fiction. As Fokkema and Ibsch (1984: 134) explain in their study of modernist European authors: 'In the linearity of the chronology everything is movement and change ... only by anachronism a sphere of tranquilness and identity can occur'.[10] The status of observer – think of Proust's *A la Recherche du Temps Perdu* – is typical of the modernist narrator.

The narrative strategy of phrasing how things are seen and experienced can be further understood by referring to an instrument coined by modernist Polish writer Czeslaw Milosz (1911–2004) as the 'telescopic eye'. In his memoirs, *Native Realm: A search for self-definition* ([1959] 2002: 2–3), Milosz defines it as follows:

> There is a new organ, which we may call the telescopic eye, which perceives simultaneously not only different points of the globe but also different moments of time; the motion picture created it in all my contemporaries ... New images canceled out none of the old and, strictly speaking, I do not see them in chronological order as if on a strip of film, but in parallel, colliding with one another, overlapping.

The telescopic eye makes it possible to experience the simultaneity of times and places, of personal and historical events, of the solitary and collective observation.[11] And this eye is what Nooteboom also uses, for instance in the novel *All Souls' Day* (2002), in which the protagonist, photographer and documentary maker Arthur Daane travels to Berlin:

> He read the city like a book, a story of unseen buildings swallowed up by history – Gestapo torture chambers, the barren stretch of land where Hitler's plane had been able to land on the very last day, everything told in a continuous, almost chanted recitative. (Nooteboom 2002: 12)

The sensitivity to recognize the empty spots is much more important than to see what *is*. The emptiness is full of absences, of things gone by, war scenes still conceivable. Although obviously both Milosz and Nooteboom are strongly influenced by the cruel facts of the Second World War, the telescopic eye or gaze as such is not necessarily associated with tragic, world-changing events and places. Reporting on a trip to Venice, a similar simultaneousness is experienced and depicted as both anachronism and timelessness. While observing, interpreting and imagining are regular activities for the tourist, in the work of the modernist author these activities are consciously connected to the layering of time, place and image, and as such to

---

10   'In de lineariteit van de chronologie is alles beweging en verandering, niets is blijvend. Alleen door het anachronisme kan een toestand van rust en identiteit optreden' (Fokkema and Ibsch 1984: 134). Original: 'In the linearity of chronology all is movement and change, nothing is permanent. It is only through anachronism that a state of tranquility and identity can emerge'.

11   This is similar to Bakhtin's ideas of the chronotope, 'the intrinsic connectedness of temporal and spatial relationships that are intrinsically expressed in literature' ([1981] 2004: 84) – a specific organization of space-time, determining a particular identity or genre.

a complex experience of a reality in which the subject as spectator finds himself being connected to other subjects and phenomena from previous times.

The Travel Writer as Actor: Tourist Imagination

At this point we want to bring in another perspective on travel: its playful nature. Again, the concept of play in tourism studies is anything but new, but we are interested in the parallels that can be drawn with play-perspectives in literary studies. Play in tourism studies is used in a dual sense: it not only applies to the tourist, who in a sense is playing, and whose travels are often a matter of hedonism and fun; it also applies to tourism as being a form of play in itself – a performance by both hosts and visitors of tourist sites.[12] In literary studies, and particularly in Nooteboom's oeuvre, we encounter another sense of play: the conscious conjuring up of a reality, the play of envisioning something that is not there. Against this specific backdrop, the concept of the *homo ludens*, as first discussed by Dutch historian Johan Huizinga (1872–1914), may be instructive. In *Homo Ludens: A study of the play element in culture* ([1938] 1949), Huizinga considers play a primary category of life, and offsets the *homo ludens* against the *homo faber*: the creating human being, focused on work and production. Play entails a separation from the common life in place and duration (time): a main characteristic of play is:

> that it is free, is in fact freedom. A second characteristic is closely connected with this, namely, that play is not 'ordinary' or 'real' life. It is rather a stepping out of 'real' life into a temporary sphere of activity with a disposition all its own. (Huizinga [1938] 1949: 8)

In line with Urry's idea of tourism as a limited breaking with established routines and practices of everyday life, Huizinga, long before the invention of tourism studies, emphasizes that the *homo ludens* is very much aware of his deliberately transforming the ordinary circumstances in reality. The play places the player in a world other than the normal one, even though, at:

> any moment 'ordinary life' may reassert its rights either by an impact from without, which interrupts the game, or by an offence against the rules, or else from within, by a collapse of the play spirit, a sobering, a disenchantment. (Huizinga [1938] 1949: 21)

---

12   Sheller and Urry (2004: 1) put forward that tourism is not just about encountering, but also about *performing* places: 'Places have multiple contested meanings that often produce disruptions and disjunctures. Tourism mobilities involve complex combinations of movement and stillness, realities and fantasies, play and work'.

In the context of Nooteboom's travel writings, Huizinga's concept of the *homo ludens* is particularly fascinating when reading about the traveller imagining and representing things as they are conceived of, things *not* as they are:

> There is no question of first conceiving something as lifeless and bodiless and then expressing it as something that has body, parts and passions. No; the thing perceived is conceived as having life and movement in the first place, and such is the primary expression of it, which is no afterthought. Personification in this sense arises as soon as the need is felt to communicate one's perceptions to others. Conceptions are thus born as acts of the imagination. (Huizinga [1938] 1949: 136)

Huizinga emphasizes something that is typical of Nooteboom's travel writing and that precedes Urry's concepts of the playing and gazing tourist. Although the tourist mainly participates in a staged play of tourism, and is influenced by media images, Huizinga underlines the concept of imagination without control but nevertheless based on knowledge, recognition and awareness: the imagination is a creative *act*, and at the same time 'spontaneously' felt. This is exactly what is understood in 'tourist imagination' suggesting 'a creative potential inherent in free movement between different spheres of life' (Crouch et al. 2006: 2). The imagination is 'taken from the everyday world into the tourist activity but equally may be brought back from the tourist world as an enhanced imaginative facility' (Crouch et al. 2006: 3). It may be used to appropriate fictions in support of the physical mobility of travel but, at the same time, travel may be the inspiration of fiction. However, this is never totally unbounded or free flowing.

Nooteboom's texts are fictionalized descriptions of reality and vice versa. The following description of the Irish Aran islands – just one example of many – provides a good illustration of this. The writer travels to the island:

> simultaneously in a book and in the real world ... The man who clips my ticket for the boat is the same one as two years previously, someone who could have played Death in the Bergman film *The Seventh Seal*. He is reading a book by Bruce Chatwin. (Nooteboom 2007: 80)

The writer as traveller is playing simultaneously on various levels: describing his journey, memorizing a previous one, referring to a book and a film that both have connections to the scene he is depicting. The experience of travel is confined to a cycle of anticipation and retrospection (Crouch et al. 2006: 1).

Nooteboom fits perfectly in the modernist discourse that influenced Huizinga and Milosz as well: on the one side, modernism is rooted in the idea of the intermingling of times, places and intertextual frames; on the other, it is based on a fundamental reflection on writing itself. Modernism involves a concern with consciousness, time and the nature of knowledge (Butler [1990] 2004: 67), and can be understood as 'a shift from aestheticism, which appears apolitical in its emphasis on beauty, toward an aesthetic politics, an art that recognizes its embodiment and its responsibilities within history' (Riquelme [1990] 2004: 106). The memory on which modernism focuses is not merely personal but also cultural and historical. As such, all modernist writings recognize the cultural memory and the historical realities of contemporary life, as well as the process by which present realities have come into being (Riquelme [1990] 2004: 109). Nooteboom is particularly clear in his description of the embodiment of time:

> It happens with every trip, or rather, it happens to me on each extended journey. The time I spend away from home stagnates, coagulates, becomes a sort of mass that closes up behind me. Then I'm off, under the sway of a different order, the order of travel, the elusive element of not belonging, of collecting what is different. [...] I am extended by everything I see, consume, amass. (Nooteboom [1992] 1997: 207)

To reiterate, Nooteboom uses what we call the telescopic eye in order to see various things at the same time, to purposely perceive different layers of reality. What he sees is both real and goes beyond the subjective, time- and context-bound perception of things. The traveller as *homo ludens* is aware of where and what he is, but is also able to lose himself in another time and place, to leave his Dutch background and connectedness and see what is happening in another place, another past, another present. For the author, it is not so much about himself as it is about the collective experience of those who came before him. The playful gaze brings the real and imagined past into being. The literary travel author thus shows how categories of play and gaze, as used in tourism studies, might be rethought. To the author-as-tourist, travelling is a deliberate manipulation of the gaze in order to recreate images of the past and present. Remarkably, in Nooteboom's work (as in Proust's or other European modernists) there is no place for the future.

Modern Pilgrim and Nomad

Let us now focus on a more in-depth analysis of Nooteboom's travel essays in order to show how the concepts of *homo ludens* and the telescopic eye are connected, and how imaginary proximity emerges as the writer identifies with different travel figures. From his extensive oeuvre we have chosen two texts as data: *Roads to Santiago* ([1992] 1997) and *Nomad's Hotel* (2007), because we consider them representative of Nooteboom's travel writing (not all of it has been translated into English), and they offer us two different but connected types of travellers: the pilgrim and the nomad. The pilgrim is the traveller for whom 'only streets make sense, not the houses' (Bauman 1996: 20). This is a historical and European-based category of traveller. The pilgrim had to disconnect himself from social structures in order to find a line to God. Wherever one moved, one was *in a place*, as Bauman explains, and this spiritual dislocation has to be interpreted as structure:

The world of pilgrims – of identity *builders* – must be orderly, determined, predictable, ensured; but above all it must be a kind of world in which footprints are engraved for good, so that the trace and the record of past travels are kept and preserved. (Bauman 1996: 23)

Nooteboom's essay 'In the footsteps of Don Quixote – the roads of la Mancha', from *Roads to Santiago: A modern-day pilgrimage though Spain* ([1992] 1997), definitely fits Bauman's characterization of the pilgrim: the literary travel author walks in the footsteps of a spiritual predecessor. We clearly see how imaginary proximity is articulated here, switching from what the writer-traveller experiences to what is conjured up in his imagination. The essay introduces Miguel de Cervantes seated at his desk, 50 years old and creating his hero Don Quixote as a portrait of himself. Nooteboom, in the position of I-narrator, claims that everyone knows what the hero looked like, but that there is no trustworthy depiction of his creator. This observation shows how the author as *homo ludens* makes room for a serious 'contest between the imaginary and the real' (Nooteboom [1992] 1997: 95). Nooteboom envisions the missing pictures. Visiting the house of the Spanish writer, Nooteboom is transported from his own time and place: 'I do not need to hear the wheels to know how they will sound on the big cobblestones' (Nooteboom [1992] 1997: 97). He even realizes that 'there is nothing for the imagination to do, one is drawn into ancient times without resistance' (Nooteboom [1992] 1997: 101). This not only signals that the play between the real and the imagined is out of control – unbounded as Crouch et al. (2006) explain as one is transported into history – it also emphasizes that experiencing the difference between now and then is beyond cognition. This becomes even clearer when the writer visits the home of Dulcinea – a character that never existed in reality. Nooteboom observes: 'after a while it is hard to tell whether you are travelling in a book or in the real world' (Nooteboom [1992] 1997: 102). It is here that we become very much aware of the *vertigo* of the play of travelling, mixing historical reality and fantasy, distancing and belonging: 'to enter a house that once belonged to someone who never existed is no small matter' (Nooteboom [1992] 1997: 103).

Not surprisingly, the most crucial passage in the essay is when the writer pays a visit to the windmills in the hills of La Mancha:

The first one we see, standing in battle formation that afternoon on a long range of hills near Consuegra, offers firm proof that the Knight of the Sad Countenance was right. If you can't see that, you are crazy yourself. The light is false, a leaden gray streaked with brass like the backdrop of a tragic opera. And of course they are not windmills but men wildly flailing their arms, dangerous warriors, high-born knights. (Nooteboom [1992] 1997: 100)

Here the travel writer is not in the ordinary world, but in the world of Cervantes' imagination. La Mancha is a material world of tangible things, but it also has a 'dream-like, unconscionable quality, where nothing is as it seems' (Nooteboom

[1992] 1997: 101). However, the traveller, in writing his essay, makes the dream concrete again and puts the frame of reality on the fantasies of Cervantes by deliberately showing that he cannot but *believe* in the fabulations of his predecessor: 'If you can't see that, you are crazy yourself' (Nooteboom [1992] 1997: 100). Huizinga emphasized that play has to do with contest and performance, and this is precisely what we encounter in Nooteboom's essay. It is a contest between writers, between reality and fantasy, and between words: 'who in the end can be said to be the creator of the flesh-and-blood Don we see before us when we read the book?' (Nooteboom [1992] 1997: 104).

The second work we focus on is *Nomad's Hotel: Travels in time and space* (2007), a collection of travel essays in which we see the author taking the role of another travel figure: the *nomad*. This type of traveller lacks the ordered movement of the pilgrim, determined by the route he has to take; the nomad, by contrast, is free to live and go wherever he wants. Pilgrim and nomad can be understood in terms of the opposite poles of restriction and unboundedness (Crouch et al. 2006: 1–12). The nomad might seem to be the more unbounded figure, the pilgrim being subjected to the spiritual order, but what we read in these texts could just as easily be interpreted the other way around, as the pilgrim is unbounded in his imagination of the mystery and the nomad remains constrained to his own identity. Let us elaborate on this.

The aim of Nooteboom's travels through Spain was to follow the footsteps of the Christian pilgrims walking to Santiago de Compostela 'parcourir la terre pour pratiquer la méditation et se rapprocher de Dieu'[13] (Nooteboom 2007: 2). The traveller in *Nomad's Hotel*, conversely, makes a 'journey alone in a world controlled by others' (Nooteboom 2007: 3). No matter how solitary this traveller is, he will always be surrounded by other people. A hotel would appear to be a fitting place for the nomad; a temporary home where one books a room, meets people, abides by the rules – but everything takes place in passing, all of it is quite ephemeral. Nooteboom explicates why he chose to use the displaced travel figure of the nomad as follows:

> Anyone who is constantly travelling is always somewhere else, and therefore always absent. This holds good for oneself, and it holds good for others, the friends; for although it is true that you are 'somewhere else', and that, consequently, there is somewhere you are *not*, there is one place where you *are* constantly, all the time, namely with 'yourself'. (Nooteboom 2007: 2)

Nomadic travelling implies a social deficit, a deliberately not being able to speak to the ones 'at home'.[14] While the modern pilgrim moving through Spain has the prospect of *arriving* in Santiago as a stronghold for his identity, the only stable

---

13   'Travel the earth to practice meditation and get closer to God' (Nooteboom 2007: 2).

14   This loss of communication is much less important in most current-day travel, in which the internet and mobile phones allow one to 'keep in touch' with home.

factor to the nomad is to be with oneself in the company of strangers. The hotel is a temporary haven where one can withdraw for the night, without any long-lasting attachment to the world. Not being attached is the ultimate condition for the traveller as nomad. This becomes clearer when Nooteboom describes a piece of waste land near the house of his youth in Rijswijk, which he called 'the Land'. For the child this was 'a dangerous place that I filled with my fears and fantasies' (Nooteboom 2007: 93). Nowadays, he realizes, the world has become 'the Land', as some places fill him with overwhelming excitement, since he is not able to understand the signs, languages and lives. This 'state of zero-gravity' in the complete unknown is a pleasant one because it gives the writer the opportunity to disconnect from the social person he is at home. In a completely foreign place like Morocco for instance, Nooteboom feels he could 'as easily be from Ohio' as his own personal traits have become indistinct: 'For what I see, the little that I am capable of seeing, is in fact something other than what I see, just as what I hear is not information, only language that I cannot understand' (Nooteboom 2007: 94). It is this loss of identity and consequently the loss of understanding signs that coincides with the entrance of fiction. The faraway place is so strange that one has the feeling it cannot be real, Nooteboom argues in another pivotal passage, when he is sitting on a bench in a Gambian office:

> I am not sitting here at all. It is a play by an African Pinter, for which I have been engaged at a huge sum. Shortly, it will be time for the interval, then we will all rise, gauge the applause and go and have a beer in the canteen. (Nooteboom 2007: 29)

Because of the place's sharp contrast to home, one can only start thinking about it in familiar terms – and that is when it becomes the play of the *homo ludens*. The nomad thinks up the borders of fact and fiction, when reality exposes itself in such an overwhelming manner that it cannot be understood.

Conclusion and Discussion

What this chapter aims to have shown is that several concepts from tourism studies are thought through in the work of a contemporary modernist author. The debate between tourism and literary studies can be stimulated when focusing on the articulation of the literary author as traveller, on the emergence of a hyper-real world as a consciously imagined historical reality. Pilgrim and nomad, play and gaze, actor and spectator are connected in travel writing projects focusing on the subject's engagement with what is imagined. As Mieke Bal notes: 'Subjectivity is a messy mix of cognition and emotion, aesthetic and sensuous preference, understanding and sentiment' (Bal 1999: 64), and Nooteboom seems to be aware of this when he consciously transforms reality into imagination and fictionalizes environment and embodiment.

As we have argued, play is not merely a hedonistic leisure activity or a pervasive process enveloping the tourist and his environment. Rather, by introducing Johan Huizinga's concept of the *homo ludens*, we saw that play is a *necessary* imaginative state of mind exemplified in Nooteboom's writing. The *homo ludens* fits in a modernist discourse in which the aestheticization of reality is performed, breaking down the boundaries between past and present. This play is not only performed for the sake of play, but also brings out certain aspects of truth. The *homo ludens* is an apt figure to describe the writer as a bi-dimensional traveller who is not just re-creating, but also playing when he is the modern pilgrim *en route* as well as the nomad on his own in between all the signs, symbols and customs permeating global tourism. Through the serious play, the author seeks to radically disconnect himself from reality through imagination – and vice versa. His corporeal proximity to travel sites is always accompanied by an imaginary proximity understood as the adopting of roles of historical travel figures in order to appropriate the places visited. By pulling on and shedding the skin of different travel figures, the writer seeks to get closer to the places he goes to see. We suggested a rhetorical instrument that performs such play: the telescopic eye sensitive to the simultaneity of experiences in time locked on to a certain place.

Nooteboom gazes, witnesses and reflects on his activity as a travelling and reporting author. A question we have not brought up until now is whether or not tourists use his work as a travel guide. Is Nooteboom's work read as an account of personal experiences, does it stimulate tourists to adopt Nooteboom's gazing and imaginative techniques in their own travels? In other words: is the literary text concretized by the reader/tourist and are we thus confronted with yet another dimension of 'tourist imagination'? There are a number of references to Cees Nooteboom on the Dutch community travel website 'waarbenjij.nu' (whereareyounow.com has different national sites in various languages) – a refined Google search yields about 55 results.[15] These can be characterized as implicit intertextual references. The blogging tourists either use explicit quotations, or refer to a topic or theme that Nooteboom has described: such as 'evening in Isfahan' or 'last train to Mandalay'. Some of them compare themselves, or are compared, to the writer in terms of writing style or quality. These references to Nooteboom's texts help to locate the tourists as reader or consumer, but cannot be understood as accounts of a stimulated imaginative experience. None of the tourists seems to be aware of the imaginary proximity that makes one see things from another time. The contemporary blogging tourist, experiencing his own rather than a historical involvement, does not have the filtered awareness of the modernist author. Imaginary proximity is not something every tourist can experience or be prompted or invited to experience. The modernist code only suits those writers who are susceptible to it.

---

15 A refined Google search was performed by using advanced operators for searching a specific website and the exact name of the author (site: waarbenjij.nu 'cees nooteboom').

References

Bakhtin, M. [1981] 2004. Time and of the chronotope in the novel: Notes toward a historical poetics, in *The Dialogic Imagination: Four essays*, edited by M. Holquist, trans. C. Emerson and M. Holquist. Austin: University of Texas Press, 84–258.

Bal, M. 1999. *Quoting Caravaggio: Contemporary art, preposterous history*. Chicago: The University of Chicago Press.

Bal, M. 2002. *Travelling Concepts in the Humanities: A rough guide*. Toronto: University of Toronto Press.

Bal, M. 2008. Heterochronotopia, in *Migratory Settings*, edited by M. Aydemir and A. Rotas. Amsterdam: Rodopi, 35–56.

Bauman, Z. 1996. From pilgrim to tourist – or a short history of identity, in *Questions of Cultural Identity*, edited by S. Hall and P. du Gay. London: SAGE, 18–36.

Bell, C. and Lyall, J. 2006. 'I was here': Pixelated evidence, in *The Media and the Tourist Imagination*, edited by D. Crouch, R. Jackson and S. Thompson. London: Routledge, 135–43.

Brokken, J. 1984. De voorbije passages van Cees Nooteboom, in *Over Cees Nooteboom: Beschouwingen en Interviews*, edited by D. Cartens. Zutphen: Koninklijke Wöhrmann.

Butler, C. [1990] 2004. Joyce the modernist, in *The Cambridge Companion to James Joyce*, edited by D. Attridge, 2nd edition. Cambridge: Cambridge University Press, 67–86.

Cartens, D. 2006. Een uiterste strengheid door stilte, in *In het Oog van de Storm: De Wereld van Cees Nooteboom*, edited by S. van der Gaauw. Amsterdam: Uitgeverij Atlas, 164–75.

Craik, J. 1997. The culture of tourism, in *Touring Cultures: Transformations of travel and theory*, edited by C. Rojek and J. Urry. London: Routledge, 113–36.

Crouch, D., Jackson, R. and Thompson, F. 2006. *The Media and the Tourist Imagination*. London: Routledge.

Dijkgraaf, M. 2009. *Nooteboom en de Anderen*. Amsterdam: De Bezige Bij.

Fokkema, D. and Ibsch, E. 1984. *Het Modernisme in de Europese Letterkunde*. Amsterdam: Uitgeverij De Arbeiderspers.

Hotel Nooteboom: Een Reis In Woord En Beeld (dir. Heinz Peter Schwerfel, 2007).

Huizinga, J. [1938] 1949. *Homo Ludens: A study of the play-element in culture*. London: Routledge.

Milosz, C. [1959] 2002. *Native Realm: A search for self-definition*. New York: Farrar, Straus and Giroux.

Nooteboom, C. [1955] 1988. *Philip and the Others*, trans. A. Dixon. Baton Rouge: Louisiana State University Press.

Nooteboom, C. [1992] 1997. *Roads to Santiago*, trans. I. Rilke. San Diego: Harcourt.

Nooteboom, C. 2002. *All Souls' Day*, trans. S. Massotty. London: Pan Macmillan.

Nooteboom, C. 2007. *Nomad's Hotel: Travels in time and space*, trans. A. Kelland. London: Harvill Secker.

Nooteboom, C. 2009. *Het Raadsel van het Licht, Met een Inleiding van Susanne Schaber*. Amsterdam: De Bezige Bij.

Riquelme, J.P. [1990] 2004. *Stephen Hero* and *A Portrait of the Artist as a Young Man*: Transforming the nightmare of history, in *The Cambridge Companion to James Joyce*, edited by D. Attridge, 2nd edition. Cambridge: Cambridge University Press, 103–21.

Rojek, C. 1997. Indexing, dragging and the social construction of tourist sights, in *Touring Cultures: Transformations of travel and theory*, edited by C. Rojek and J. Urry. London: Routledge, 52–74.

Rojek, C. and Urry, J. 1996. Transformations of travel and theory, in *Touring Cultures: Transformations of travel and theory*, edited by C. Rojek and J. Urry. London: Routledge, 1–19.

Sheller, M. and Urry, J. 2004. *Tourism Mobilities: Places to play, places in play*. London: Routledge.

Sontag, S. 2003. *Regarding the Pain of Others*. London: Penguin.

Urry, J. 2000. *Sociology Beyond Societies*. London: Routledge.

Urry, J. 2002a. *The Tourist Gaze*, 2nd edition. London: SAGE.

Urry, J. 2002b. Mobility and proximity. *Sociology*, 36(2), 255–74.

Chapter 8

Making Spain: The Spanish Imaginary in Travel Writing since the Second World War

Steve Watson

Spain and the Spanish have a place in the British imagination that goes beyond historical connections, mass tourism and a shared European polity. Indeed the contemporary European nation that is Spain is not in any way a part of the collection and accretion of meaning that I refer to here as the *Spanish imaginary*. This is a separate place, mythic, timeless and exotic, the source of endless explorations and discoveries that bring us no closer to understanding the Spain that *is*, but which nevertheless through cultural and institutional means construct, sustain and reproduce a Spain as *made* in the northern imagination. The Spanish imaginary has a long antecedence in the writings of northern travellers and its origins can be detected in the records of traders and ambassadors (Mitchell 2004), but most influentially in those of Richard Ford and Washington Irving in the nineteenth century. Since then, each successive wave of travellers has reproduced and enlarged upon it until in the post-Second World War period it reached its peak with easier, quicker travel facilitated by new roads and motorized transport and, eventually, air travel.

The concept of the imaginary used in this chapter is borrowed from Charles Taylor (2004), who conceives of modern social imaginaries as common and coherent understandings of social surroundings 'carried in images, stories, and legends'. For Taylor, the *social imaginary* is painted on a large canvas, the 'background' onto which the social world is both projected and projected from, and enabling a 'repertory' of collective actions to be actualized and understood (2004: 24–5). My borrowing of this concept is to adapt its use in understanding the way a repertory of signifiers relating to Spain has been drawn up and out of a collective northern response to that country, and the way that nearly two centuries of travel writing have sustained and reproduced it as a defining concept of Spain: the Spanish imaginary.

My purpose in this chapter is to present three essential features of the Spanish imaginary as it has been represented regularly and consistently in travel writing since the Second World War: the broadly affective, the cognitive and the distanced, the latter providing the basis for an overarching sense of 'otherness' that in the case of Spain makes it appear sometimes to be only nominally European, often exotic and frequently oriental. In using the term 'broadly affective' I am deliberately bundling together the pre-cognitive aspects of engagement (i.e. affect) currently understood through non-representational theory in cultural geography as an embodied response (Thien 2005, Pile 2010), with the more expressive and emotional responses of the travel writers concerned. This broadly affective component of the imaginary is represented in the sensuality, absorption and fascination expressed by these writers, combined with a kind of wariness and distaste often sparked, for example, by reflections on the violence of the corrida, the horrors of the Civil War or even those more visceral, unknowable or threatening aspects of its orientalism.

The cognitive aspect is expressed in a desire to discover and reveal, to describe and assimilate, especially through history and the art of the past, architecture and the landscape. The history of the *reconquest* is particularly favoured, and frequent reference is made to it in somewhat triumphant language as the recovery of Christian civilization from retreating Islam. Yet there is just enough of Islam left to be unsettling, a source of fascination, intrigue and mystery and defining cultural distance; a need to stand somehow in relation to this imaginary Spain, but always separate from it in a way that contrasts with its geographical closeness.

Using travel writing as a key to unlock this discourse, I examine the ways in which the Spanish imaginary is manifest in northern perceptions and also the implications of this for the way that these meanings are reflected in contemporary representations of Spain for travellers and tourists. I argue, furthermore, that the imaginary has come to replace other, more local concepts of identity and cultural practice.

The Origins of the Spanish Imaginary

It is difficult to think of the Alhambra without thinking of Washington Irving, as if without his reflections on the brilliant exoticisms of its Moorish past it would mean less to us now than it does. For Irving, it was a period which, though long in years, was short-lived in its historic significance, especially once the Catholic Monarchs had re-conquered it. Thus the Moorish presence in Spain took, as he put it, 'no permanent root in the soil it embellished'. 'Never was the annihilation of people more complete than that of the Morisco-Spaniards' 'Where are they?' he asks rather plaintively ([1832] 1985: 53–4).

Spain, of course, has long been perceived as a junction of East and West, and it can be cast perhaps rather too easily as an example of Edward Said's *Orientalism*, a European invention and ultimately a means of control and self definition by contrast with an alien other (Said 1978). 'The orient', he says, was 'a place of romance, exotic beings, haunting memories and landscapes, remarkable experiences' (1978: 1). Irving's description of the Alhambra Palace corresponds neatly with this description, where Orientalism is a way of Europe coming to terms with the orient through this 'otherness'. Some of the sources quoted by Said were travellers who contributed to what he describes as an *imaginative geography* that began with a vision of Islam as a lasting trauma, crystallized first in the invasion of the Iberian Peninsula by the Moors in 711, and afterwards in the sense of a

European Christian civilization in constant danger from the Ottoman East. The abandonment of Rhodes by the Knights Hospitaller in 1523 might be seen as a formative moment in that reflexive cultural anxiety.

I would like to argue here, however, that what I call the Spanish imaginary is actually a more complex cultural construction than that described by the Orientalist perspective. Whilst the imaginary was certainly fostered in the northern European consciousness and projected in the relatively modern literature discussed here, it has, in the burgeoning of tourism, tourism marketing and the representational practices associated with it, become assimilated into the discursive realm of Spanish identity, which is reproduced now as 'real Spain'. This, in turn, is based on an appropriation of the otherness associated with Moorish Spain into that same discursive realm. I cannot hope to demonstrate that conclusively here, however, as my analysis is confined to the contribution made by travel writing in the post-war period, so my concern is to demonstrate facets of the imaginary and the way it works in this particular representational medium. By the end of my period, around 1975 and the end of the dictatorship, mass tourism under the impetus of the policy of *desarrollo*[1] had largely superseded individual travel as the principal means of engaging with Spain, and in overall terms the country had also entered the industrial and social modernity that other European countries had already experienced for two decades.

As an example of Orientalism, the process of assimilation represented by the Spanish imaginary is thus more complex and nuanced than Said's description. In establishing a dominant narrative it is not simply a 'domestication of the exotic' (Said 1978: 60) entailing a limited vocabulary and imagery, but also a coming to terms with an 'Other' that is within contemporary Europe rather than one which was pressing from outside those natural and cultural boundaries. What interests me most, however, is the contribution that travel writing has made to the construction of a contemporary heritage discourse in Spain, not only in the northern imagination, but now also in Spain itself.

There are a number of reasons why I have chosen this 30-year period from the end of the Second World War to Franco's death in 1975. The first point is that the otherness of Spain could hardly have achieved a greater intensity than it did in this period. Whilst Western Europe was basking in the reconstruction and technological development of the post-war period, and Eastern Europe was achieving an intimation of this by another route, Spain appeared mired in both a distant past and in the aftermath of its recent Civil War, and was struggling to achieve anywhere near the same kind of economic and technological progress (Cebrian and Lopez 2004). For Northwestern Europe, the nightmare of war was over and even the possibility of a nuclear Armageddon could at least be expunged from the quotidian consciousness. So whilst *Europa* blinked in the unaccustomed light of a modernity conditioned by the shiny new politics of social democracy and

---

1 *Desarrollo* refers to planned development under Franco, in which tourism played a major part.

emergent consumerism, Spain slumbered on, despite its geographical proximity. As travel writer and journalist Jan Morris put it in 1964, '[t]his time-lag still makes Spain an anachronism among the nations. Her industrial Revolution is really only happening now, and in many ways she retains the simplicity, even the innocence, of a pastoral nation' (Morris 1964: 26). Whilst the same could be said of Greece, and certainly of Crete, Spain was conspicuously *closer* to the new Europe.

As for the writers themselves, simplicity and innocence combined with something elemental, violence and exoticism are common themes, often reflecting the pre-war influence of Ernest Hemingway and his obsession with bull fighting as famously portrayed in *Death in the Afternoon*, which was first published in 1932. They also frequently reproduce Gerald Brenan's view that '[s]outh of the Pyrenees one finds a society which puts the deeper needs of human nature before the technical organization that is required to provide a higher standard of living', and in a clear expression of the imaginary he goes on: 'This is a land that nourishes at the same time the sense for poetry and the sense for reality, and neither of these accords with the utilitarian outlook' (1957: 12). Spain's otherness, therefore, could not have been more *other* than in the 30 years after the Second World War, but what the travel writers of this period demonstrated more than anything else, was that this difference was not external and distant but, paradoxically, within Europe and close to Britain, the country for which it seemed to hold most fascination. Nor must we forget the changes that made such travel writing possible, the use of the motor car in particular, which assumed a much greater significance in the post-war period and all of this is placed in sharp relief by what happened next: the mature stage of mass tourism from the 1970s, when Spain itself ceased to be seen as anything other than a holiday leisure destination (Barke et al. 1996, Pack 2006).

There is also an important historical context that provides a diet of preconceptions for the writers in this period. The nineteenth-century perception of Spain was dominated by the Englishman Richard Ford and the American Washington Irving, with George Borrow adding another rich layer of experience in 1843 (Borrow [1843] 1906). Together these early travellers provided a rich northern perspective that influenced every subsequent writer, either directly or through the developing imaginary. Ford's *Handbook* ([1845] 1966) and his later *Gatherings from Spain* ([1846] 2000) were intended to provide a wealth of useful practical information for travellers, with tips about dealing with avaricious inn-keepers, how to provide for a horse and how to avoid the depredations of bandits. As such it also provides an early and compelling contribution to the Spanish Imaginary. To be sure, there are earlier accounts, principally those of courtiers, ambassadors and tradesmen (see, for example, D'Aulnoy ([1691] 1930); Townend (1791) and Fischer (1802)) and others roughly contemporary with Ford, such as Mackenzie (1831 and 1836), Roscoe (1837), Rochfort Scott (1838), Wallis (1850), Clarke (1851) and Hoskins (1851). But Ford is the first to paint a compelling and influential Spain of the imaginary, and one that is still recognizable today. His main rival in this regard is Washington Irving, a young American lawyer who, for the sake of his health, travelled to Andalucia and 'rediscovered' Seville and Granada for northern tourists, and specifically the Alhambra in Granada as a place of enchantment. His fine-grained account of its people and dilapidated splendour brings to the North Atlantic audience for the first time a romantic account of mystery and imagination to match Ford's rather superior and dismissive practicalities (Irving [1832] 1985). The second half of the nineteenth century saw an explosion of publications on travel in Spain, that continued up until the First World War and included the monumental and beautifully illustrated books of Wigram (1906) and Calvert (1908).

In the twentieth century, Gerald Brenan and Ernest Hemingway helped to establish what Mitchell (2004: 117–18) later described as the *blood and sand* image that so impressed Brenan's Bloomsbury circle. The onset of the Spanish Civil War in 1936 saw two further literary notables arriving in Spain, fighting for the Republican side and writing about their experiences, George Orwell ([1938] 2007) and Laurie Lee (1971). Lee returned after the Second World War to lay his ghosts in a short but elegiac masterpiece *A Rose for Winter* ([1955] 2003) and so he joins the group that is my subject here. Space does not permit an examination of all of those other writers who shaped the imaginary in the first half of the twentieth century, but they include in no particular order of merit: Somerset Maugham ([1935] 1971) writing from Seville just before the Civil War, Gertrude Bone (1938) and her artist husband were touring the country by car as it began, and produced a handsome illustrated account of their journey, and there are two journalistic accounts of note: Clara Laughlin (1931), a Chicago travel journalist, produced an excellent guide book with some travel writer's insights in 1931, and the remarkable Australian journalist Nina Murdoch (1935) whose book glows with intelligence, humour and engagement and anticipates much in more recent styles of travel writing. All of these would repay further investigation, but for now they are important scene setters, prefiguring what was to follow after the watershed of the wars, and each of them contributing to what had already become the Spanish imaginary.

Post-War Travel and the Spanish Imaginary

After the Second World War, travellers were understandably slow to return after what had been a hiatus of nearly ten years. And yet it was the 1950s that saw the apotheosis of travel writing in Spain and it seems to have lost its appeal for them when the first plane-loads arrived on early package holidays, in the early 1960s. The annual numbers of inbound tourists increased from one million in 1950 to about 35 million at the end of the period (Pack 2006). The trend is reflected in the production of tourist guidebooks. The first *Blue Guides* to Spain were published in 1929 and 1930, just before Clara Laughlin's more personal account, and were not revised until 1964 (Muirhead 1964). In the 1950s a trickle of guidebooks appeared including the early Williamson's Green Guide (Williamson 1950), Cooper's (1952) *Your Holiday in Spain and Portugal*, Bransby's (1953) *A Fortnight in Spain*, Paris-based Nagel's Guide (Martineau 1954) John Way's (1956) *Good Companion Guide*, Hope Samson's (undated) *Spain*, part of the *Everybody's Pocket Travel Guide* series, appears to belong to the middle of the decade. While all of these books still have the characteristics of early travel guides, rather than travel books, they contribute much in their own way to the imaginary, especially in respect of otherness. H. John Way, for example, is at pains to explain Spain's differences from the rest of Europe:

> In no other European country do you feel so thoroughly that you are abroad. Spain is 'different'. It belongs, one feels, almost to another continent, and in some respects to another age. Much of this land and its way of life still remains in the eighteenth century-and where the twentieth century intrudes it does so uncertainly, as though it were unwanted. (Way 1956: 10)

Orientalism is a constant presence and a way of explaining these essentialized differences, as Hope Samson makes clear:

> In assessing the position of women in Spain it should be borne in mind that for seven centuries Moslem and Spaniard lived side by side and the way of life of one was largely influenced by the proximity of the other. Thus it is not surprising to find that the Arab concept of male superiority has remained to this day. (undated: 47)

Other guides pointed out the importance of tradition and protocol, and the awful consequences of wearing shorts away from the beach or a bikini, as opposed to a one-piece swimsuit, on it. In the background were the Civil Guard, those sinister guardians of the fascist state with their guns and funny hats. Whilst such valuable information was becoming more freely available, the writers of guidebooks seemed keen to replace the long tradition of travel writing that had preceded them. Gordon Cooper, for example, recognized that there had been 'a flood of new travel books about Spain, most are too chatty and personal to be of real value' (1952: 38), although he singled out Sacheverell Sitwell (1950) and H.V. Morton (1955) as honourable exceptions. The guidebook writers were, however, happy enough to express an opinion or two when the occasion or the issue demanded. Cooper, for example, is more of a latter-day Richard Ford, than an objective purveyor of facts. Witness his views on the language issue: 'I have previously remarked that I journeyed exhaustively through Spain without any knowledge whatsoever of the Spanish tongue – apart, of course, from a few necessary phrases that I picked up' (1952: 39–40).

Although too chatty and personal in Cooper's explorer's eyes, the travel writers proper are marked firstly by their diversity. Three are returnees from earlier times, the novelist V.S. Pritchett first visited and wrote about his travels in the 1920s and 1930s and returned in the early 1950s, publishing *The Spanish Temper* in 1954.

His, perhaps, is one of the books that Cooper was complaining about, because it starts with the following statement:

> This is a personal book and not primarily a work of information. It assumes the
> reader has at any rate read his Guide. I write because, of all the foreign countries
> I have known, Spain is the one that has made the strongest impression on me.
> (Pritchett 1954: 7)

Few views, however, could be more personal than those of Gerald Brenan, who famously settled in a small village in the Alpujarras Mountains in the south in the 1920s, left during the 1930s and the war period and later returned, to live more comfortably near Malaga. Here, he became something of a living legend for those who followed in his footsteps, with a visit to his house being an essential part of the itinerary for writers like Nina Murdoch. Another returnee was Laurie Lee, who in 1951 revisited the places that he had known in the Civil War, and the people with whom he had fought, or at least those that had survived. His account of this visit, *A Rose for Winter*, has already been mentioned and is a haunting and lyrical account of an imaginary Spain that now seems as lost in time as Irving's in *Tales of the Alhambra*. This was a sensual African place separated by eons, from post-war Europe. He says, for example of the peasants at Castillo, that:

> in their salty, sunburnt eyes, in the twist of their copper lips, and in their silences,
> one saw what they could not say – a savage past, an inglorious present, a future
> choked with unmentionable hopes. (Lee [1955] 2003: 103)

Over half of the books published in this period we might describe as literary or even scholarly in style and intent. For Sacheverell Sitwell, for example, the arts and architecture were the main focus of attention, proceeding 'from province to province of the entire country dealing with its monuments in turn' (1950: xi). Its monuments duly dealt with, Sitwell affords himself some reflections on the less tangible aspects of his Spanish journey, not least in Seville where, though lulled by the afternoon heat and the hypnotic sights and sounds of the Feria, he is transfixed by the soft complexions of the young girls 'ravishing to behold' (1950: 12).

Others, such as Bernard Newman (1966), we might describe as occupying the more popular end of the travel writing genre, although his approach is largely a journalistic travelogue, he does manage the unique distinction of opening his book with an interview with Franco. As well as journalists, there were novelists, amateur travel writers, a sociologist (Fraser 1973), the founder of a language school in Cordoba (Haycraft 1958), and Richard Wright ([1957] 1995), a black American author whose marginality in his own country finds some resonance with that of Spain in Europe. But these broad categories hide a great deal of variety and difference. For example, of the amateurs, one, W.T. Blake (1957), was a retired major and devout admirer of Franco, another, George Rainbird (1952), was an inveterate amateur traveller whose main concern was to find the cheapest lunch or hotel. Reading his book you feel you are being constantly winked at and given the inside track, along with helpful tips on how to deal with 'the Spaniard' in any given situation. Aimé Tschiffely (1952), a Swiss famous for his 'long rides' on horseback in the Americas, travelled around the whole country on a motorbike in 1950, through the debris of the Civil War, and his anecdotal style provides a wealth of detailed description and insight. Another amateur, Penelope Chetwode (1963), the wife of the poet John Betjeman, rode on horseback around a corner of Andalucia for a few weeks in 1961, finding and staying in cheap posadas, and mixing with the local people that she met on the way. Her commentary is lighter in tone than most, more familiar and more contemporary. She also charts the beginning of the period of change and modernization and the early results of development.

Women figure significantly in this literature. They include Rose Macaulay ([1949] 1973), the earliest of the post-war travellers who, in 1948, and in her mid-sixties, drove through Spain alone, and with the eyes of a classical scholar. Her account combines the sensual pleasures of the table and bathing in the sea with a rigorous and analytical eye for architecture and historical reference, the affective and the cognitive in perfect balance. I have mentioned already the redoubtable Penelope Chetwode, and to these must be added the novelist Madelaine Duke (1957) and the journalist Honor Tracey (1957), both of whom, like Chetwode and Murdoch, have a fresher and more contemporary style than most of their male counterparts.

Travelling the Imaginary

My analysis of this 'primary' material is based on what the authors experienced, what they discovered and revealed, and finally what they revealed about their own feelings of both distance and familiarity. I have then attempted to link this to their relationship with the imaginary, the extent to which they merely reflect it or actively reproduced it. Richard Wright provides a pretext for such reflections:

> Frankly, I had not been prepared for what I had encountered. Yet I could not feel
> that the fault was mine. I had diligently waded through scores of volumes by
> Spanish authorities and scholars to provide myself with some background against
> which I could measure and inform the reality that I would discover. But the more
> that I had probed and looked and listened, the more obvious it became to me that
> my trek to Barcelona, Madrid, Granada and Seville had not been a voyage that
> I could by any means describe as having taken me through the precincts of the
> Western World. Though Spain was geographically a part of Europe, it had had
> just enough Western aspects of life to make me feel a little at home. But it was not
> the West. Well, what then was it? (Wright [1957] 1995: 227)

Most of these authors travelled south, having entered Spain after a journey through France. There were alternatives, however, such as arriving in a southern port and travelling north, but the typical pattern is to enter in the northeast, travel south clockwise, leaving in the northwest. Only one of them arrived in the south and travelled north, the journalist Honor Tracey. As she crossed the border she made it very clear that she was prepared for the difference. Left behind were 'order, efficiency, cleanliness, peace and fair play' (1957: 7). There is a very common expression, however, not just of travelling south but of descent, or perhaps immersion, measured by the growing Moorish influence south of Valencia. When Rose Macaulay reaches Valencia from the north her expectations are more than met: 'Everywhere are Moorish towns and villages, place names, mosques, minarets, irrigation channels and watermills. The language has Arab words, much of the music and song is African by descent' ([1949] 1973: 80).

Almost every book provides a map showing the route taken, the map itself an account of what Judith Adler describes as being empirically knowable, so that the itinerary 'translates the spatial order of a map into a temporal sequence, defining proximity and distance in terms of time and feasibility' (1979: 1367). This feasibility is conditioned primarily by the mode of transport, which for most of these writers was a motor car and the freedom thus afforded from the long accustomed linearities of the railway. Though unreliable by contemporary standards these cars diminished space with their speed and made complex itineraries viable for the first time. The car itself, of course, was a symbol of difference from the land through which it was driven, a capsule within which the traveller was isolated and protected by the metal skin of the vehicle, a cultural shell of modernity.

There are times, says Honor Tracey, when 'the foreigner seems to be sailing comfortably in a private craft through oceans of misery' (1957: 16). In the early period petrol was often hard to find, and rationed; the roads were in poor shape, not having been repaired since before the Civil War. Car owners therefore relied a great deal on the reputation of the manufacturer and the proximity of mechanics and agents who could provide the necessary attention and spare parts. Cars were stabled like horses and tended with copious amounts of grease and oil to maintain them on the journey. Perhaps because of this they often became personalities in themselves, offering not merely transport, but protection and reassurance. Wilson MacArthur (1953) described himself as an 'autonomad' and his car, which he called 'Huberta', was treated with a reverence that his ever-present wife might have envied. Huberta even chose their hotel in Madrid, 'nosing through the crowds, pulled up of her own accord outside the Hotel Comercio, a handsome stone building on a corner, with great wooden shutters and an inviting brightness within' (1953: 52).

Drivers often found themselves almost alone on the road and when they stopped in towns and villages, as MacArthur did in Almeria in 1952, they would attract a crowd, not just of curious children, but adults too (1953: 42). The rarity of cars brought risks of its own and W.T. Blake reports, with great pride, that during the whole tour:

> We were successful in not knocking down a single person, but we were twice run into by men who stepped off the pavement and walked into the side of the car.

On several occasions slight damage happened to cyclists who fell off in front of us in fright at the sound of a horn, though we pulled up long before we reached them. (1957: 40)

Later he remarks that the pedestrians of Spain are terrible jay-walkers, 'one never knows what they are likely to do' (1957: 80), although walking into the side of his car or making him stop abruptly were clearly sources of annoyance and frustration. The developed countries of Europe were using their vehicles as time capsules, visiting their own lost arcadia, the presence of the car drawing out a mutual fascination of one with the other.

The Cognitive and the Imaginary

The cognitive dimension here is linked to attempts to understand Spanish ethnicity and the vestiges of original Iberian peoples, Celts, Romans, Visigoths but especially, of course, the Moors. The Moors *are* the orient in the Spanish imaginary and as such they are sought everywhere by these writers, as if as tokens of long gone exotic otherness they are talismanic representations of the reality of Spain's difference. For Morton, the Moorish invasion of 711 was Spain's defining moment:

> It is the event which distinguishes her early history from that of other European
> countries; it has placed a dark, enduring gleam in the eyes of her women and has
> given that plaintive eastern undercurrent to her music; among other things it has
> possibly planted that streak of cruelty in Spanish hearts which is regularly sated
> on Sunday afternoons. (1955: 101)

This is the Spanish imaginary writ large and clearly linked to a Moorish heritage that formed a constant preoccupation often expressed descriptions of the people and their distinctive looks, especially in Andalucia, which in the terms of the imaginary has almost come to stand for Spain as a whole. Pritchett is typical in drawing attention to physical features and the differences with those of northern Europe. Here, he de-humanizes them with his account of the classic Spanish type: 'Grave, dark, sallow, a little heavy sometimes; and there is the small monkey-ish type, quick, melancholy, mischievous' (1954: 73). For Morris, the men are swarthy and skinny, the older ones 'with fringed beards like marabouts' (1964: 78). Sitwell describes the Muslim appearance of women at Vejer de la Frontera near Cadiz (1950: 38) and, indeed, the women generally are likely to be cast as even more Moorish because of their clothing and behaviour:

> when some old lady wanders into the grocery store and spots a stranger there,
> you will notice that she takes the corner of her black headscarf between her
> teeth, and holds it there defensively-precisely as the women of Egypt ... (Morris
> 1964: 78–9)

And MacArthur (1953: 48): '[s]o, before the stranger, the peasant woman in remoter parts of Andalucia may still hide her face, the head-shawl serving as veil; and the greetings you receive are translated directly from the Arabic'. Some of these essentializing narratives bordered on the comical: George Rainbird, for example, offered the following:

> Every now and again we met a peasant woman, hand on hip, with a basket of oranges on her head. She walked with the magnificent poise and grace that only come to those who have balanced things on their heads from childhood. (1952: 87)

Morris, for whom the 'timeless quality of Spanish life still [felt] very Muslim' (1964: 79), even complained when guidebooks mentioned certain surviving Moorish customs in remote villages only to find, on arrival, nothing unusual except that, 'in a properly oriental way, hidden legacies of magic, pederasty, or high living that make the East feel pleasantly at hand' (1964: 79). She is content later, in Cadiz, where she finds two children in mock battle: '"I am the Christian caballero", said the girl brightly, hitching her helmet up. The boy, however, had more sense of history. "I am the others!" he darkly replied, and bent his scimitar between his hands' (1964: 81).

In this way travellers thus sought to comprehend what Pritchett (1954) called the 'Spanish temper' in relation to their understanding of history and the co-mingling of different cultures. The people of Spain, in true orientalist fashion, are abbreviated to a limited and familiar range of characteristics that can then be held to explain various and important differences between Spain and the north. Copious reference is made to 'the Spaniard'. The use of the definite article seems old fashioned, condescending, de-humanizing even, but it enabled things to be said that might otherwise require expansion and a deeper understanding and, of course, it emphasized distance and difference. Wilson MacArthur, for example, is told by a Spaniard that it will be a long time before the country is ready for democracy, but is the lack of a democratic instinct all bad? Not according to MacArthur, who justifies his view on the grounds that the Spaniard is such an individualist. If Spain ever became democratic there would need to be as many political parties as there were people (1953: 206).

Art and architecture were also the natural province of the traveller in Spain, a tradition that went back to the nineteenth century with antiquarian travellers. The gothic architecture of the north, perhaps most graphically described in the cathedral at Burgos, is contrasted with the mosque-cathedrals of the south and especially at Seville and most visually at Cordoba. All of this had to be noted, taxonomized, contextualized, historicized and understood, this knowledge channelled into the image of Spain and the Spanish as 'a part' according to Sitwell, 'and an important part of the old and dwindling Europe' (1950: 129).

The Affective and Emotional Imaginary

The bullfight and the flamenco arguably belong to traditions other than the Moorish, but they are also linked to a distant past, vestigial remnants barely remembered. The bullfight attracted opprobrium from many of the writers because of its cruelty to horses (at that time) as well as to bulls. But here are expressions of the affective element of the writers' engagement. The strong feelings elicited by the corrida and flamenco, and the exotic darkness of both are balanced by the lightness and sweetness of Moorish essences and the 'vistas of amazing loveliness' that MacArthur sees in the gardens of the Alcazar in Seville (1953: 236). Nina Murdoch had already provided the most affecting description of Seville in the 1930s: 'Seville is like a laughing woman in a summer frock come in from raiding the garden with her arms full of flowers' (1935: 123), and subsequent writers were more than equal to the task of both feeling and expressing such delights. Spain accosts all of the senses, but it begins, for George Rainbird (1952), with the visual: 'All along the road mimosa trees were brilliant with yellow blossom; whilst red, white, pink and variegated camellias bloomed in every cottage garden, their waxen flowers supremely lovely to our waxen eyes' (1952: 87). Other sensations soon follow. 'No land in Europe', says Sacheverell Sitwell in 1950, 'probably no land in the civilized world, has so violent a personality, so strong a flavour, as that of Spain' (1950: 11); and even he, the archetypal traveller antiquarian, is not immune from the showy sensuousness of the Feria, Seville's springtime festival:

> As you walk home and look back for the last time, leaving the lights and music behind you, your breath will be caught with orange blossom, and falling asleep, forgetful of the hour, you may think, as I do, that the Feria of Seville must be the most beautiful public spectacle in the world today. (1950: 43)

For Jan Morris, Spanishness itself, whatever it is, is 'a pungent substance that floats around you the moment you cross the Spanish frontier' (1964: 31).

The affective response was always conditioned by the experience of polarities, familiarity and strangeness, proximity and otherness; modernity and pre-modernity; beauty and violence; exoticism and dirt; the wealth of culture and the poverty of people, the 'killing poverty', as Honor Tracey (1957: 16) called it. W.T. Blake is at once fascinated and repelled by the presence of beggars in large numbers:

> The tourist districts invaded by Americans are thickly inhabited by these pests. They are spoilt by the American visitors who encourage them to scramble for coins and do not seem to object to having their sleeves twitched and grimy hands and sore covered faces thrust in front of them at regular intervals. (1957: 23)

V.S. Pritchett, who spent more time in Spain than most of these writers and whose experience of it spanned several decades, was perhaps the most expansive in his reflections on its affective register:

> ... Spain is the old and necessary enemy of the West. There we learn our history upside down and see life exposed to the skin. Neither in France nor in Italy can one be so frankly frightened. All the hungers of life are blankly stated there. We see the primitive hungers we live by and yet, by a curious feat of stoicism, fatalism and lethargy, the passions of human nature are sceptically contained. (1954: 7)

For Richard Wright, the climate and landscape are a constant source of affective experience and emotional consequence. The sun is 'brutal', rocks are jagged and fantastically sculptured, and 'naked promontories' 'jutted' into a 'flat blue unbending sky'. When he finally sees an industrial chimney he compares it to an exclamation mark 'emphasising how far Spain had fallen to the rear of her sister European nations' ([1957] 1995: 136).

If we try to interpret what these writers contributed to the Spanish imaginary we can see that though varied in their purpose and experience, they acted consistently to both reflect and sustain it. Partly this involved the production of the essentialized narrative that is evocative of Said's Orientalism. This is a Spain for the twentieth century, one that helped to define, by contrast, contemporary European modernity. They identified an 'Other' within, but distanced by the differentials built into European post-war reconstruction and development. They revealed these differences and identified them as the essentialisms of Spain that they had already been prepared for by a century or so of earlier writing. I have called this the Spanish imaginary, and these writers used the post-war condition of Spain to revivify it for the modern age. One writer, however, seemed immune to the imaginary. Robert Hugill, a school teacher from Durham in northern England, simply described what he saw and did during his north–south walking tour of the country and did so, apparently, with an open mind. Instead of imposing his own and other preconceptions on Spain he allowed Spain to impose its presence on him:

> I wasn't the same person who'd seen the Spanish shore across the Bay of Biscay a little over two months ago. I'd become, I hoped, a little wiser than before, more tolerant and more compassionate, and after what I'd seen of this country and its people (especially its people) that I'd be able to look at my own through more discerning eyes. (1967: 182)

If Hugill contributed anything to the Spanish imaginary, it was precisely that it was just that, an imaginary, pervasive, but not necessary, readily available but not required, an essence of place but in no sense inherent in it. On the contrary, the imaginary worked in moments of engagement, emerging in moments of intensity, connecting with knowledge and experience to reproduce its core meanings. The imaginary is thus a performance, spatially bounded and recognizable in Crouch's (2010) idea of flirtation with space, which he has also expressed in the cultural moments of tourism:

> Performativity acts and happens in in dynamic interplay among sensory feelings, imagination, sensuality and desire, expressiveness and meaning making. Moreover, the character of process in the relationality of performativities and objects we can feel, touch and reflect upon operates multiple effects, time and space. (2012: 23)

Hugill, it seems, found his own imaginary in Spain.

For social anthropologists like Dean MacCannell (1999) the Spanish imaginary could be seen simply as a short cut to 'authenticity' for discontented moderns whose daily life was infused with artifice and alienation. Certainly, all those aspects of the imaginary that are elemental and affective can be seen as discursive routes to an imagined authenticity, and there we find another of those polarities: imagination and reality, in a subtle and reciprocal dependency. The travel writers made constant reference to these elemental realities as they saw them. Pritchett was impatient at the time spent in France on the way to his goal: 'the prolonged sight of France annoys; one is impatient for the drama of the frontier and for the violent contrasts, the discontent and indifference of Spain (Pritchett 1954: 11).

Conclusions: The Imaginary Re-Imagined

By 1960, things had begun to change. Mass tourism, under Franco's urging, had begun to take hold on the Costas in the south and east. And so the imaginary began to fade from view, replaced by the tangibilities of the tourist industry: the high-rise hotels, bars and nightclubs, the tackiness of the promenade and the trade in cheap souvenirs. The Spanish imaginary was lost in northern stereotypes and expressed in a single word like 'Manana' muttered in deprecatory tones and with knowing looks, part of the limited repertoire of signifiers of Spain and the Spanish, along with bullfights, donkeys and sangria. The writers discussed here mostly fled before the tourist hordes. Through the 1960s and 1970s Spain became less imaginary and readily available as a network of built-up coastal resorts to anyone and everyone. Spain was no longer for the traveller, but for the package tourist for whom the recreation of homely familiarities in the sunshine was more important than difference and exoticism, which were either regarded with suspicion like the food or became the butt of jokes about lazy or lascivious waiters. The delightful towns and the coast so beloved of Rose Macaulay disappeared under concrete, in a matter of a few years. Those writers' descriptions of places such as Nerja, Torremolinos and Benidorm are strange to us now; villages to them, high-rise urban sprawls to us.

So where is the imaginary now? Well, perhaps surprisingly, it has not gone away. The Moorish aspects for example are now assimilated into a new representation of Spain designed to attract a different kind of tourist segment: this is 'Real Spain', and marketing campaigns that seek to attract higher spending cultural tourists with an appeal to the cognitive and affective dimensions of the Spanish imaginary linked to intimations of authenticity.

The Spanish imaginary has been a powerful definitional force in the representation of Spain not traditionally by the Spanish themselves but by northerners who perceive and value its otherness with shades or orientalist sentiment. Never was the imaginary stronger than in the period after the Second World War, when Spain lagged behind many of its northern European neighbours. Travel writers luxuriated in its strangeness and its exoticism and revelled in their discovery (or rediscovery) of its ancient secrets. They described both its history and it arts and they related their experience of its warmth, its light and shade, its sounds and scents, its tastes and its temper. Through their rose-tinted sunglasses they saw what they wanted to see and at the end of each day they wrote up their journals like explorers and collectors in their own private paradise. When they left, Spain was transformed into what must have seemed like its historical destiny as a pleasure ground for northern European mass tourists delivered from the air. And now it is re-imagined, but this time by marketers using the travel writers' language and imagination. The economic significance of international tourism make it so, and it can be no surprise that the offer of *Real Spain* relies as much on the imaginary as it does on any more local sense of place or identity.

Perhaps Irving was right when he regretted the complete passing of the Moorish people from Spain. What's left, after all, is no more than imaginary.

References

Adler, J. 1979. Tourism as performed art. *American Journal of Sociology*, 94(6), 1366–91.

Barke, M., Towner J. and Newton, M.T. (eds) 1996. *Tourism in Spain: Critical issues*. Wallingford: CAB International.

Blake, W.T. 1957. *Spanish Journey or Springtime in Spain*. London: Alvin Redman.

Bone, G. 1938. *Days in Old Spain*. London: Macmillan and Co.

Borrow, G. [1843] 1906. *The Bible in Spain*. London: J.M. Dent and Son Ltd.

Bransby, L. 1953. *A Fortnight in Spain*. London: Perrival Marshal.

Brenan, G. 1957. *South from Granada: A sojourn in southern Spain*. London: Penguin Modern Classics.

Calvert, A.F. 1908. *Southern Spain*. London: A & C Black.

Cebrian, M. and Lopez, S. 2004. Economic growth, technology transfer and convergence in Spain, 1960–1973, in *Technology and Human Capital in*

Historical Perspective, edited by J. Ljundberg and J.P. Smits. Basingstoke: Palgrave Macmillan, 1–33.

Chetwode, P. 1963. *Two Middle-Aged Ladies in Andalusia*. London: John Murray.

Clarke, W.G. 1851. *Gazpacho: Or, summer months in Spain*. London: John W. Parker and Son.

Cooper, G. 1952. *Your Holiday in Spain and Portugal*. London: Alvin Redman Ltd.

Crouch, D. 2010. *Flirting With Space, Journeys and Creativity*. Farnham: Ashgate.

Crouch, D. 2012. Meaning, encounter and performativity: Threads and moments of spacetimes in doing tourism, in *The Cultural Moment in Tourism*, edited by L. Smith, E. Waterton and S. Watson. London: Routledge, 20–37.

D'Aulnoy, Madame, [1691] 1930. *Travels into Spain*, edited by Sir E. Denison Ross and Eileen Power, London: George Routledge and Sons.

Duke, M. 1957. *Beyond the Pillars of Hercules, A Spanish Journey*. London: Evans Brothers Ltd.

Fischer, F.A. 1802. *Travels in Spain in 1797 and 1798. With an Appendix on the method of travelling in that country*. London: A. Strahan for T.N. Longman and O. Rees.

Ford, R. [1845] 1966. *Handbook for Travellers in Spain*. London: Centaur Press.

Ford, R. [1846] 2000. *Gatherings From Spain*. London: Pallas Athene.

Fraser, R. 1973. *The Pueblo, A Mountain Village on the Costa Del Sol*. London: Allen Lane.

Haycraft, J. 1958. *Babel in Spain*. London: The Travel Book Club.

Hope Samson, E. undated. *Everybody's Pocket Travel Guide to Spain*. London: W. Foulsham and Co. Ltd.

Hoskins, G.A. 1851. *Spain as it Is*, in 2 volumes. London: Colburn and Co.

Hugill, R. 1967. *I Travelled Through Spain*. Wimbledon: Vernon and Yates.

Irving, W. [1832] 1985. *Tales of the Alhambra*. Granada: Miguel Sanchez.

Laughlin, C.E. 1931. *So You're Going to Spain*. London: Methuen and Co. Ltd.

Lee, L. 1971. *As I Walked Out One Midsummer Morning*. London: Penguin Books.

Lee, L. [1955] 2003. *A Rose For Winter, Travels in Andalucia*. London: Vintage.

MacArthur, W. 1953. *Autonomad in Spain*. London: Cassell and Company Ltd.

Macaulay, R. [1949] 1973. *Fabled Shore, from the Pyrenees to Portugal*. London: Hamish Hamilton.

MacCannell, D. 1999. *The Tourist, A New Theory of the Leisure Class*, 2nd edition. Berkeley: University of California Press.

Mackenzie, A.S. 1831. *A Year in Spain, by a Young American*. London: John Murray.

Mackenzie, A.S. 1836. *Spain Revisited*. New York: Harper and Brothers.

Martineau, G.R. 1954. *Spain* (The Nagel Travel Guide series). Paris: Les Editions Nagel.

Morton, H.V. 1955. *A Stranger in Spain*. London: Methuen and Co.

Mitchell, D. 2004. *Travellers in Spain, An Illustrated Anthology*. Málaga: Ediciones Santana.

Morris, J. 1964. *Spain*. London: Faber and Faber.

Muirhead, L.R. (ed.) 1964. *The Blue Guide to Southern Spain with Gibraltar, Ceuta and Tangier*, revised and enlarged by John H. Harvey. London: Ernest Benn Ltd. (see also, *the Blue Guide to Northern Spain*).

Murdoch, N. 1935. *She Travelled Alone in Spain*. London: George G. Harrap and Co. Ltd.

Newman, B. 1966. *Spain Revisited*. London: Herbert Jenkins.

Orwell, G. [1938] 2007. *Homage to Catalonia*. London: Penguin Books.

Pack, S.D. 2006. *Tourism and Dictatorship: Europe's peaceful invasion of Franco's Spain*. New York: Palgrave Macmillan.

Pile, S. 2010. Emotions and affect in recent human geography. *Transactions of the Institute of British Geographers*, 35(1), 5–20.

Pritchett, V.S. 1954. *The Spanish Temper*. London: Chatto and Windus.

Rainbird, G. 1952. *Escape to Sunshine*. London: Collins.

Rochfort, S., Capt. C. 1838. *Excursions in the Mountains of Ronda and Granada, with Characteristic Sketches of the Inhabitants of the South of Spain*. London: Henry Colburn.

Roscoe, T. 1837. *The Tourist in Spain*. London: R. Jennings and Co.

Said, E.W. 1978. *Orientalism*. London: Routledge and Kegan Paul.

Sitwell, S. 1950. *Spain*. London: Batsford.

Somerset Maugham, W. [1935] 1971. *Don Fernando*. London: Heinemann.

Taylor, C. 2004. *Modern Social Imaginaries*. Durham, NC: Duke University Press.

Thien, D. 2005. After or beyond feeling? A consideration of affect and emotion in geography. *Area*, 37(4), 450–6.

Townend, J. 1791. *A Journey through Spain in the Years 1986 and 1787: With particular attention to the agriculture, manufacturers, commerce, population, taxes and revenu*. London: C. Dilly, in the Poultry.

Tracy, H. 1957. *Silk Hats and No Breakfast: Notes on a Spanish journey*. London: Methuen and Co.

Tschiffely, A. 1952. *Round and About Spain*. London: Hodder & Stoughton.

Wallis, S.T. 1850. *Glimpses of Spain, or, Notes of an Unfinished Tour*. London: Sampson Low.

Way, H.J. 1956. *The Good Companion Guide No. 5, Spain*. London: Nicholas Vane.

Wigram, E.T.A. 1906. *Northern Spain*. London: Adam and Charles Black.

Williamson, H.W.S. 1950. *The Tourist Guide-Book of Spain*. London: British American Publishing Company.

Wright, R. [1957] 1995. *Pagan Spain*. New York: Harper Perennial.

PART III
Visual, Media, Representation

Chapter 9

'Where all the Lines of the Map Converge': Werner Herzog's Ekstatic Imagination and Performative Thresholds

Gabriella Calchi-Novati

> This place works almost as a natural selection for people that have this intention
> to jump off the margin of the map, and we all meet here *where all the lines of the
> map converge*.
>
> – Herzog 2009[1]

> The *signature* is the place where the gesture of reading and that of writing invert
> their relation and enter into a zone of undecidability. Here reading becomes writing,
> and writing is wholly resolved into reading.
>
> – Agamben 2009: 56 (my emphasis)

Time, the Fabric of Imagination

In its etymological meaning, the term *imagination* carries within itself the
Latin word *imago*, image. Italian philosopher Giorgio Agamben, discussing the
concept of the image, refers back to the work of Aby Warburg and his idea of
Pathosformel[2] – 'formula of pathos' – wherein the term *formula*, contextualized
within the artistic realm, 'implies that it is impossible to distinguish between
creation and performance, between the original and its representation' (Agamben
1999: 89–103). Aesthetic and literary formulae, Agamben elucidates, 'are hybrids
of matter and form, of creation and performance, of primeness and repetition'
(Agamben 2007: 17).[3] But what is that whose form is matter, and whose origin is
its own becoming, if not time? Time, which for Agamben, is the distinct 'fabric
of images' and 'the actual paradigm of contemporary life' (Agamben 2007: 18;
10). Time in itself always implies thinking: we cannot conceive of time without

---

1   Quotes from the film *Encounters at the End of the World* are from the 'Dialogue
Transcript' of the film, available online at: http://www.script-o rama.com/movie_scripts/a1/
encounters-at-the-end-of-the-world-script.html.

2   Agamben discusses at length the importance of the work of German thinker and
art historian Aby Warburg on the study of images, or rather 'iconology', in his 1975 essay
entitled 'Warburg and the nameless science', published in Agamben (1999).

3   The nymph is one of these very aesthetic formualae that Agamben articulates in detail.

thinking time, without conjuring up a conceptual movement, through which we paradoxically attempt to catch time in its unattainable stillness. It is important to note also that Walter Benjamin illustrates such a 'movement of thinking' in his method called *Dialektik im Stillstand* – dialectic at a standstill. He sustains that what belongs to thinking is 'the movement as well as the arrest of thought', adding that 'where thinking comes to a standstill in a constellation saturated with tensions – there the dialectical image appears. It is the *caesura* in the movement of thought' (Benjamin 1999: 475: N10a, 3, my emphasis). Drawing from Benjamin, Agamben discusses the concept of *caesura* in his short text 'L'idea della cesura'[4] in which he starts by quoting a distich composed by the Italian poet Sandro Penna. In those two short verses, Agamben claims that the synthesis between content and form, between the metric caesura and the arrest of thought, takes place. Agamben, moreover, explains that for Penna 'the element that arrests the metrical momentum of the voice, the *caesura* of the poetic verse, is thinking' (Agamben 2002: 23). In addition to this, the philosopher says that 'the rhythmic transport that moves the impetus of the verse, is empty as it is solely the transport of itself. And it is in this emptiness that, as *pure word*, the caesura, for a little time, thinks' (Agamben 2002: 24).

In this chapter, I seek to show that imagination inhabits such a *caesura*, whether it be aural or visual. It is only in such a pause that images arise, and along with them, the movement of imagination, or what I call *ekstatic imagination*. Thus, I will employ Werner Herzog's documentary of physical and metaphysical travelling, *Encounters at the End of the World* (2007)[5] as a philosophical means to investigate the instances in which imagination becomes *ekstatic*. Over the past 40 years, Herzog has taken viewers on many cinematic and allegorical journeys through his documentaries and films. *Encounters* brings us to the Antarctic, where we encounter the community of those who are gathered under the aegis of the National Science Foundation. In McMurdo Station, which looks, Herzog suggests, 'like a future space settlement', we meet philosophers, ex-PhD students, volcanologists, ecologists, glaciologists, who all have in common the desire to escape from civilization. They are 'the full-time dreamers and part-time workers' who populate McMurdo Station, to explore, in their very personal ways, the meaning of life and its probable approaching extinction.

However, before getting to the heart of the matter, I would like to rehearse some of Elaine Scarry's claims in relation to imagination, for I believe that they will help me to introduce and frame my idea of *ekstatic imagination*. In *The Body in Pain* (Scarry 1998: 161), while 'uncovering the structure of torture', and thus exposing the different performative aspects of pain, Scarry sustains that there is a fundamental difference between pain and imagination. She claims that pain is a state anomalous to imagination, for:

---

4   The idea of caesura.

5   *Encounters at the End of the World* is the only one of Herzog's films to be nominated for an Academy Award.

> While pain is a state remarkable of being wholly without objects, the imagination
> is remarkable for being the only state that is wholly its objects. There is in
> imagining no activity, no 'state', no experienceable condition or felt-occurrence
> separate from the objects: the only evidence that one is 'imagining' is that
> imaginary objects appear in the mind ... Although the gerund 'imagining' assumes
> an activity, and although in some philosophical contexts it is described as though
> it were made up of both an intentional act and an intentional object, in fact ...
> it is impossible to imagine without imagining something. (Scarry 1998: 161–2)

Therefore, according to Scarry, imagination is but its own imagined objects, which
appear within imagination without any mental activity, in a stillness of thinking,
so to speak. Drawing on such a claim, I would like to propose an alternative
reading of imagination, one that moves towards an *outside*, rather than towards
its own inside, as proposed by Scarry. Instead of remaining anchored to its inner
imagined object, which 'happened to have been taken as a representable instance
of imagining' (Scarry 1998: 163), *ekstatic imagination* is, on the contrary, always
already in transit. Let us now consider in a closer fashion the concept of *transit* in
the context of imagination and travelling.

'Ekstatic Imagination': Imagination *in Transit*

In his 2007 text *Ninfe*, Agamben suggests that any time we are 'working' with
images it means that we are 'at a crossroads between, not only the corporeal and
the incorporeal, but also, and more importantly, between the individual and the
collective' (Agamben 2007: 53). Being at a crossroads suggests in itself dwelling
in the realm of potentiality, for both the choice and the actualization of the choice
(the 'where should I go next?' choice) have yet still to happen. Imagination thus
is not only a movement of thought that produces images, but also, and more
crucially, a conceptual movement that in itself is pure potentiality. For Agamben
'imagination circumscribes a space in which we are not thinking yet, in which
thought becomes possible solely through an impossibility of thinking' (Agamben
2007: 52). But what is that space in which we are open to thinking, but not in
fact thinking yet? What is that space in which we can think exactly through the
impossibility of thinking, if not time?

Therefore, my concept of *ekstatic imagination* does not refer to a movement
in space, but rather to a movement in time, to a transit in a time that timelessly
inhabits a caesura, a pause, and in so doing becomes always-already present. The
opening images of the film *Encounters at the End of the World* are under water, or
as Herzog puts it, under the frozen sky, where divers are exploring with torches
the incommensurably blue waters of Antarctica. The ice seen from beneath looks
like a sky whose clouds are so low that one could actually touch them. The quiet
that pervades those waters sets the meditative tone of our travelling to a continent
that 'does not have languages', and yet speaks the universal language of silence.

The aural and visual *caesura* of pausing, in which stillness is that which performs, transitions us, the viewers, into the plane, flying towards the South Pole. Herzog and the other 'professional dreamers' are heading towards the Antarctic community of McMurdo Station. Located on the frozen ice of Ross Island, this station is the headquarters of the National Science Foundation, which sponsored the making of *Encounters*. On the plane Herzog, through his voice-over commentary, which seems to grant us whispered access into his thoughts, asks: 'who were the people I was going to meet in Antarctica at the end of the world? What were their dreams?' Such a question is what the German director attempts to address throughout the whole film. That very same question would never be fully answered.

After flying into 'the unknown, a seemingly endless void', Herzog eventually lands at the South Pole to meet the people who work at McMurdo Station, the largest human settlement in Antarctica. Upon arrival, we are shown a grey depressing landscape, something similar to 'a ugly mining town, filled with caterpillars, and noisy construction sites'. At this point, the director, with his characteristic child-like curiosity, wants to know 'who are the people who drive the heavy machinery and what brought them to Antarctica?'. Who are the *encounters at the end of the world* that we are about to experience?

Stefan Pashow, forklift driver and philosopher, tells the camera that he has been travelling in his imagination since, as a child, he read the *Odyssey*, a book that made him fall in love with the world. In order to answer more specifically Herzog's question on the reasons that brought him to McMurdo Station, Stefan replies that, that place 'works almost as a natural selection for the people who have this intention to jump off the margin of the map' so that in the end they 'all meet [t]here, where all the lines of the map converge'. I would claim that 'bordering' is this singular point, where *all the lines of the map converge*.

Agamben reminds us that, according to Immanuel Kant, 'singularity borders all possibility and thus receives its *omnimoda determinatio* ... only by means of this *bordering*' (Agamben 2005: 67, emphasis in original). 'What is in question in this *bordering*', Agamben explains, is the concept of '*threshold*', which is a 'point of contact with an external space that must remain empty' (Agamben 2005: 67–8). The concept of *threshold* in Agamben's philosophy is similar to the one of *caesura*. In both concepts, *potentiality* is that which is at stake. Image and thus imagination inhabit such a zone of arrest, which is 'a *threshold* between stillness and movement' (Agamben 2007: 28). In other words, imagination is *ekstatic*, that is to say in transit, not in relation to physical movement, as I have already pointed out, but in relation to a metaphysical one. 'The life of images', Agamben suggests, 'does not occur in a simple stillness, nor in the subsequent regaining of movement, but in a *pause* charged with the tension between stillness and movement' (Agamben 2007: 29).

Already in *De Memoria et Reminiscentia*, Aristotle addresses the crucial interconnection that exists between memory, imagination and time. He shows that whenever we are dealing with imagination we are, in fact, dealing with *thresholds*:

It is necessary to cognize magnitude and movement by the same faculty by which time is also cognized ... When a person actualizes his memory for the fact that he has seen, heard or learned something, he senses in addition that he did this earlier; and the concepts of 'earlier' and 'later' belong in time ... Those things that are essentially the objects of memory are also such of which there is imagination. (Bloch 2007: 29)

The perception of time, thus, is the *conditio sine qua non* for both memory and imagination to occur. While memory makes us perceive that what we are remembering occurred at a certain moment in a past temporal tense; imagination pushes our thinking towards a future temporal tense, potential and yet to be actualized: a temporal *tense in transit*.

Stillness and Silence: Performative Thresholds

Herzog's *Encounters* calls for such a temporal tense. Spectators are implicitly asked to be patient, to sit and wait for the images to unravel in the moment of their unravelling. For this reason, I would claim that *Encounters* can be seen as a visual score that the viewers themselves have to bring to life, through their own imagination, as happens with music whose score is, in itself, silent and indeed very different from the performed piece. Herzog's *Encounters* is reminiscent of avant-garde art-works such as John Cage's musical composition *3'44"* (1952), and Yves Klein's creative attempts to tangibly represent the void through the employment of the colour blue. Similarly to these works, *Encounters* needs to be experienced several times, to be able to see what is at first invisible and to hear what erroneously sounds at first like silence. Cage, regarding the audience's experience of *3'44"*, says that:

> What they thought was silence, because they didn't know how to listen, was full of accidental sounds. You could hear the wind stirring outside during the first movement. During the second, raindrops began pattering the roof, and during the third, the people themselves made all kinds of interesting sounds as they talked or walked out. (Gann 2010: 4)

In 1958, a column from *Le Monde* summarized the press reaction to Klein's work on the void:

> 'Revolution through the Void' (*Arts*); 'Exhibition of White' (*La Croix*); 'Long live Nothing!' (*Noir et blanc*): this is how the press saw Yves Klein's latest exhibition ... 'Where are the paintings?' asks the visitor who has ventured into this tabernacle; Klein's response goes further, when all is said and done, than his joke: 'In his journal, Delacroix set great store by the concept of the indefinable.

I make it my essential material, systematically using it: the painting, by dint of being indefinable, makes itself absence'. (Riout 2010: 75)

I claim that in Cage, Klein and Herzog's work, it is what resides in the interstices of silence and absence that performs. Herzog's documentary depicts not just stillness and silence, but rather that which *pauses* between movements and sounds. Through his expansive camera shots, Herzog allows us to linger on the vibrant stillness of life, which in *Encounters* is metaphorically represented by the Antarctic icebergs, described as being 'a dynamic living entity'.[6]

By travelling over the sidereal realm of the South Pole, not only do we witness the monochromatic void of thousands of kilometres of ice, but we also listen to the unusual *non-sound* of the 'underwater recording of seal calls': a sound that is at the same time 'the most amazing and inorganic sound' that one could ever imagine.

In one of Herzog's previous documentaries, *Grizzly Man* (2005),[7] he claimed that what he tries to reach in his work is an 'ecstatic truth' by 'stepping outside of "humanness" and into ecstasy'. I would argue that in *Encounters*, Herzog is able to reach several of these moments of *ecstatic truth*, for instance when the divers, in total silence, dive into the freezing waters of Antarctica. Herzog reflecting on the divers' comments:

> To me, the divers look like astronauts floating in space. But their work is extremely dangerous. They are diving without tethers to give them more free range. But here you can't trust a compass. So close to the magnetic pole, the needle would point straight up or straight down. Somehow, you have to find your way back to the exit hole or you are trapped under the ceiling of ice.

Divers, as we see in *Encounters*, do not speak at all in their routine; their language is made of ritualistic gestures that make them look as though 'they were priests preparing for mass'. 'Under the ice', Herzog says,

> The divers find themselves into a separate reality, where space and time acquire a strange new dimension. Those few who have experienced the world under the frozen sky often speak of it as going down into the 'cathedral'.

It is of note that the soundtrack of the film, besides the recordings of the seals' calls, is comprised of religious choral music, which enables *ekstatic imagination* to take

---

6 These are the words that, in *Encounters*, glaciologist Douglas MacAyel uses to describe the icebergs in Antarctica, adding that they look like still entities, but they are all shifting north.

7 *Grizzly Man* traces the life and death of animal activist Timothy Treadwell, who spent 13 years in what he called 'the grizzly maze'. In October 2003 Treadwell and Amie Huguenard, his girlfriend, were killed by a grizzly bear in the Katmai National Park and Reserve.

place also on an aural level. In an interview, Herzog states that the experience of the 'cathedral', and of Antarctica as a whole, is imbued by religious feelings of awe. The director, through a quasi-poetic stream-of-consciousness, admits that:

> The music, of course, points it [the religious feeling] out – Russian Orthodox Church choirs – and all of a sudden, you have this feeling of a strange sacrality of these places. And of course, sometimes you are into the most unbelievable things, like these long carved tunnels in the ice, under the very south, mathematically true South Pole; corridors endlessly long and at the end of one of those corridors, and it's 70 degrees below zero, and somebody has carved some sort of a shrine into the ice [with frozen pop-corn and paper flowers], and you find a deep frozen sturgeon there ... Nobody could even invent it. I could not even invent such a thing. It's either pure ecstasy, or pure science fiction, or pure Zen! (Greenbaum Kasson 2008: n.p.)

I find extremely appropriate Herzog's mention of Zen when he describes Antarctica. Zen, as we know, is that branch of Buddhism that emphasizes the values of present moments and meditation as the means to attain the experience of them. *Encounters*, thus, can be considered a meditative piece too, since we are called to the 'here and now' of our *ekstatic imagination*, as though we were experiencing in the first person the breathing of life as such. What I mean by this is that in *Encounters*, for example, when the divers are under the ice, the only movement that we perceive is their breathing, which is visually translated into tangible bubbles. These bubbles, in the seeming stillness of the southern waters disappear into one another becoming one big bubble that resembles a living fluorescent organism squeezed under the ice.

These bubbles for me are the visual emblem of the concept of *ekstatic imagination*. In *ekstatic imagination*, thinking becomes the metaphorical locus where creation, reproduction and proposition turn into a fluid dialectic movement. This movement is *a priori* the 'coming and going of thinking', the continuous crossing of a threshold that pushes thinking from the inside to the outside, and back to the inside once more. I see the movement of thinking as an oscillatory movement, similar to the one of breathing, where we inhale and exhale, just to inhale again, immediately after a minute pause that always occurs in between. It is on that very pause that *ekstatic imagination* takes place. We pause on that threshold in-between the exhaled breath and the about-to-be-inhaled one. Like those intellectuals who pace back and forth while they are thinking, only to suddenly stop, when they have stumbled on the moment of conceptual creation. *Cogito ergo sum*, Descartes used to say: I think therefore I am.

Crucial to the actualization of my idea of *ekstatic imagination* is the Cartesian *cogito*. Before moving forward, let us briefly reflect upon the etymology of the Latin verb *cogitare*, which comes from the fusion of the following two terms: *cum* and *agito*. While the former means 'with, together', the latter, being the first person of the present tense of the verb *agitare – to move*, suggests *movement*. Therefore, the term *cogito* implies within itself a *movement-with*, where the *with* gestures towards the *threshold* that in Agamben's thought is the 'being-thus', namely, not being like this or that thing, but just the *thus*. As in the Italian term *cosi*, which Agamben refers to, we *are* the adverb *thus*, that is to say, in constant transit from A *to* B, which sees us pausing exactly on the *to* that is between A and B.

Conclusion

I propose that Herzog's documentary *Encounters at the End of the World* opens, philosophically speaking, a visual and aural access to the concept of *threshold*, for it enables the viewers' imagination to pause and dwell in what Agamben calls the '*outside*', that is, *where all the lines of the map converge*. What Herzog presents the viewers with, through mesmerizing images and soothing words, is in fact the innermost performative nature of *threshold*.

Performativity, as it is known, is a term that was firstly theorized within the linguistic realm. In fact, it was John Langshaw Austin, who in 1955 in a series of lectures delivered at Harvard University – which appeared in book form in 1962 as *How to Do Things With Words* – first began to develop his theory of constative versus performative utterances. While constatives are those sentences whose meaning can be considered either true or false, such as 'the bottle is on the table'; there are other sentences that do much more than what they just say: these are what Austin refers to as 'performatives'.[8] A performative utterance is for example 'I do' spoken as part of the wedding ceremony, or 'I name this ship the *Queen Elizabeth*' proclaimed by smashing a bottle against the bow of the boat. Austin clarifies that 'in these examples ... to utter the sentence (in, of course, the appropriate circumstances) is not to *describe* my doing of what I should be said in so uttering to be doing or to state that I am doing it: it is to do it', so that 'the issuing of the utterance is the performing of an action' (Austin 1975: 6–7). Austin, moreover, elucidates that, as soon as we realize that what is most important is 'not the sentence but the issuing of an utterance in a speech-situation, there can hardly be any longer a possibility of not seeing that stating is performing an act' (Austin 1975: 138–9). But what is a performative threshold?

It is a threshold that is but its own potentiality, which can never find a factual actualization, but solely an imagined one. At the end of his documentaries in fact, Herzog leaves the audience with questions rather than answers, with an active desire 'to jump off the margin of the map' rather than a passive satisfaction of owning the map. His films, whether they show distant lands or forgotten caves, are not meant to merely inform but rather to captivate the mind's eye, to make us wonder and

---

8   In note 3 (Austin 1975: 6), we read Austin's explanation of his preference for the term 'performative' over 'performatory'. He says: 'formerly I used "performatory": but "performative" is to be preferred as shorter, less ugly, more tractable, and more traditional in formation'.

wander over the *threshold* of the map itself. Agamben claims that the *threshold* is 'not another thing with respect to the limit' but rather, it is 'the experience of the limit itself, the experience of being-*within* an outside' (Agamben 2005: 68), thus when we look at Herzog's work through this critical lens, we access what I would refer to as Herzog's 'cinematic *signature*', a zone of indistinction where the creativities of the artist and the viewer merge, becoming one.

I will conclude my speculation on imagined travels and travelling imagination, by advancing that works such as Herzog's transform the *signature*'s 'zone of undecidability' into a locus where 'the movement of freedom', which Foucault attributes to imagination, takes place (Agamben 2009: 103). It is such a 'movement of freedom' that grants us a glimpse into not just 'another space, but rather, [into] the passage, the exteriority that gives it access' (Agamben 2009: 103), in a word, the secret *eidos* – the face – of travel as such. And if we agree with Jean Baudrillard that 'the secret' is 'the seductive, initiatory quality of that which cannot be said because it makes no sense, and of that which is not said even though it gets around' (Baudrillard 1990: 79), we could advance that the desire to be *where all the lines of the map converge* is the secret that travel and imagination share.

Note

Translation of Italian texts into English is by the author if not indicated otherwise.

References

Agamben, G. 1999. *Potentialities: Collected essays in philosophy*, edited by D. Heller-Roazen, trans. D. Heller-Roazen. Stanford: Stanford University Press.

Agamben, G. 2002. Idea della cesura, in G. Agamben, *Idea della Prosa*. Macerata: Quodlibet, 23–4.

Agamben, G. 2005. *The Coming Community*, edited by S. Buckley, M. Hardt and B. Massumi, trans. M. Hardt. Minneapolis: University of Minnesota Press.

Agamben, G. 2007. *Ninfe*. Torino: Bollati Boringhieri.

Agamben, G. 2009. *Signature of All Things: On method*, trans. L.D'Isanto and K. Attell. New York: Zone Books.

Austin, J.L. 1975. *How to Do Things With Words: The William James Lectures delivered at Harvard University in 1955*, 2nd edition, edited by J.O. Urmson and M. Sbisa. Oxford: Oxford University Press.

Baudrillard, J. 1990. *Seduction*, trans. B. Singer. New York: St. Martin's Press.

Benjamin, W. 1999. *The Arcades Project*. Cambridge, MA: Harvard University Press.

Bloch, D. 2007. *Aristotle on Memory and Recollection: Text, translation, interpretation, and reception in Western scholasticism.* Leiden: Brill Academic Publishers.

Gann, K. 2010. *No Such Thing as Silence. John Cage's 4'33".* Yale: Yale University Press.

Greenbaum Kasson, E. 2008. *Ecstasy on Ice: Werner Herzog's 'Encounters at the End of the World'. documentary.org.* Available at: http://www.documentary.org/content/ecstasy-ice-werner-herzogs-encounters-end-world [accessed: 28 September 2012].

Riout, D. 2010. *Yves Klein: Expressing the immaterial,* trans. C. Petridis. Paris: Edition Dialecta.

Scarry, E. 1998. *The Body in Pain: The making and unmaking of the world.* New York: Oxford University Press.

Film References

Encounters at the End of the World (dir. Werner Herzog, 2009).
Grizzly Man (dir. Werner Herzog, 2007).

Chapter 10
Toys on the Move:
Vicarious Travel, Imagination
and the Case of Travelling Toy Mascots

Shanna Robinson

For an industry fundamentally fuelled by the desire to experience difference – spatially, culturally or socially – it is surprising that tourism literature has largely overlooked the role imagination plays in travel practice and encounters. In addition to proposing theoretical justification for an increased emphasis on the imaginative and vicarious, this chapter will argue that these non-corporeal elements of travel experience constitute a touristic encounter in their own right, regardless of whether they are actually integrated with going 'somewhere' or 'elsewhere' in a physical sense. Empirical evidence supporting this premise will be provided through a case study focusing on travelling with a stuffed animal or toy. Along with a description of the practice, the chapter will consider the ways in which taking photos of the toy, sharing these images and the visualization of a potential audience constitute highly valued components of the experience.

Framed broadly as an example of experimenting with the multifarious possibilities of travel and journeying, this study of travelling toys will present two key challenges to the premise that touristic experience is inherently bound to some kind of physical journey. Firstly, I will assert that individuals place a high value on imaginative components of touristic encounters, and that this has been dealt with inadequately by tourism scholarship to date. Secondly, I will argue that people utilize the travel encounters of others to vicariously experience something outside of their own personal, physical space. These two challenges will be framed in terms of imaginative mobilities (Urry 2007), exemplifying the importance of the performance of embodied experimental tourist encounters in terms of the imaginative and vicarious, while also tracing the cultural logics that both encourage and enable this behaviour.

Travel, Imagination and Vicarious Experience

The imagination is a ubiquitous and central feature of mental life. It pervades nearly every mental operation. It never rests, day and night ... It plays a constitutive role in memory, perception (seeing-as) dreaming, believing, meaning – as well as high-level creativity. (McGinn 2004: 163)

Drawing on McGinn's (2004) analysis of imagination, Staiff (2013) explores the complex permutations of the imaginary and cinematic in relation to touristic experience of Roman heritage sites. Staiff notes how the fluid, slippery nature of imagination sits alongside an often unexplored assumption of its centrality in everyday human experience. In addition to articulating the inextricable interplay between imagination and the experiential, Staiff emphasizes paradoxical qualities of imagination, noting that it is 'an embodied and intensely personal experience that seems to operate in a way not simply tied to the somatic', simultaneously 'unbounded by time and space in its inner manifestation of psychological states, but is rooted in the time-space moment of the person imagining' (2013: 86–7). While Staiff observes that there is some difficulty in locating scholarly works focused on interconnections between heritage, heritage representation and the imagination, this observation could equally be extended to the broader field of tourism research. Imagination and touristic experience has received only sporadic, inconsistent attention to date. Indeed, if 'imagining' is envisaged as an embodied practice constituting a kind of tourism experience in its own right, there is a noticeable absence of literature on the subject (but see for example Salazar 2010, 2012).

One way in which the nexus between tourism, imagination and vicarious experience have been considered is through studies primarily utilizing a media-focused perspective. Cinema and television have often been considered as exemplary of these intersecting points (see, for example, Morkham and Staiff 2002, Crouch 2003, Davin 2005, Waade 2006, Molz 2009, Staiff 2013). In addition, IMAX cinema has also attracted detailed attention as a specific case (Griffiths 2006, Wearing et al. 2010). Other studies of touristic experience and imagination have focused on their relationship with virtual travel and cyber-tourism (Prideaux 2002; Book 2003, Molz 2004).

Interconnections between imagination, the media and travel have often been conceived of as tourism imaginaries, particularly as a way to imagine other-ness (for example, places and cultures). Relying on a similar philosophical foundation to the work of de Botton (2002), the recent work of Salazar (2010, 2012) and Su (2010) conceptualize this process of othering as part of a broader system of tourism imaginaries in which our lived worlds are 'increasingly constructed through fantasies and fabrications that first must be imagined in order to be realized' (Salazar 2010: 8). As Salazar (2010: 14) elaborates:

stories, images and desires, running the gamut from essentialised, mythologised and exoticised imaginaries of the Other to more realistic frames of reference, function as the motor setting the tourism machinery in motion.

Lengkeek (2000: 14) supports this central premise of tourism imaginaries, stating that:

imagination as a projection of possibilities can bring people to the point where they go in search of sensory experiences that have, in everyday life, been consigned to the margins or rejected all together because they do not fit in.

This drive of tourism imaginaries as a key motivator for travel is developed further by Crouch et al. (2005) as being reliant on modes of consuming difference: part of an overall imaginative process of understanding and making sense of the world and our place within it. Crouch et al. (2005) augment their interpretation through specific attention to the complex interplay between tourism and the media, while simultaneously recognizing the centrality of the imagination in this relationship. The contextual importance of an embodied perspective is also emphasized when they state that 'the activity of tourism itself makes sense only as an imaginative process which involves certain comprehension of the world and enthuses a distinctive emotional engagement with it' (Crouch et al. 2005: 1). Crouch et al. (2005: 1) go on to note that embodiment is relevant 'even if the experience of tourism is only confined to a cycle of anticipation, activity and retrospection'.

Setting aside for a moment this entanglement of imagination, media representations, anticipation and corporeal experience of place, what the conceptualization of tourism imaginaries has failed to consider to date is what is going on at the time of the imagining. Although Salazar notes that 'reading novels, playing games, watching movies, telling stories, daydreaming, planning a vacation, etc. – involve imagining or entering into the imaginings of others' (Salazar 2010: 5), connections between imagination, vicariousness and the embodied experience of imaginative journeying are not made explicit. Indeed, the studies that consider tourism imaginaries generally do not spend any time in thinking through what the process of imagination *actually* involves. How is it done? Where is the person situated? What is their posture? What is actually going on in this imaginative process?

Imaginative Mobilities and Embodied Touristic Experience

One of the ways in which contemporary society has been characterized is as an increasingly fluid, liquid form of modernity, in which social interactions have been transformed from previous eras through an accelerated kind of 'time-space' compression and a shift from 'solid, fixed modernity' (Bauman 2000, Urry and Larsen 2011). Providing an arena in which to explore this complexity is one of the key benefits of the mobilities paradigm (Urry 2007). In addition to acting as a lens through which the swift flows of tourists and travellers moving around the globe can be studied and made sense of, mobilities also allows for consideration of both the representational and the embodied, particularly in terms of contextualizing travel imagination and vicarious experience.

In his schema for the mobilities paradigm, Urry (2007) identifies five 'interdependent' mobilities, including: corporeal travel, the physical movement of objects, virtual travel, communicative travel and imaginative travel. A tantalizing glimpse of the potential of imaginative mobilities is provided when Urry (2007: 169) echoes Morkham and Staiff (2002), stating that: 'there have been many other forms of imaginative travel, as people "travel" elsewhere through memories, texts, guidebooks and brochures, travel writing, photos, postcards, radio and film'. Although Urry admits that his analysis is restricted primarily to interconnections with physical travel, it is still disappointing that he limits his conceptualization of imaginative travel to 'images of places and peoples appearing on and moving across multiple print and visual media' (particularly television and radio) (Urry 2007: 47). In addition, the division of imaginative travel into two categories (either generative of the desire to travel corporeally, or as a method of enhancing a journey that is already being undertaken) provides only a limited scope for considering the pervasive and powerful nature of imaginative mobilities. Despite the limitations to this two-fold approach, the premise that imaginative mobilities are fundamental to the way in which we experience contemporary travel is a useful starting point for infusing the analysis in this chapter with a more nuanced interpretation of the travelling toy phenomenon.

Imagination infiltrates every aspect of tourism experience. In terms of tourism imaginaries it is vital in shaping how other places, spaces and cultures are conceptualized. It plays a role in how individuals interact with others when they travel (both locals and other travellers), and it has an impact on the value placed on experiences or the cultural capital accrued from journeying. I will argue, however, that beyond this, imaginative journeying can be conceived of as a significant, embodied experience in its own right, even when the contextual framework of a specific, corporeal journey to a tourism destination is absent. This is not to suggest that an imaginative journey discounts or is devoid of a corporeal component, or that the physical is somehow 'switched off' in these circumstances. Like the myriad of imaginative processes that we experience and engage in on a day-to-day basis, those that are interwoven with our tourist encounters permeate our waking, and portions of our sleeping, consciousness in a complex and inseparable manner. Similarly, imagination, memory and fantasy interweave into our everyday existence, rather than existing in a vacuum on their own (McGinn 2004, Staiff 2013). By focusing on the imaginative and vicarious components of travel, my assertion is not that the physical is somehow a less vital component of the experience being described. Rather, through a consistent privileging of the corporeal in tourism research, the imaginative components of travel are not extended an adequate level of consideration (even if taking into account recent research that considers the sensorial or embodied aspects of tourism experience: for example, Coleman and Crang 2002, Crouch 2003, Crouch et al. 2005). There thus is an opportunity to develop a more complex understanding of imaginative mobilities and vicariousness in relation to embodied tourism experience.

Photo-sharing and the 'Travelling Toys' Group: Toy Mascots on Flickr

A contemporary example of the intersection between imagination, vicariousness and touristic experience is the practice of taking a toy travelling. In a sense, toys have been travelling, in the guise of characters from children's books and television programs, for many decades now. And while it is impossible to know the first time that an individual took a toy travelling with them, the recent proliferation of media forms – in particular, social media – has increased the visibility of this practice beyond what was previously apparent. A travelling toy may have its own website or blog, a Twitter following or a Facebook page. Travel agents for toys have appeared in the past decade, as well as hosting programmes for toys, where owners can send their toy to a host who then takes the toy travelling and posts images – and the toy – back to the owner.

The case study presented in this chapter is taken from a larger research project that sought to describe and analyse the myriad of different representations of travelling toys across a broad range of media, including books, film and social media. This research also aimed at accounting for the embodied nature of the travelling toy phenomenon, incorporating survey results from individuals who actively participate in the practice, as well as analysis of commentary from blog sites, discussion forums and comments sections from newspaper articles on the topic. Two particular dimensions of this larger project will be discussed in this chapter. Firstly, an analysis of photo-sharing website Flickr, one of the more popular spaces where travelling toy mascots are evident, will be presented to exemplify one of the most popular manifestations of sharing images of travelling toys. Secondly, the results of a short survey of Flickr members will be incorporated into discussion of themes that emerged from analysis of photos on Flickr, in order to supplement the representational analysis with a more nuanced account of embodied experience, as well as motivation.

For those uploading pictures (rather than simply viewing) to Flickr, the website operates in two ways: either on an individual level or on a group level. On an individual level, images are uploaded and belong to a person's photostream. Those uploading photos to the site also have the option to join (or create) groups that oscillate around a shared interest of some kind. Images from the individual's photostream can then be tagged – or connected – to the collection of images of the larger group.

In order to conduct an analysis of travelling toy photos on Flickr, search parameters based on the key words of 'toy' and 'travel' or 'mascot' and 'travel' were set in order to identify groups that had been created to share images of travelling toys. Of the 139 specific groups identified by these search parameters, the most popular – 'Traveling Toys' – was chosen to be the focus of this study as it consisted of both the highest number of members (2,257) and the highest number of images uploaded and shared (31,000). The 'Traveling Toys' group was over seven times larger than the next largest group in terms of membership numbers, and provided a clear description of the type of member that the group aimed to attract, stating on its *Group Info* page:

Do you take on your trips a reminder of home? Do you take photographs of a toy
on your vacations? This group is about your oddball travel companions *a la* the
garden gnome in the movie Amélie ... (Flickr 2012a)

Rather than analyse each of the 31,000 images from the 'Traveling Toys' group,
this study sought to identify coherent, recurring trends from a sample of the images.
To procure this sample, the five most recent pages of photos were examined.
With around 350 images per page, the total sample size was approximately 1,750
images. The resultant analysis focused specifically on images shared by group
members, considering the framing and structure of images, as well as methods by
which the photographer demonstrated their own personality and creativity.

While a number of interesting issues were discernible from the study of photos
in the 'Travelling Toys' group on Flickr, a focus solely on visual representations
risked leaving others under-explored. Thus, to supplement the findings of this initial
analysis, a short survey was created to generate more multifaceted results. The survey
comprised nine questions, which focused on possible motivations for taking a toy
travelling, descriptions of what was happening at the time of photographing the toy,
and how images taken were subsequently used or shared. The survey was open for a
period of one month in 2012, and invitations were circulated on the Flickr message
boards of 'groups' that share images of travelling toys. A total of 18 participants took
part in this time-frame, providing a small but valuable data-set.

Capturing the Moment: Photographic Trends in Depicting Travelling Toys

The first distinct photographic trend identified in the group 'Travelling Toys' revolves
around those images that anthropomorphize the toy, particularly exemplified
through posing toys to imitate human behaviour. For example, toys were depicted
engaging in a variety of sensorial behaviours, including 'eating' breakfast on the
Eurostar, 'smelling' the blossom trees in Japan, or 'gazing' at a beautiful view
(see, for example, Figure 10.1). In addition to these behaviours, the toys are also
photographed in physically active poses: for example, perusing maps and planning
the journey ahead, riding a bicycle or pointing at famous sites. As well as 'engaging'
in human-like experiences, toys are given a voice through captions or comments
underneath images. This voice is often composed in first-person, as the toy describes
their tourist experiences. For example, the caption underneath a photograph of a toy
dog (dressed in a cable-knit sweater, with a leather backpack) on a train, states:

> I made it onto the train! There was a bit of drama where I got separated from my
> travelling buddy in the London Underground, but we got it together in the end.
> Also, they gave me breakfast on the train! And I got a nice view of the English
> countryside on my way to France. (Flickr 2012b)

Comments below this photo from the vicarious audience of the Flickr site also
iterate concern, speculating that the toy 'must have been scared' and 'what a

Figure 10.1 A popular anthropomorphizing technique observed was having the toy gaze at a view or landscape
Source: Flickr 2012c (Photo courtesy of www.ansgar.nl).

relief' it must have been to be reunited with their owner. This ascription of human emotions (and a human voice) as a process of anthropomorphizing the toy is a distinct feature of the travelling toy trend, and illustrative of the centrality of imagination in this type of touristic experience.

Responses to the short survey highlight that the anthropomorphism is an important, imaginative component of the overall experience. For example, when asked to describe how they preferred to set up travel encounters for their toy, one participant responded that meal times were a favourite time to take photographs of their toy, and that they also liked to stage shots in which the toy was 'looking at the view from [the] car windscreen' (Kim). Another response to the same question was that the toy 'picked' the shots, and that as the human companion, the participant was merely a 'side-kick on the adventure' (Sam). According to Epley et al. (2007), the tendency to infuse human characteristics, motivations, intentions or emotions into non-human agents, is both a common and varied practice. In particular, they emphasize that people are most likely to anthropomorphize when there is a perceived lack of social connection to other humans, or as a way of developing an understanding of the behaviour of others (Epley et al. 2007). While illustrating the centrality of imagination and vicariousness, the inclination to anthropomorphize toys – both by the owner and the viewer – is also evidence of a desire to creatively and imaginatively engage with travel spaces and touristic encounters.

Figure 10.2 Skipper at the main square in Antwerp
Source: Flickr 2012d (Photo courtesy of www.travelbuddiesaroundtheworld.com).

The second trend in the types of images shared in the 'Traveling Toys' group are those that feature toys visiting famous landmarks or engaging in tourism behaviours that are generally consistent with processes of 'accumulating' experiences that are valued in the context of travelling, highlighting the connection between the

Figure 10.3 This photo from user Discret_incognito78 is characterized by considerable attention to framing, photographic skill and a sense of creative aestheticism
Source: Flickr 2012e (Photo courtesy of Arnaud Brecht).

phenomenon of the travelling toy and broader cultural logics of tourism. For example, photos depicting toys visiting famous tourist sites included 'Dexter' the toy chipmunk at Monument Valley, USA, a panda bear 'strolling' in Red Square in Moscow, Russia, a teddy checking out 'Stari Most' in Bosnia, or Skipper the penguin at Antwerp's main square (see Figure 10.2). Similarly, images of penguin Skipper, at a tropical beach in Penang, Malaysia, and a toy rabbit at the thermal baths in Budapest, Hungary, illustrate toys engaging in tourist behaviours that are considered to be desirable or hold some kind of intrinsic value.

Supporting this premise were responses from participants regarding how they preferred to set up travel encounters for their toys. Thirty-three per cent of those surveyed responded that they deliberately tried to capture images of their toy at famous monuments, while an additional 22 per cent indicated that they would do so, if they happened to have the toy there at the right moment. Other evidence of a preoccupation with accumulating travelling-based cultural capital included one respondent, Dale, who stated their mission was to take photos of their toy in every state in the US, or Drew, whose ambition was to take photos of their toy in every country that doesn't have a McDonald's.

The third trend in the sample of images from the 'Traveling Toys' group was that which focused on displaying the photographer's capability and creativity, rather than simply depicting the toy at a tourist location. This type of image often (though not always) placed the toy off-centre in the frame, with the background of the shot commonly blurred or out-of-focus, thus capturing the artistic aesthetic of the photographer (see Figure 10.3). Despite this styling, captions for the photos often made reference to the location of the shot, as a method of identifying and denoting a particular image as being worthy of attention. In response to the question '*What is your favourite thing about travelling with your toy*', one respondent stated that it 'adds a dimension to the trip … keeping [a] photographic eye engaged looking for photographic opportunities' (Kim). Another stated that 'it shakes up what you expect from a photo, and makes a shot artistic and unique' (Frankie).

These three trends identified in the analysis of photos on Flickr align with a number of themes central to current investigations into tourism practice, including modes of gazing, playing with spaces of mobility, and embodied tourism encounters, as discussed in more detail below.

Toy Travel Photography and Disrupting Modes of Gazing

The example of photographing, sharing, commenting on, and viewing images of travelling toys on Flickr upsets the argument that travel photography is inherently based on (re-)producing modes of gazing or viewing. Some analyses of tourism photography (focusing on brochures and guidebooks, for example) consider how the deliberate framing of images, and the inclusion of certain components of visual culture, play a significant role regarding expectations that tourists have (Jenkins 2003, Young 2008). Crang (1997), developing the work of Albers and James (1988) on this topic, highlights how the creation of expectation develops an environment where the photographic images circulating become more significant than the site itself. Although Crang (1997: 361) is critical of the way in which this kind of perspective fails to adequately account for the actual embodied experience of taking (or viewing) travel photography, and 'the intersection of gazes between the tourist, the observer, the observed and the later viewers of any pictures', this discussion raises a point of divergence in relation to the travelling toy mascot and travel photography. In this case study, the presence of the toy in the photographic frame disrupts the presumption that a certain aspect of an image should be looked at, or is valuable.

These images also serve to exemplify the argument made by Crang (1997) that photography, and particularly travel images, can be considered a form of 'symbolic capture'. Building on Bourdieu's discussion of habitus, Crang (1997: 366) argues that taking travel photographs is a type of 'visual accumulation [that] accords with the expectations already embedded in touristic activities and travels as a way of recounting and making sense of events'. In this context, the practice of photographing toys while travelling can be considered a way of making sense of the travel encounter, while simultaneously accumulating a specific type of symbolic capital whose value is recognized and shared amongst a select group of individuals who participate and share experiences of that practice.

Vicarious Travel and Playing with Spaces of Mobility

In a study that applies the mobilities framework to forms of non-corporeal travel, while also extending beyond the more commonly used media-based examples of television and cinema discussed earlier in this chapter, Molz (2004) analyses the ways in which individuals, as viewers, use round-the-world websites to engage and play with the idea of travel. By placing concerns with embodiment at the centre of the touristic experience, she asserts that 'websites not only constitute a new kind of tourist destination where people can play online, but they also have implications for how we think about the meaning of corporeal travel ...' (Molz 2004: 169). Indeed, this framing of websites as a space in which not only the traveller, but also viewers-as-travellers, can challenge the existing dichotomous relationship between physical and non-physical travel is one that resonates particularly well with travelling toys and this study of sharing images on Flickr.

Responses to the survey by Flickr members indicate that a determining factor of photographing travelling toys is how – in the moment of capturing the image – the photographer is imagining and planning to share these experiences with family and friends, as well as the broader travelling toy community. For example, when asked '*What is your favourite thing about travelling with your toy?*', one survey respondent claimed that they liked to 'hang up pictures of the toy in different locations on the wall at home' (Ashley). Ashley reflected that in doing so, visitors to their home were invited to take part in the toy's journey and that the images were generally considered 'an interesting talking point'. Similarly, another respondent claimed that 'it is nice to think of all the people looking at Hampers [the toy] on Flickr' (Cameron), and that they hoped this imagined audience found their images 'interesting' and 'inspiring'. The imagining of this vicarious audience was thus taken into consideration when choosing what elements to incorporate in their photography.

Seventy-two per cent of participants in the survey indicated that they like to share 'stories' of their toy's travel. This was apparent, both visually through chronologically photographing the toy's journey, as well as textually through captions. Providing further evidence that the viewer or audience is a fundamental component of the Flickr experience, this emphasis on story-sharing across a virtual interface also indicates that there is a kind of virtual sociality occurring in the Flickr space. Blurring between 'real' and virtual spaces occurs, and both the photographer and the viewer play with vicarious experience: either through imagining the experience of the toy, or engaging in a kind of virtual relationship with the toy. The sharing of these 'stories' on Flickr also served to transform 'an individual experience to a collective experience' (Molz 2004: 177), reaching an audience that is (potentially) spatially and temporally distant (Crang 1999).

Visuality, Embodiment and Creative Sharing

As far back as the 1970s, the imbrications of photographic practice and tourism were noted by Sontag in her seminal work on photography, where she stated that 'the camera is a device which makes real what one is experiencing ... it seems positively unnatural to travel for pleasure without taking a camera along' (Sontag 1979: 9). In the decades since, tourism scholarship has focused heavily on the role of the representational in terms of tourism photography (some examples include Urbain 1989, Scarles 2004, Davin 2005), as well as broad conceptualizations of the visual in tourism (for example, Crouch and Lübbren 2003, Urry and Larsen 2011). In addition, in the past 15 years, emerging interpretations of tourism and photography have taken into account the embodied, performative nature of the practice (Crang 1997, 1999, Coleman and Crang 2002, Waterton and Watson 2010). While it is beyond the scope of this project to review the extensive literature on the topic of tourism, photography and the visual, the recent work of Crang (1997, 1999) and Scarles (2009) establish a basis for understanding the embodied practice of photographing (and sharing photographs of) travelling toys.

Scarles asserts that there is a need to renegotiate the visual in relation to tourism, proposing a move away from the understanding of tourism as 'a series of predetermined, linear and static stages we pass through' (2009: 465). In her thorough interpretation of ways in which the visual can be considered part of a process of 'becoming', Scarles builds on the work of Coleman and Crang (2002) and Franklin and Crang (2001) to propose that there are 'fluid interplays' in which the visual, as well as visual practice, illuminates the 'process of becoming' (2009: 465). Visual practice is thus conceptualized as something that exists 'through the fusion of all senses as tourists move through place imaginatively and experientially' (Scarles 2009: 466). This recognition of the importance of the interplay between the imagination and experience is, although implicit in a number of theoretical studies and perspectives in tourism theory, rarely articulated in such a clear manner. Scarles elaborates on this process by saying that:

> moving through the vortex of the visual, tourists create spaces of dislocation
> as imagined and abstract spaces emerge in a swirling connection of real and
> imaginary, self and other. Consequently, tourists become re(positioned) within
> the photographed subject as they are consumed by the visual, as it is consumed
> by them. They become imaginative voyagers, enlivening photographed subjects
> and making place legible. (2009: 472)

Crang (1997), in his insightful analysis of the role of the practice of producing the visual, similarly emphasizes that utilizing vision to pay attention to the 'active, embodied world' can help overcome too prominent a focus on images and pictures at the expense of bodily experiences. He states that 'so far, more attention has been paid to the representations than the practices that create these representations' (Crang 1997: 359) and asserts that one of the overlooked functions of tourism photography is the ability of the practice to allow the tourist to actually take part in, rather than simply reflect on, the world.

While Flickr provides clear examples of how representational trends play out in the case of the travelling toys, what was happening in the actual moment of photography was more clearly elucidated through responses to the survey. One respondent indicated that it enabled them to 'see the world through their [the toys] eyes' (Frankie), highlighting the importance of imaginative processes of anthropomorphism (as discussed earlier in this chapter). Another stated that their favourite aspect of travelling with a toy was 'setting up the scenes for photos and watching people's reactions' (Morgan). Overall, 33 per cent of participants felt that the photographic moment facilitated meeting other travellers, and that this was important. For example, individuals' responses in the survey included 'he is a great conversation starter in a group of tourists' (Drew), 'it's just good fun and a laugh' (Morgan), and 'it's a great way to start chatting with people – although some will think you are weird!' (Sam). This emphasis on a performance for, as well as anticipated first-hand interaction with, an audience indicates value is placed on a sense of playfulness and generating a kind of sociality. Similarly, the desire for interaction with an audience suggests a need for public legitimization of interaction between an adult and a toy: something that is generally only considered acceptable in specific contexts, such as memorializing childhood (Fleming 1996) or playing with mechanically-complex toys like robots or remote-controlled vehicles (Sugiura et al. 2012). Other responses from the survey also underlined connections to ideas around legitimization of play, including allusions to a sense of comfort that travelling with the toy provided. For example, one participant said 'It keeps homesickness at bay … its [*sic*] also very comforting, when you are in another country that you've never been, to have something familiar to you' (Kim). Another responded that 'sometimes you just need a rabbit' (Jamie), while another stated that 'it just gives a bit of whimsy to the experience, something that is taken away from the mass tourist experience these days' (Ashley).

Conclusion

In order for understandings of travel to correspond with how it is actually practised in contemporary society, emphasis needs to be extended beyond the corporeal to include the often overlooked imaginative and vicarious components of touristic experiences. Initially, discussion of tourism imaginaries exposed an opening for further consideration of the intersections between travel, the imaginary and vicariousness. Urry's (2007) conceptualization of imaginative mobilities then provided the beginnings of a theoretical framework through which the fluid components of imaginative and vicarious travel can be considered, while simultaneously taking into account various forms and methods of representation.

Through discussion of the ways that individuals who travel with toys deliberately anthropomorphize their toys (and the toys' experiences) in a creative, whimsical manner, this study has exposed an area of tourist experience where imagination is both highly visible and valued. Similarly, expression of a desire to see the world through the eyes of the toys by survey respondents exemplifies this assessment. The sharing of images of travelling toys, as well consideration and visualization of a vicarious audience by the photographer was also found to be an important aspect of the phenomenon, simultaneously highlighting how viewers use the travel encounters of others to vicariously experience something outside their own personal, physical space. Enhancing the perspective of imaginative mobilities, the approaches of Crang (1997), Molz (2004) and Scarles (2009) allowed for the performative, embodied experience of both journeying with, and taking photos of, travelling toys, particularly in relation to survey responses that focused on the moment of photography. The very nature of taking a toy travelling is reliant on imaginative processes, and this case study demonstrates that the vicarious sharing and consumption of images is a vital component of the overall experience. The travelling toy phenomenon is also intrinsically related to the value placed on certain types of touristic experience, and can thus be considered symptomatic of a broader cultural logic that the tourism industry leaves little outlet for individual experimentation, individuality and creativity.

While this study provides empirical evidence of the importance of imagination and vicarious experience, openings for future research are also apparent through gaps in current literature. For example, it was beyond the scope of this study to investigate the embodied encounters of the Flickr audience (rather than active members who upload images), and in particular, the ways in which *their* sense of imagination is activated through the process of viewing, vicariously experiencing the journeys of others as a kind of virtual traveller. Particular connections and relationships that this audience develops with specific travelling toys could also be a fruitful area of examination, as could the implications of this kind of virtual, imaginative journeying in relation to types of mobile sociality (Molz 2004). Similarly, there is potential for a more detailed investigation of connections between imaginative mobilities, a sense of play and creativity, as well as touristic experimentation undertaken in order to engage in unique or unusual forms of travel.

References

Albers, P.C. and James, W.R. 1988. Travel photography: A methodological approach. *Annals of Tourism Research*, 15(1), 134–58.

Bauman, Z. 2000. *Liquid Modernity*. Cambridge: Polity Press.

Book, B. 2003. *Traveling through Cyberspace: Tourism and photography in virtual worlds*. Paper to the Tourism and Photography: Still Visions – Changing Lives conference, Sheffield, UK, 20–23 July 2003.

Coleman, S. and Crang, M. 2002. *Tourism: Between place and performance*. Oxford: Berghahn Books.

Crang, M. 1997. Picturing practices: Research through the tourist gaze. *Progress in Human Geography*, 21(3), 359–73.

Crang, M. 1999. Knowing, tourism and practices of vision, in *Leisure/Tourism Geographies: Leisure practices and geographical knowledges*, edited by D. Crouch. London: Routledge, 238–56.

Crouch, D. 2003. Spacing, performing, and becoming: Tangles in the mundane. *Environment and Planning A*, 35(11), 1945–60.

Crouch, D. and Lübbren, N. (eds) 2003. *Visual Culture and Tourism*. Oxford and New York: Berg.

Crouch, D., Jackson, R. and Thompson, F. (eds) 2005. *The Media and the Tourist Imagination*. London and New York: Routledge.

Davin, S. 2005. Tourists and television viewers: Some similarities, in *The Media and the Tourist Imagination: Converging cultures*, edited by D. Crouch, R. Jackson and F. Thompson. Abingdon: Routledge, 170–182.

de Botton, A. 2002. *The Art of Travel*. London: Penguin.

Epley, N., Waytz, A. and Cacioppo, J. 2007. On seeing human: A three-factor theory of anthropomorphism. *Psychological Review*, 114(4), 864–86.

Fleming, D. 1996. *Powerplay: Toys as popular culture*. Manchester and New York: Manchester University Press.

Flickr. 2012a. *Flickr: Traveling Toys Group Page*. [Online]. Available at: http://www.flickr.com/groups/travellingtoys/#group-info [accessed: 10 June 2012].

Flickr. 2012b. *Flickr: Travelling Toys Group – Doggy Wishbone – Off to Paris*. [Online]. Available at: http://www.flickr.com/photos/doggywishbone/7365235978/in/pool-90095671@N00 [accessed: 10 June 2012].

Flickr. 2012c. *Photostream of '.ansgar' – Balvenie Castle*. [Online]. Available at: http://www.flickr.com/photos/ansgarspeller/7197339082/in/photostream [accessed: 20 January 2013].

Flickr. 2012d. *Photostream of 'Travel buddies around the world' – Skipper in Antwerp*. [Online]. Available at: http://www.flickr.com/photos/85018210@N07/8193084139/in/photostream [accessed: 20 January 2013].

Flickr. 2012e. *Photostream of 'discret_incognito78' – Dark Malgus monte la rue Foyatier*. [Online]. Available at: http://www.flickr.com/photos/discret/8066811272/in/pool-travellingtoys [accessed: 20 January 2013].

Franklin, A. and Crang, M. 2001. The trouble with tourism and travel theory? *Tourist Studies*, 1, 5–22.

Griffiths, A. 2006. Time traveling IMAX style: Tales from the giant screen, in *Virtual Voyages: Cinema and travel*, edited by J. Ruoff. Durham, NC and London: Duke University Press, 238–58.

Jenkins, O. 2003. Photography and travel brochures: The circle of representation. *Tourism Geographies*, 5(3), 305–28.

Lengkeek, J. 2000. Imagination and differences in tourist experience. *World Leisure Journal*, 42(3), 11–17.

McGinn, C. 2004. *Mindsight: Image, dream, meaning*. Cambridge, MA: Harvard University Press.

Molz, J.G. 2004. Playing online and between the lines: round-the-world websites as virtual places to play, in *Tourism Mobilities: Places to play, places in play*, edited by M. Sheller and J. Urry. London: Routledge, 169–80.

Molz, J.G. 2009. Representing pace in tourism mobilities: Staycations, slow travel and 'The Amazing Race'. *Journal of Tourism and Cultural Change*, 7(4), 270–286.

Morkham, B. and Staiff, R. 2002. The cinematic tourist: Perception and subjectivity, in *The Tourist as a Metaphor of the Social World*, edited by G.M.S. Dann. Wallingford and New York: CABI Publishing, 297–316.

Prideaux, B. 2002. The cybertourist. In *The Tourist as a Metaphor of the Social World*, edited by G. Dann. Wallingford: CABI Publishing, 317–39.

Salazar, N.B. 2010. *Envisioning Eden: Mobilizing imaginaries in tourism and beyond*. New York: Berghahn Books.

Salazar, N.B. 2012. Tourism imaginaries: A conceptual approach. *Annals of Tourism Research*, 39(2), 863–82.

Scarles, C. 2004. Mediating landscapes: The processes and practices of image construction in tourist brochures of Scotland. *Tourist Studies*, 4(1), 43–67.

Scarles, C. 2009. Becoming tourist: Renegotiating the visual in the tourist experience. *Environment and Planning D: Society and Space*, 27(3), 465–88.

Sontag, S. 1979. *On Photography*. London: Penguin Books.

Staiff, R. 2013. Swords, sandals and togas: The cinematic imaginary and the tourist experiences of Roman heritage sites, in *Heritage and Tourism: Place, encounter, engagement*, edited by R. Bushell, R. Staiff and S. Watson. London: Routledge, 85–102.

Su, X. 2010. The imagination of place and tourism consumption: A case study of Lijiang ancient town. *Tourism Geographies*, 12(3), 412–34.

Sugiura, Y., Lee, C., Ogata, M. and Withana, Y. 2012. PINOKY: A ring that animates your plush toys. *Proceedings of the SIGCHI Conference on Human Factors in Computing Systems*, 725–34.

Urbain, J.D. 1989. The tourist adventure and his images. *Annals of Tourism Research*, 16(1), 106–18.

Urry, J. 2007. *Mobilities*. Cambridge: Polity Press.

Urry, J. and Larsen, J. 2011. *The Tourist Gaze 3.0*. London: SAGE.

Waade, A.M. 2006. Armchair travelling with Pilot Guides, in *Geographies of Communication: The spatial turn in media studies*, edited by J. Falikheimer and A. Jansson. Goteburg: Nordicom, 155–68.

Waterton, E. and Watson, S. (eds) 2010. *Culture, Heritage and Representation: Perspectives on visuality and the past*. Farnham: Ashgate.

Wearing, S., Stevenson, D. and Young, T. 2010. *Tourist Cultures: Identity, place and the traveller*. London: SAGE.

Young, T. 2008. Mediating volunteer tourism alternatives: Guidebook representations of travel experiences in Aboriginal Australia, in *Journeys of Discovery in Volunteer Tourism: International case study perspectives*, edited by K.D. Lyons and S. Wearing. Wallingford: CABI, 195–209.

Chapter 11
MT Promises:
Science Fictional Travel Technologies and the
Making and Unmaking of Corporeal Identity

Sean Williams

The history of transportation is the history of mankind.

– Harrison 1973: vii

It is difficult to refute the proposition that revolutions in transport technologies have far-reaching effects on society: the domestication of the horse caused no less upheaval than the take-off of the first long-haul jet aircraft. But what might lie in the future as transportation achieves new degrees of instantaneity and convenience? Science fiction (SF) is uniquely enabled to hypothesize about the impacts of such imagined technologies, and Harry Harrison is just one of many authors to examine the science fictional trope of the Matter Transmitter – 'MT' as he dubbed it, deriving the abbreviation in the same fashion that 'TV' comes from television (Harrison 1973: x).

Conceiving new means of going ever farther was a prevailing concern of scientific romances in the late nineteenth century, such as Jules Verne's ([1870] 1993) *Twenty Thousand Leagues Under the Sea* and H.G. Wells' (1895) *The Time Machine*. As Bignell (1999: 91–2) argues, such early proto-SF narratives were written:

> amid a long-standing fascination with visually based representational devices in the late nineteenth century, exemplified by the dioramas, panoramas and other proto-cinematic devices of the period ... These devices were enthralling because they transported the spectator to alien places and alien times by means of visual technologies.

Like the rocket ships and time machines 'invented' at the same time, MT remains a well-known and frequently utilized means of fictional transportation: 'a device that can dematerialize a thing – even a living body – into a pattern of information that it transmits as a beam and rematerializes at another location' (Livingston 2006: 79). Immortalized by *Star Trek*'s catchphrase, 'Beam me up, Scotty', its historical antecedents are extensive. In the Christian New Testament, the 'Spirit of the Lord' is credited with the rapid relocation of the disciple Philip 30-odd miles from Gaza to the coastal city of Azotus (Acts 8: 39–40), while the Quran records a magical transportation of the throne of the Queen of Sheba from southern Arabia to the feet of King Solomon in his temple in Israel (27: 38–40); the Talmud also contains several incidents of miraculous travel between two places by wonder-working rabbis (BT Sanhedrin 95). All evince an enduring and aspirational fascination with the idea of instantaneous transportation that has survived despite all claims to its impossibility since the Scientific Revolution (Bendle 2002: 54–5).

The publication of Edward Page Mitchell's (1877) story *The Man Without a Body* demarcates a key transition in the expression of this age-old idea. The year before, the first performance of Richard Wagner's opera *Götterdämerung* featured a helm that instantly transported Siegfried to 'far-off lands', and later, significantly, allowed him to change form (Wagner [1876] 1999: 13). The Tarnhelm's nature is clearly supernatural, with no explanation offered for its function or purpose except that it is 'the cunningest work' of the Niblung, a race of dwarfs (Wagner [1876] 1999: 13). The device in *The Man Without a Body*, on the other hand, exploits scientific terms and metaphors to make the fantastical seem technically plausible:

> Matter is made up of molecules and molecules, in their turn, are made up of atoms ... Their dissolution may be accomplished by chemical affinity or by a sufficiently strong electric current ... There [is] no reason why matter could not be telegraphed, or to be etymologically accurate, 'telepomped'. (Mitchell 1877: n.p.)

Reference to the Scientific Method lends the device further credence, with an account of the inventor's initial attempts to send simple compounds 'such as quartz, starch and water' from one room to another, followed successfully by a postage stamp (Mitchell 1877: n.p.). The first living thing transmitted is a captured cat that 'disappeared in a twinkling' and arrives 'alive and purring, although somewhat astonished' (Mitchell 1877: n.p.). Despite being armed with 'all the truth and logic of stern science', the aptly named Professor Dummkopf attempts to transmit himself without checking that his batteries contain sufficient power to complete the process (Mitchell 1877: n.p.). The batteries expire before his journey is complete, leaving him the eponymous figure of the story, his body lost forever.

Mitchell's neologism for the device, 'Telepomp', did not endure, but his story did assemble a formula for simple MT narratives that remains current today. The wonder of instantaneous travel (in this case only modestly imagined across the Atlantic to London) is evoked by the use of scientific imagery, language and method. At the same time, the initial success of the protagonist is undone by his failure to fully examine the technology's implications, reflecting an undercurrent of late nineteenth-century concerns about the impacts of real technologies, such as electricity. The Telepomp thus signals a clear break from the fantastical Tarnhelms of the past, and opens up entirely new narrative possibilities for the future. As well as establishing a 'scientific' framework for a trope that had previously been represented as supernatural, Mitchell's story posed a larger philosophical anxiety that would come to underpin many later fictional treatments of MT: although new technologies can take us to familiar places more quickly than ever before, or to places where we have never been, they also create the potential of human error or misuse.

In the decades immediately following Mitchell's ground-breaking story came Robert Duncan Milne's ([1885] 1980) *Professor Vehr's Electrical Experiment*, Fred T. Jane's (1897) *To Venus in Five Seconds: An account of the strange disappearance of Thomas Plummer, pillmaker*, Garrett P. Serviss's (1900) *The Moon Metal*, William Warren's ([1904] 2010) *The Nemesis of the Vibratory Theory*, and Guillaume Appollinaire's ([1910] 1968) *Remote Projection*. Sir Arthur Conan Doyle dabbled with the trope twice, in *The Mystery of Cloomber* (1889) and *The Disintegration Machine* (1929), the latter most clearly in Mitchell's new mode. By the dawn of science fiction in the 1930s, MT was well established as a means of moving characters across the surface of the Earth and beyond.[1] The expansive possibilities of MT were also occasionally imagined in terms of threat, for it offered the possibility of bringing what lies beyond the Earth much closer to home, as in Edmond Hamilton's ([1927] 1967) *The Moon Menace*.

This is a characteristic of science fiction stories noted by Rose (1981: 3):

[they] either portray a world that is in some respect different from our own, as for instance in stories set in the future or on other planets, or, alternatively, they describe the impact of some strange element upon our world, as in alien-invasion stories or evolutionary fables.

MT, like other tropes of SF, is able to operate as the narrative facilitator in both scenarios, by removing protagonists from their familiar environments or by introducing details that do not belong to those environments (including MT itself, in many instances). So can time machines, and in a narrative sense the two devices often function identically.[2] Each 'takes us from our known world into an unknown world', or into unknown locations within our world (Wolfe 1979: 18). Each is in essence a simply-conceived trope that can result in startling, even paradoxical, outcomes. For instance, time travel challenges conventional notions of causality by looping protagonists back across their own timelines, thus appearing to duplicate them (Stableford 2004: 219).[3] The other iconic means of travelling from A to B in

---

1   SF's Golden Age is usually said to begin in 1931, when influential editor Hugo Gernsback and early champion of MT became editor of *Astounding*, the longest running continually published SF magazine in the world.

2   The two tropes arguably share a common creator: four years after Edward Page Mitchell wrote *The Man Without a Body* (1877), he anonymously published one of the earliest technological time travel stories, *The Clock That Went Backward* ([1881] 2011).

3   Parallel universe stories can perform a similar feat. Instead of taking the protagonist to another time in this universe, however, they take them to the same time but in a different universe, where they encounter subtly different versions of themselves. Time travel and parallel universe stories are therefore key means of exploring the unheimlich in SF, often relying on MT to perform the critical act of dislocation.

SF, the spaceship, is 'at once habitat, womb and vehicle, [giving] mankind [*sic*] the means to appropriate the unknown without sacrificing any of the comforts of home' (Wolfe 1979: 85). MT, by omitting the space between A and B, uniquely extends the traveller's reach '[t]o the rim of the universe and then beyond' in one elegant step, thereby removing the need for habitat and womb entirely (Silverberg 1988: 182). As Clarke and Baxter ([1997] 2000: 951) ironically ask, '[w]hat [is] a spaceship, after all, but plumbing'?

Unlike time travel and other forms of travel through unconventional dimensions, MT is usually presented by its fictional inventor as a revolution in mass-transport that will replace planes, trains and automobiles in a single bold stroke. Spaceships are not immune from replacement, either. As early as 1897 MT is employed to move protagonists to worlds beyond our own, with Venus and the Moon the first to be visited, perhaps because they are the brightest objects in the night sky. Mars soon followed, with Edgar Rice Burroughs' *A Princess of Mars* showing in 1917 just how easily transport to the Red Planet could be imagined. Critical to the acceptance of these devices is the immediacy of transmission and the relative comfort they offer. Instead of motion across great distances taking days or weeks – or millennia in the case of interstellar voyages – it occurs instantaneously, taking its lead from the telegraph and related technologies. Similarly, the usual discomforts of travel are exchanged for faintly electrical tingling feelings (if any at all) and maybe the odd spark of light. Travel is thus rescripted as an exercise in convenience rather than something to be endured.

This foregrounding of convenience is evident in the places visited, also. Some stories introduced relatively hostile worlds, such as one covered entirely in mud in Joe Haldeman's (1976) *Mindbridge*, but compared to narratives concerned with exploration and territorial expansion, such as the heavily spaceship-populated sub-genres of planetary romance or space opera, it is notable that the environments of most worlds visited by MT are more or less indistinguishable to our own, as in Robert Heinlein's (1955) *Tunnel in the Sky*. When users have the ability to choose their destinations – destinations that are but a step or two removed from home, after all – home-*like* is the usual choice. Unlike time machines and spaceships, then, MT is not frequently a facilitator of adventure, but a means of conveniently accessing the familiar.

Or so it might seem at first glance. The commonest place visited by MT might be much like home for the protagonists, but the *idea* of home itself is radically reconceived. This re-conception arises in response to far more than just the superseding of existing transport systems. In some narratives, for instance, the permeability of borders threatens the sovereignty and security of individual nations. Mass-movement of population leads to cities becoming abandoned museums in a world of meadows and flowers. Hotels are turned into 'continuity clubs' that look the same everywhere all over the world, or they are no longer needed at all (Niven [1974] 1975: 63). Rusting bridges and crumbling highways are re-imagined as sites of commerce or conservation. Gene pools become mixed, blurring racial boundaries and making immediate that which once seemed culturally remote. MT '[covers] the earth like a great clean cape, standardizing language, dress, customs, and ambitions' (Sturgeon [1954] 1979: 122).

Economies large and small are another aspect of society transformed by the presence of MT. William Warren imagines live cattle sent from the plains to Chicago, where they are killed and served later the same day in New York. In John Brunner's (1973) *You'll Take the High Road*, the advertising budget of *Transmatter Inc.* is exceeded only by those of the threatened automobile and fuel industries. Such business opportunities are overshadowed by narratives in which capitalism as a whole comes under threat from one possible side-effect of MT, the possibility of creating any number of perfect copies: 'If what is actually being transmitted is encoded information rather than a package of "dissociated matter", then matter transmitters might better be regarded as matter duplicators', a prospect that bodes well for the poor and starving but not necessarily for the rich (Stableford 2004: 219). Negative consequences for the West caused by the mass-duplication of manufactured goods and the end of value can be found in numerous stories, such as George O. Smith's (1945) *Pandora's Millions*, in which the only way to stave off economic collapse is to discover a new substance that cannot be copied.

Perhaps not surprisingly, in the inter-war and post-Second World War years the dystopic possibilities of societal transformation wrought by MT are imagined as arising less from the technology itself than from the capacity 'of Man [sic] to use the machines of Man to bring about the destruction of Man' (Van Vogt [1942] 1952: 266). In *The Disintegration Machine*, Arthur Conan Doyle's protagonist warns:

> I need not enlarge upon the revolutionary character of such an invention, nor of its extreme importance as a potential weapon of war. A force which could disintegrate a battleship, or turn a battalion ... into a collection of atoms, would dominate the world. (Doyle 1929)

However, it is less often the technology's utility as a weapon of mass-destruction but more prosaically its effectiveness in enabling crime, corruption or surveillance that expresses the fear of humanity's capacity to wreak harm or exploit power. In numerous fictions MT is ingeniously used to fake a second coming of the Messiah, dispose of evidence, flee the scene of a crime, commit murder, motivate organized crime, smuggle, kidnap, evade border controls and take revenge on a cheating spouse. Likewise, MT can be used by police to control movement, plant incriminating evidence, and provide inescapable prisons.

Not least amongst the social transformations effected by the deployment of MT is that on the spatiality of everyday life. Space-hopping doorways allow homes to cover vast distances, such as the domiciles in Dan Simmons' (1989) *Hyperion* that might have a bedroom on Earth, a living room on Mars and a kitchen on a world orbiting a distant star, foregrounding the quotidian occupation of interstellar space. People might in one week sleep in 'seven beds on seven continents' simply by travelling from one end of their house to another (Brunner [1974] 1977: 102). Isaac Asimov ([1954] 1969: 259) takes the idea further, suggesting that people might never leave their houses at all: 'Each house was a secluded little castle, the Door of which had entry anywhere the world over where other Doors existed.'

This new function of the doorway – to privilege access to enclosed spaces across the outside world and to domesticate the distant – drives narratives in which socially 'normal' people are exposed to unpredictable nature for the first time. The dark shadows of such tales are those in which MT fails, leaving inhabitants trapped in their homes with no means of exit or of emptying their high-tech toilets.

In a world where MT is commonplace, therefore, humanity's perception and occupation of space is irrevocably changed. The distance between transmitters matters less than the number one dials to move from one to the other, rendering traditional maps irrelevant.[4] Tourist destinations and points of sudden interest may be overrun thanks to sudden ease of access, while mementoes of exciting events, such as handkerchiefs dipped in the blood of a murdered celebrity, can spread around the world as quickly as gossip on the internet. Daily commutes cross time-zones at will: the opening paragraph of *Nobody's Home* by Joanna Russ (1975: 235) shows a woman working at the North Pole, attending family business near the Red Sea, going to dinner in New Delhi, taking a nap in Queensland, then watching the sun rise over the Carolinas. Indeed, the concept of 'daily' is itself undermined: in the opening pages of Larry Niven's (1970) *Ringworld*, the protagonist is shown circling the Earth in order to stay ahead of midnight, thereby extending his two-hundredth birthday as long as humanly possible.

Changing spatial and temporal relationships necessitates a change in notions of speed, since velocity is determined by the relationship of distance over time. If travel time is reduced to zero and the distance between two booths is effectively collapsed to zero, then MT does much more than allow humanity to achieve 'the ultimate velocity' (Bendle 2002: 55). MT erases *the journey* entirely from human experience, fundamentally altering our relationship with the spaces around us, and not always for the better. As the protagonist of *Transing Syndrome* discovers, the eradication of the journey leaves in its place the ironic impression of being trapped in inertia: 'But you were always here, here when you stepped in and here when you stepped out, gone was the feeling of motion, of going anywhere' (Von Trojan 1985: 10). Henceforth, there is only *destination*, and all destinations appear the same.

This collapse of social distance is an intrinsic function of the trope, potentially creating a profoundly claustrophobic milieu in which everyone in the world is in immediate contact with everyone else, friends and strangers alike. In Larry Niven's ([1974] 1975) *A Kind of Murder*, a criminal is driven to his crime by

---

4   In such a world, the mapping of location no longer entails the concept of movement in spatial-temporal terms, since the relationship between origin and destination is collapsed into immediately accessible points of social contact.

constant proximity to other people, while *Doctor Fogg* agonizes over failures of communication that persist even in the face of physical proximity:

> though we travel on light waves, yet we will be separated; and so, as between planets, is it between you and me. There is you, and there is I and there is a third which is separation. (Matson 1929: 116)

The spatial rearrangement of the world under the homogenizing umbrella of MT necessitates a complete re-evaluation of what it means to be 'individual'. Can MT's process of disintegration and reintegration combined with a complete reconfiguration of society allow the retention of a sense of 'unique self'?

Identity as a concept that can no longer be described in terms of surface and depth but as something more dispersed, and thereby subject to the possibilities of unbuilding and remaking, has been a theme of MT stories from the very first appearance of the trope. 'A man is the same man', stated Edward Page Mitchell in 1877, 'although there is not an atom in his body which was there five years before' (1877: n.p.), predating a now-common philosophical argument by a full century. As Livingston (2006: 79) describes it:

> A living body [is] more like a transporter beam than like a solid inert object. As most people know, our bodies are in constant flux at the cellular level, where cells are continually disintegrating and being replicated ... The living body is a pattern of information, a fact and a fiction, something continuously being made and unmade.

In stories deploying the trope of MT, anxieties regarding the fluidity of individual identity are often expressed through speculations about what happens between leaving and arriving, when a person's physical identity has been most overtly transformed into a non-material state. In John Brunner's (1980) *The Infinitive of Go*, transmitted humans pass through mysterious 'rho' space, while in Joshua Green's (1965) *The Loafers of Refuge* it is called the 'space-that-has-no-time' or 'the nothingness and timelessness that was sub-space' (Green 1965: 72, 104). '[M]y body was Lord knows where', says Professor Dummkopf in Mitchell's (1877: n.p.) *The Man Without a Body*, perhaps propelled as 'a molecular cloud ... into the cosmos' like Professor Challenger's in *The Disintegration Machine* (Doyle 1929: n.p.). The fragility of psychological permanence in the grip of such a technology is frequently highlighted alongside physical impermanence:

> There is a moment in which we do not exist, there is a moment in which we inhabit all space and time, and only the instinctive chemistry of the cells carrying its imprint enables us to become what we were, where we want to be. (Malzberg 1974: 101)

For the travellers in Stephen King's ([1981] 1985) *The Jaunt*, that *between* moment stretches too long for humans to endure, so they must be sedated or else driven mad – or is this psychosis driven by the paradox of existing in a state of non-existence? Whatever the reason, it is clear that MT places traditional notions of identity under intense pressure.

The notion of an 'imaginary elsewhere' or 'electronic nowhere' antagonistic to the self is one frequently raised in connection with modern media, particularly television (Friedberg 1993: 2, Sconce 2000: 132). Like the early scientific romances that were inspired by visually representational devices of their time, MT has maintained a close engagement with TV that runs deeper than Harry Harrison's neologism. The relationship stretches back decades before the trope first appeared on the small screen – not with *Star Trek* in 1966 but *Flash Gordon* in 1955, *Outer Limits* in 1963 and *Doctor Who* in 1964 – when the metaphor of displacement was invoked to sell the experience of owning a TV set:

> As the development of television accelerated in the 1930s and the experimental
> technology became more widely known to the public, both scientifically 'factual'
> predictions and wildly 'fictional' prognostications of a future with television
> emphasized the new medium's astonishing qualities of visual presence in terms
> of electronic transportation. Television was to alternatively transport viewers
> into another world and transport other worlds into the home. (Sconce 2000: 127)

Later, shows such as *The Twilight Zone* featured stories involving *actual* transportation via TV to such familiarly imagined locations as the Wild West. Another example of the recursive MT/TV relationship is the *Doctor Who* serial 'The Keys of Marinus' (1964), which featured 'travel dials' that allowed the wearer to instantaneously move from place to place, much like remote controls.

While TV serials most often use MT as a simple means of moving characters around, modernist and postmodernist writers found it a powerful trope for exploring themes of alienation and the politics of fragmentation. Alfred Bester's (1956) *The Stars My Destination* is a substantial work in this mode, as is Barry M. Malzberg's (1974) *Guernica Night*. Both works explore radically re-imagined psychological landscapes brought into being by society's embrace of MT. Such dystopic futures paved the way for the 'cyberpunk' movement of the 1980s in the same way that virtual reality promised a literal and imminent disconnect between the psychological and the physical. De facto MT – whereby the material of a person is not transported or recreated at all, but instead the data comprising their thoughts, personality and memories are relocated into a 'virtual' reality – has been a commonplace trope since William Gibson's (1984) *Neuromancer* in the mid-1980s and captured popular consciousness via *The Matrix* in 1999.

Once the illusion of concreteness has been abandoned and a person has been transformed into information, nothing in theory stops that information being altered. The technologies of postmodernity may highlight the anxieties that accompany physical breakdown, but these appear even in the trope's earliest instances, a century before cyberpunk and postmodernism. *The Man Without a Body* presents the inventor as destroyed by his own creation, his head a shrivelled fossil 'much affected by the ravages of decay' (Mitchell 1877).[5] In slightly later *fin de siècle* tales, small flecks of gold find their way by 'atomic bombardment' into the bodies of bystanders (Serviss 1900) or terrible penalties arise from 'failure to observe the substantial condition of scientific law – penalties which threaten absolute annihilation' (Milne [1885] 1980: 86). Foreshadowing modern information theory, which holds that bits of information are inevitably lost or distorted whenever information is transferred in quantity from one place to another, early writers imagined that the process of MT might change the material body's essential integrity, such as 'the hair of the body being on an entirely different vibration to the living organic tissues [allowing it therefore to] be included or excluded at will' (Doyle 1929: n.p.); or *Rabbits to the Moon*, in which 'skeletons … are always lagging behind and have to be integrated later' (Banks 1959: 110).

Even if operated properly, MT is portrayed as a technology vulnerable to causing unwanted physical mutation. A guinea pig test subject arrives dead in Sir Arthur C. Clarke's first published story *Travel by Wire!*; later, in the same story, people require plastic surgery to correct errors in transmission. George Langelaan's ([1957] 1980) classic *The Fly* shows the first object to be transported, an ashtray, arriving back to front; subsequently the first living subject, a cat, disappears, only to later compound the grief caused to the inventor by his accidental hybridization with an insect. In Brunner's *You'll take the High Road*, 'scrambled-in-transit' accident rates are not released for fear of how the public will react: 'Sometimes they open up the delivery terminal and all they find inside is a kind of borscht' (Brunner 1973: 124). One of the most relentless portrayals of the potential risks of MT appears in Jack Wodhams' ([1967] 1970) *There is a Crooked Man*, which contains a traveller arriving radically rearranged, a scientist multiply duplicated at the expense of other travellers (who disappear), a heterosexual couple that swaps bodies in order to prop up a failing marriage, limbs switching in error from person to person, and a suggestion that it is possible to become allergic to the process. Less dramatically, accruing gradual cellular changes as a result of frequent matter transmission – like repeatedly photocopying a photocopy until nothing remains but a blur – is a persistent thread in Kurt von Trojan's (1985) *Transing Syndrome*, named after the phobia of using MT. This fear of physical mutilation is difficult to shake even in narratives where safety is not overtly a concern, since 'in an infinite universe, there is an infinity of choice, and someone at some time will crawl out of these machines … a monster' (Malzberg 1974: 101).

---

5   Were there any doubts that this story is at heart concerned with physicality, the Professor's slow disintegration, starting with his feet and working slowly upwards, he conscious all the while, soon dispels them – that, and the bizarre conclusion of the tale, wherein his head is given a new body scavenged from a moa skeleton, dressed up and sent wandering through Central Park in an outlandish outfit comprised of cultural detritus found at the back of the museum (Mitchell 1877).

The gothic possibilities of enlisting emergent scientific technologies to extend the body's physical limitations are of course neither new nor confined to science fiction, and are perhaps most famously explored in the nineteenth-century classics of Mary Shelley's (1818) *Frankenstein* and Robert Louis Stevenson's (1886) *The Strange Case of Dr Jekyll and Mr Hyde*. Yet the imagined double risk of disembodiment and mutation uniquely enables the trope of MT to challenge normative ideas of individuality, existence and consciousness. This was first highlighted in 1910 by Appollinaire's character Baron d'Ormesan, who creates numerous independent physical copies of himself, some of whom go on to father children, but all of whom die when one of them is shot, leaving behind a 'profusion of corpses' – 841 in all (Appollinaire [1910] 1968: 102). Did these bodies all belong to the same man, or were they individual beings in their own right? Similar thought-experiments frequently appear in cognitive philosophy texts, such as Douglas R. Hofstadter and Daniel C. Dennett's (1982) *The Mind's I*. These speculations into the ramifications of MT are nearly always identical in plot: a subject enters a booth, is disintegrated and re-created in another booth. Is this re-creation the same person as the original or not? If the original is *not* disintegrated, are there now two of the same person or two separate individuals? Hofstadter and Dennett's iteration of MT is described as a 'murdering twinmaker' simply for operating the way it is supposed to (Hofstadter and Dennet 1982: 4).

Perhaps this is why, although MT shares no methods of operation with claustrophobic spaceships, the overwhelmingly predominant architectural representation of MT is as a booth. This cramped space *might* function as a symbolic prophylactic against incipient agoraphobia or even outright Pascalian terror. However, given the process of destruction and re-creation that occurs within, there is likely an extra symbolic level in operation. 'Freud would have found its implications thrilling', quip Pohl and Williamson (1973: 49), describing their 'tachyon transporter box' as 'another womb – with a completely different set of birth traumas'.

Womb, or temporary coffin? The possibility of creating individual back-ups that can be rebooted or 'resurrected' in the case of sudden death is a key variation on this reimagining of the self as something both plastic and reproducible. The matter of the soul cannot be avoided in these stories: Clifford Simak's *Way Station* portrays the animating force of interstellar travellers as jumping instantaneously from duplicate to duplicate, leaving 'a long trail of dead' behind (Simak 1963: 63). However, given the trope's (and the genre's) primary dismissal of the supernatural, any discussion of such matters tends to focus more on the technology's impact on organized religion rather than on the effects on the individual. MT is frequently described by the superstitious or ignorant as dangerous in the spiritual sense or by the Pope as a '*diabolical* invention' worthy of interdiction (Brunner 1973: 124, emphasis in original). Alternatively, as in Thomas Marcinko's *Heretics*, the transmission and duplication of missionary priests may become a papal mandate. But regardless of its implications for spiritual or psychological rescripting, the technology of MT itself is characteristically value-neutral: while it may sometimes give rise to destructive effects, such possibilities arise from the randomness of error or accident, or from the deliberate decisions of the people who use it. Technologies may facilitate changes for better or for worse, but unlike people, they carry no power of intention.

It is clear, then, that MT's portrayal as the deliverer of a transport revolution conceals more far-reaching concerns about social change, identity transformation and embodiment. In this sense, thanks to the seamless process of disintegration and reintegration that lies at MT's heart, MT stories are not simply about revolutions in transport any more than MT itself simply moves people around. Its capacity for challenging our understandings of both social order and individual identity gives the trope enormous scope, demonstrated in a long tradition of fictional imaginings which encompass utopic possibilities as well as their dystopic shadows. Without speculation on the broader transformations that such a technology would inevitably entail, MT merely becomes a magical instrument in disguise, no different to the flying carpets or seven league boots of legend. When this occurs, as it often does in franchises like *Star Trek*, *Doctor Who* or *Halo*, the trope has exited the realm of science fiction and entered pure fantasy.

But even Richard Wagner in 1876 recognized the possibilities for transmogrification contained within his fantastical Tarnhelm. When Siegfried dons it and takes the physical form of Gunther, Lord of the Gibichungs, the connection between spatial collapse and the collapse of identity is made explicit. Both Tarnhelm and Telepomp serve as potent symbols of the post-Telegraph age of immediacy and immateriality, and a reminder that travel does much more than simply broaden the mind.

References

Appollinaire, G. [1910] 1968. Remote projection. *The Magazine of Fantasy and Science Fiction*, July, translated by R.I. Hall, 93–102.
Asimov, I. [1954] 1969. It's such a beautiful day, in *Nightfall and Other Stories*. New York: Doubleday, 245–67.
Banks, R.E. 1959. Rabbits to the moon. *The Magazine of Fantasy and Science Fiction*, July, 106–18.
Bendle, M.F. 2002. Teleportation, cyborgs and the posthuman ideology. *Social Semiotics*, 12(1), 45–62.
Bester, A. 1956. *The Stars My Destination*. London: Sidgwick and Jackson.
Bignell, J. 1999. Another time, another space: Modernity, subjectivity and *The Time Machine*, in *Alien Identities: Exploring difference in film and fiction*, edited by D. Cartmell, I.Q. Hunter, H. Kaye and I. Whelehan. London: Pluto, 87–103.
Brunner, J. 1973. You'll take the high road, in *Three Trips in Time and Space*, edited by R. Silverberg. New York: Dell, 86–158.
Brunner, J. [1974] 1977. *Web of Everywhere*. London: NEL.

Brunner, J. 1980. *The Infinitive of Go*. New York: Ballantine.

Burroughs, E.R. 1917. *A Princess of Mars*. Chicago: McClurg.

Clarke, A.C. [1937] 2000. Travel by wire!, in *The Collected Stories*. London: Victor Gollancz, 1–4.

Clarke, A.C. and Baxter, S. [1997] 2000. The wire continuum, in *The Collected Stories*. London: Victor Gollancz, 948–64.

Doyle, A.C. 1889. *The Mystery of Cloomber* [Online: Project Gutenberg]. Available at: http://www.gutenberg.org/ebooks/7964 [accessed: 16 October 2011].

Doyle, A.C. 1929. *The Disintegration Machine* [Online: Project Gutenberg Australia]. Available at: http://gutenberg.net.au/ebooks06/0601391h.html [accessed: 1 October 2011].

Friedberg, A. 1993. *Window Shopping: Cinema and the postmodern*. Berkeley: University of California Press.

Gibson, W. 1984. *Neuromancer*. New York: Ace.

Green, J. 1965. *The Loafers of Refuge*. London: Victor Gollancz.

Haldeman, J. 1976. *Mindbridge*. New York: St Martin's.

Hamilton, E. [1927] 1967. The moon menace. *Famous Science Fiction*, 1(2), 11–39.

Harrison, H. [1970] 1973. *One Step From Earth*. Devon: Readers Union.

Heinlein, R. 1955. *Tunnel in the Sky*. New York: Scribner's.

Hofstadter, D.R. and Dennett, D.C. 1982. *The Mind's I: Fantasies and reflections on self and soul*. New York: Bantam.

Jane, F.T. 1897. *To Venus in Five Seconds: An account of the strange disappearance of Thomas Plummer, pillmaker*. London: A.D. Innes.

King, S. [1981] 1985. The jaunt, in *Skeleton Crew*. New York: Putnam, 237–65.

Langelaan, G. [1957] 1980. The fly, in *They Came from Outer Space*, edited by J. Wynorski. New York: Doubleday, 239–73.

Livingston, I. 2006. *Between Science and Literature: An introduction to autopoetics*. Champaign: Illinois University Press.

Malzberg, B.N. 1974. *Guernica Night*. New York: Bobbs-Merrill.

Matson, N. 1929. *Doctor Fogg*. New York: Macmillan.

Milne, R.D. [1885] 1980. Professor Vehr's electrical experiment, in *Science Fiction in Old San Francisco Volume II: Into the sun and other stories*. Rhode Island: Donald M. Grant, 83–94.

Mitchell, E.P. 1877. The man without a body. *The Tachypomp and Other Stories* [Online]. Available at: http://www.forgottenfutures.com/game/ff9/tachypmp.htm [accessed: 12 October 2012].

Mitchell, E.P. [1881] 2011. The clock that went backward, in *The Wordsworth Collection of Science Fiction*, edited by D.S. Davies. Hertfordshire: Wordsworth Editions, 887–98.

Niven, L. 1970. *Ringworld*. New York: Ballantine.

Niven, L. [1974] 1975. A kind of murder, in *A Hole In Space*. London: Futura, 53–70.

Pohl, F.P. and Williamson, J. [1973] 1974. Doomship, in *The 1974 Annual World's Best SF*, edited by Donald A. Woldheim. New York: Daw, 41–104.

Rose, M. 1981. *Alien Encounters: Anatomy of science fiction.* Cambridge, MA: Harvard University Press.

Russ, J. [1972] 1975. Nobody's home, in *Women of Wonder*, edited by Pamela Sargent. New York: Vintage, 235–56.

Sconce, J. 2000. *Haunted Media: Electronic presence from telegraphy to television.* Durham, NC and London: Duke University Press.

Serviss, G.P. 1900. *The Moon Metal* [Online: Project Gutenberg]. Available at: http://www.gutenberg.org/ebooks/8199 [accessed: 11 October 2011].

Shelley, M. 1818. *Frankenstein; or, The Modern Prometheus.* London: Lackington, Hughes, Harding, Mavor and Jones.

Silverberg, R. 1988. We are for the dark. *Isaac Asimov's Science Fiction Magazine*, October, 122–84.

Simak, C. 1963. *Way Station.* London: Victor Gollancz.

Simmons, D. 1989. *Hyperion.* New York: Doubleday.

Smith, G.O. 1945. Pandora's millions. *Astounding*, June, 7–31.

Stableford, B.M. 2004. *Historical Dictionary of Science Fiction Literature.* Lanham: Rowman & Littlefield.

Stevenson, R.L. 1886. *Strange Case of Dr Jekyll and Mr Hyde.* London: Longmans, Green and co.

Sturgeon, T. [1954] 1979. Granny won't knit, in *The Stars are the Styx*. New York: Dell, 111–70.

Van Vogt, A.E. [1942] 1952. Secret unattainable, in *Away and Beyond*. New York: Berkley, 40–79.

Verne, J. [1870] 1993. *20,000 Leagues Under the Sea*, translated by W.J. Miller and F.P. Walter. Annapolis: Naval Institute Press.

Von Trojan, K. 1985. *Transing Syndrome.* Adelaide: Rigby.

Wagner, R. [1876] 1999. *Götterdämerung* [Online]. Available at: http://homWhoe.earthlink.net/~markdlew/shw/Ring.htm, translated by F. Jameson [accessed: 12 October 2012].

Warren, W. [1904] 2010. The nemesis of the vibratory theory, in *The Space Annihilator: Early science fiction from the Argosy, 1896–1910*, edited by Gene Christie. Normal: Black Dog, 71–3.

Wells, H.G. 1895. *The Time Machine.* London: William Heinemann.

Wodhams, J. [1967] 1970. There is a crooked man, in *Analog 7*, edited by J.W. Campbell. New York: Belmont, 256–313.

Wolfe, G. 1979. *The Known and the Unknown: The iconography of science fiction.* Kent, OH: Kent State University Press.

Film and Television References

The Matrix (dir. Andy Wachowski and Larry Wachowsi, 1999).

'The Keys of Marinus', *Doctor Who* (Season 1, Serial 5, dir. John Gorrie, 1964).

PART IV
Unsettling Imaginations

Chapter 12

'It's Still in Your Body': Identity, Place and Performance in Holocaust Testimonies

Steven Cooke and Donna-Lee Frieze

Introduction

In her ground-breaking book, *Return to Auschwitz* ([1981] 1997), Kitty Hart-Moxon wrote of her return to the death camp at Auschwitz-Birkenau, where she spent a number of years as a prisoner during the Holocaust, as a visit to a place she belonged, almost a 'homecoming'. In the act of opening and closing her eyes she moves between past and present, the past laden with fear, death, mud and noise more 'real' for her than the benign present of grass and tourists. The description of her return and its emotional impact illustrates the complex relationships between imagination, memory, place and performance, all key themes of recent conceptualizations of identity and travel.

This chapter examines these issues through the videotestimony of eight Holocaust survivors: all of them Jewish, all connected with Auschwitz or Auschwitz-Birkenau (either because they were held in the camps themselves or lost close family members there), all living in Australia and all of whom had chosen, for a variety of reasons, to return to sites of atrocity during the last two decades. The analysis of videotestimony provides an opportunity to examine issues of performance, identity and place in a number of ways. As well as examining their return visit as a performative act – the motivations, experiences and emotional responses to an embodied encounter with traumatic sites and the remembering of events that happened over 50 years previously – videotestimony also allows us to analyse the performance of their storytelling and how this dynamic between performativities illustrates ideas of mobility, home, belonging and absence in the construction of identity.

Geographies of the Holocaust: Mobilities, Identity, Performance and Affect

From a seeming reluctance of geographers to research the Holocaust (Cole and Smith 1995), there has been a growing body of work on the subject informed by geographical perspectives. This research includes the geography of the historical events themselves (for example Beorn et al. 2009, Cole 2003, 2011, Danielsson 2009, Golan 2002) but also what might be termed the 'aftermath', whether it be the politics of memory (Charlesworth 2004a, 2004b, Cooke 1998, Cole 1999, Till 2005, Witcomb 2010), management of sites (Charlesworth and Addis 2002), Holocaust pedagogy within the literature on student educational visits (Charlesworth 1994) or tourist experiences to sites associated with the Holocaust (Ashworth 2002, Keil 2005).

This last category has grown with the interest in dark tourism more generally, drawing on the work of, *inter alia*, Rojek (1993), Seaton (1996), Lennon and Foley (2000), and Sharpley and Stone (2009). More recent research in tourism has focused on mobilities, foregrounding the relationship between place, emotion and identity (Creswell 2011, Kobayashi et al. 2011). Such research sees tourism as a multi-sensory, embodied and affective encounter, which traces 'an anatomy of power' (Gibson 2010: 525, see also Tolia-Kelly 2006) that is not just about the visual. Such experiences are being 'conceptualised as being simultaneously representational as well as performative and embodied' (Diekmann and Hannan 2012: 1316). These 'mobile, embodied practices are central to how we experience the world, from practices of writing and sensing, to walking and driving. Our mobilities create spaces and stories – spatial stories' (Cresswell and Merriman 2011: 5). As these authors go on to argue, a focus on mobilities also brings our attention to notions of rootedness and stillness – foregrounding notions of 'home'.

Videotestimonies provide a rich archive through which to gain sensitivity to the complex geographies of the Holocaust, particularly the engagement with material and imaginative landscapes of atrocity. Whilst some authors have suggested that the category of dark tourism excludes those who have direct connection with the sites (Lennon and Foley 2000), the boundary between tourist, pilgrim and witness has become increasingly blurred in recent years (Collins-Kreiner 2009). In this sense, videotestimonies illuminate the return visits not only as commemorative rituals, but embodied experiences which foreground the shifting boundaries between tourist, pilgrim, witness, parent, sibling and offspring. Through videotestimony we can explore the ways in which such engagements illustrate the process where the 'mnemonic power and emotional affectivity of commemoration rest[s] significantly on individual bodily participation in ritual acts' (Uusihakala 2011: 62). Videotestimonies comprise a range of signals and significations illuminated in body language, verbal language, complex ethics and mnemic traces which contrast with 'stable and unambiguous points of ethical identification' and the 'ethical security' found in some visual representations of the Holocaust, such as *Schindler's List* (Cohen 2003: 49). Videotestimony is not a hierarchically superior form of testimony compared to written or documentary testimony, but is a different mode or genre, each constructed within their own modes of storytelling. However, as examined previously by Hartman (1996), Felman and Laub (1992), Simon (2005) and more recently by Frieze (2008), videotestimony allows the viewer to observe the cracks in speech, the interruption of imagination into memory and the fissures of memory obfuscated behind protective body language and thus, in some cases, a return to stock expressions of the Holocaust.

Therefore this chapter explores the place of imagination in videotestimony; how power and agency, and ideas of tourist and host, witness and actor are performed and how useful these are in understanding the return visits. How are these sites of atrocity simultaneously here and there, imagined and material? To broaden Sheller and Urry's (2004) question: what are the *emotions* (not just pleasure) place can give that are only available through physical presence?

We chose to explore these questions by analysing videotestimonies of Holocaust survivors held online in the Shoah Foundation's Visual History Archive (VHA).[1] We were interested in Holocaust survivors who had been in, or who had close relatives in, one of the Auschwitz complex of camps, including the death camp at Birkenau, and who had then migrated to Australia post-war. We chose the Auschwitz camps because of the contraction and confusion over the name that is evident in contemporary media, and also because it is on the UNESCO World Heritage list. The name 'Auschwitz' invokes the paradigmatic evil of the Holocaust. Yet, it is often used to imply Auschwitz II (Birkenau), the largest of the three main camps, and the only camp in that complex designated purely as a death camp. Even survivors who were in Auschwitz-Birkenau confuse the specific areas in the complex within their narrative on the videotestimonies. Auschwitz/ Auschwitz-Birkenau is therefore a place that is material, grounded and fixed, and also mobile, imaginative and performed.

The testimonies in the VHA are searchable using an extensive list of categories. We filtered for country of residence, personal or family connection to Auschwitz or Auschwitz-Birkenau and for a return to the camps(s) in Poland post-war. The testimonies were then viewed in their entirety before examining in more detail their telling of their return visit. The videotestimony provided insights into the process of storytelling and an opportunity to examine survivor narratives both about what they did and experienced when they were at the camp and how they spoke about it and reinterpreted it. We were therefore able to explore 'the terrains of the imagination and the physical environment, [which] far from existing on distinct ontological levels, run into one another to the extent of being barely distinguishable' (Ingold 2010 cited in Diekmann and Hannam 2012: 1332).

Why go Back? The Presence of the Event

Returning to the sites of atrocity has often been contentious, particularly within the elite of the Melbourne Jewish community. For example, the Victorian Jewish

---

1   The Shoah Foundation archive was established in 1994 by Stephen Spielberg with the aim of collecting videotestimony from Holocaust survivors and witnesses. It now contains the largest collection of survivor testimony in the world, with over 52,000 testimonies, 90 per cent of which are from Jewish Holocaust survivors, with the rest including other victims, liberators, rescuers and aid providers, and War Crimes Trials participants. http:// dornsife.usc.edu/vhi/aboutus/ (accessed 3 July 2012).

Board of Deputies at first declined to be involved in official commemorations in Poland for the Anniversary of the Warsaw Ghetto Uprising and was reluctant to take part in the first years of the March of the Living. Many individual survivors were also reluctant to return, a response to their Holocaust experiences and perceptions of continuing Polish anti-Semitism. Although some have challenged the myth of post-war silence of Holocaust survivors (Cohen 2007), it remains a strong narrative in the testimonies (Rutland 2005, Rosen 2010).

There are complex and varied reasons why those Holocaust survivors with connections to the Auschwitz camps returned. Many are prompted by the urging of family members. For example, Olga tells her interviewer: 'I didn't have time to think about it ... my son said "mummy I have booked a place for you in Auschwitz" just before we left for London', while Bronka went because her granddaughter asked her to go (Olga 1998, Bronka 1996).[2] For Guta, the return to Poland was to primarily show her son and daughter where she and her husband grew up. In one case, the reluctance on the part of survivor was overcome through the insistence of family. Szaja had not intended to return to Poland, quite the opposite: 'I did not want to go back to Poland, I did not want to see Poland for nothing in the world' (Szaja 1997). However, he was persuaded to return by his son who wanted Szaja to show him the sites of persecution, rather than use an official guide. Indeed, various survivors return with children or grandchildren because as Hirsch and Spitzer (2002: 274) explain, 'children of refugees inherit their parents' knowledge of the fragility of place, their suspicion of home' and in the case of these survivors of Auschwitz-Birkenau gain an insight into their own and their parents' identity. Others focused on material landscapes as evidence. For example, Chaim visited so that he could prove to his wife and himself that he 'went through these things' (Chaim 1997).

Other visits are more serendipitous. Nathan is prompted to return after a chance encounter at a Jewish dinner function in Melbourne. Sitting next to him at his table was someone who knew his father during the Holocaust and remembered his death. This meeting prompted Nathan to seek the place in Poland where his father is buried. Such serendipity is also evident in Edith's visit to Auschwitz and Auschwitz-Birkenau. The initial motivation came from her husband, who had always wanted to go back to Poland. The visit was primarily to visit places associated with their pre-war lives, including Krakow. However, the day the group visited Krakow, someone mentioned that it was *Shavout*[3] (16 May 1994) which was the same day in the Jewish calendar that Edith originally arrived at Auschwitz 50 years earlier (27 May 1944). Despite her conflicting emotions, from Krakow to Oświęcim is a short distance – 'So close we can go by taxi: – So I really couldn't make myself to go, but to be here the day when I have *Yahrzeit*, the day of the ... when I came to Auschwitz, I want to go'.[4]

---

2   A list of survivors and their testimony dates is provided at the end of the chapter.
3   The Jewish harvest festival that celebrates the giving of the *Torah*.
4   *Yahrzeit* is the Yiddish word for the anniversary of a death.

Given these complex motivations, how do the survivors frame their experiences in the videotestimonies we examined? We would like to explore this by focusing on three encounters told by the survivors: with other travellers, with places of atrocity and with 'home'. These themes foreground the embodied experience of place, simultaneously material, imaginative and performed.

Embodied Encounters I: Performing Host and Guest

For all of the survivors we examined, their visit to Auschwitz I and/or Birkenau was a group experience and this context impacted on their return visit in a number of ways. For example, rather than act solely as a guide for his son around Auschwitz, Szaja insists that he and his son, Mark, join a guided tour. The motivation for joining a guided tour is Szaja's perceived inability to tell the story of the site, arguing that 'He'll explain to you maybe better than I will'. The group they joined comprised of priests, 'and as we marched and marched and marched' around the site, the guide's narrative angered Szaja. He recalls the guide stating that the group was 'walking on a ground where 6 million Poles have been murdered by Nazi Germany, by the Nazi, Nazi war machine'. The effect on Szaja is immediate and intense: 'I just stood back then, and if anybody would have stuck a knife in me, blood would not have come out.'

Szaja recalls blanking out for a short while, about 5 or 10 seconds. His son asks him what is the matter, 'and then I came back to myself'. He has a nip of whiskey from his son, and then challenges the guide, in Polish:

> Don't you tell people lies, why do you tell people lies like this. I said: 'How many Polaks were killed here in this camp? A handful' I said. [raises hand]. 'Hundred, two hundred, three hundred would be a lot. So why do you say Poles? Why don't you say Polish Jews'. He said, 'well a Jew is a Pole'. I said 'no: a Jew is not a Pole, a Jew is a Jew'. (Szaja 1997)[5]

He recounts showing his tattooed number to his guide, and said he wouldn't go back. His position as a survivor and witness, inscribed on body, legitimizes his intervention in the tour:

> And I've told them what happened, and showed him the number, and they couldn't believe it, that I'm a survivor, even the guide couldn't believe that I'm a survivor. And at the end, he called me away, the guide and he said, 'look, I have to do this, that's what our government is telling us to tell people', and I says 'well that's … that's cheating and telling the biggest lie on earth going'. (Szaja 1997)

---

5   The extracts from the testimonies have been transcribed verbatim. We have avoided the use of [*sic*], preferring instead to follow exactly the nonstandard and inconsistent verbal performances of the survivors, who are all speaking in their second language.

Nathan's visits to landscapes of atrocity also elicited an extreme and ongoing bodily reaction. He decided to travel to Poland to try and locate where his father was buried and to visit Auschwitz-Birkenau where his mother died. In his testimony he describes his joy at finding his father's grave, particularly of being able to provide locals with money to tidy up the cemetery where his father is buried. He displays a sense of elation about having the chance to clean up the neglected area. He becomes extremely upset and whilst crying he says how he is comforted that he is now aware of his father's location: 'I know [pauses to wipe his face], I know where he is' (Nathan 1997). This sense of agency disappears when he discusses his visit to Auschwitz-Birkenau. Nathan becomes noticeably uncomfortable about the place and about this visit:

> I went to Auschwitz, and I know they were there, but I couldn't stay. I, I ... you feel the earth moving [crying – and making churning movements with his hands]. I cannot really explain how it feels to be there ... I know exactly ... I found in Auschwitz, where my mother had to go ... the train came in and they put them in barracks, and she was in barrack 17. Not very far from there was already gas chambers. I've seen all that. I only stayed for a few hours ... I had to get out, I just felt everything was moving ... from that excitement I came home with an illness, I got asthma and the doctor reckons it was from stress. (Nathan 1997)

Unlike his experience finding his father's grave, there is no sense of closure for Nathan at Birkenau. Despite Hirsch and Spitzer's (2002: 260) observation that 'in the act of recollection, traumatic events are inevitably linked to their points of origin, and a physical return can thus facilitate the process of working through', Nathan continues to re-live his experiences: 'I still dream about it. You can't get rid of it, it's there. It's still in your body' (Nathan 1997).

As discussed above, Bronka's experience is also regulated by her travel companions, albeit in a very different way to Szaja. Although, like many of the other survivors discussed, she was with her daughter and granddaughter, the presence of an organized Israeli school visit structured her experience within a redemptive narrative that emphasized nationalism and the Jewish State. She was initially reluctant to go back 'because I knew I would go to pieces but I didn't' (Bronka 1996). She discusses feeling very proud of the students carrying the Israeli flag, and cries when she recalls the students signing the *Hatikvah* during a visit to the site of the Majdanek camp.[6] For Bronka, the students represent the continuation of Jewish life: 'They are my hope, our hope. Jews being Jews' (Bronka 1996). Her role within the group is clear – she describes herself as 'the soap star. I was exhibit number one' (Bronka 1996). At the end of her testimony she reads aloud her comments from the commemorative book of the trip which illustrate her redemptive experience:

---

6 The *Hatikvah* was a poem written by Naphtali Herz Imber, and has become the Israeli national anthem.

> I was grieving for people, family and friends. For lost years, for sufferings I saw,
> and experienced, and experiences, experienced ... But seeing you, marching up
> to the monument of the ashes in Majdanek, holding high above your head the
> Israeli flag, hearing you [breaks down] singing the *Hatikvah* [pause] in front
> of the ruins of the crematorium of Birkenau gave me back hope for the future.
> Seeing you crying and shocked by what you saw reassured me you would not
> forget, that it will not happen again ... I feel that we have won. (Bronka 1996)

As well as the communal experience of the visit, Bronka describes a community
of affect. Through the shared performance of the emotional experience, Bronka is
comforted by the students' demonstration of their inner transformation. For Bronka
both the visual, aural and other bodily functions are implicated in the emotions that
her visit and the memories of her experiences on the tour generate. Like Susan who
recalls in her testimony the shock of being able to 'stand on the railway as a free
person' (Susan 1997), Bronka's epiphany comes from the most basic and mundane
of everyday experience: going to the toilet: 'I went to the toilet, which I felt when
we went to the toilet in Auschwitz [during the Holocaust] I really felt that I am
not a human being anymore' (Bronka 1996). The element of narrative control she
discusses ('we have won') is confirmed by the control over her own body.

Olga also went with an organized tour. Like Szaja and Bronka, Olga performs
the role of an authentic witness, shifting from guest to host. The guide defers to her:

> And you know what, even the guide said 'You know what, Mrs H, you better tell
> the people, because you know what to tell'. So they all came to me. (Olga 1998)

However for Olga this experience, which provided an opportunity for Szaja and
Bronka to exhibit control, disrupts her experience. Olga's testimony reveals
the desire to engage with knowledge rather than the imagination. She tells her
interviewer, 'you cannot imagine a thing what you don't know' (Olga 1998),
meaning that the visitors to Birkenau cannot engage in imagination in order to
'know' what happened there in the 1940s and also that Olga needs knowledge
in order to engage with imagination. For Olga that knowledge comes from her
experiences during the Holocaust, but she denies the possibility of an imaginative
encounter for the rest of the group because they did not experience it. She describes
the tourists as 'innocents' and 'unprepared' and thus Olga becomes the leader of
the group taking over from the guide:

> terrible things they showed [them] ... because I knew, I knew ... whatever I saw
> I knew first hand [her hands are cupped close to her chest]. But these people
> were born after the war ... I was the only one in Auschwitz and my mother
> was here already in Auschwitz so it spread [the news to the guided group] so
> everybody came up to me to ask me all these questions ... They wanted to know
> everything. [Here she mimes looking at her audience on the tour, looking from
> face to face, re-enacting her performance on site]. (Olga 1998)

Olga gesticulates often with her hands, leans forward and touches her open palms to her chest. She feels her knowledge and its transmission physically. The obligation Olga feels to tell 'the innocents and the unprepared', to transmit her knowledge, is perhaps a version of ethical duty reminiscent of Emmanuel Levinas' ethical Other, where 'we venture outside the permissible limits of ... obligating forces ... to find ourselves far more obligated than we imagined' (Spargo 2006: 17). Her ethical obligation to transmit is strong. Again with her hand on her heart Olga speaks:

> You know I wanted to *grieve* [strong intonation] there very much but they [the other visitors to Auschwitz] didn't let me because the way they were asking me questions I said to myself that I have to tell these people [here her voice is soft] what happened here. (Olga 1998)

'What happened here', where the 'here' refers to Birkenau and to the hand that covers and protects the vital organ. Place for Olga is in the body. The change in status from guest to host, which has offered Szaja and Bronka an element of control, places additional obligations on Olga which disrupt the commemorative part of her visit.

Do the survivors (and the interviewers and viewers) expect that the site will help them identify with the self who was interned in the camp? As mentioned, Olga's testimony has an epistemological engagement with her return visit, thus it is imperative that knowledge of the events is transmitted to others. Olga is on a guided tour with her son but for her, '[t]he guide could only tell the stark facts. From a human point of view I could tell them [the other visitors to Birkenau] the way that when we arrived in Auschwitz' (Olga 1998). For Olga, identification becomes key and through this process the 'incomprehensible event seems to become comprehensible' (Eaglestone 2004: 22). Because of her authenticity as a survivor, Olga becomes the ultimate witness, the historical chronicler rather than a mourner. Transference of knowledge becomes a duty for Olga. A group commemorative function allows Olga to grieve but churns up her identification process. Later in the testimony, and now less animated Olga recalls lighting a *yahzeit* candle at a *yizkor* (memorial) service at crematorium four in Birkenau:

> [Olga]: It was very, very moving, very tragic, very sad because what we came back to Birkenau for? What we came back to? ... What did we come there? [the interviewer interprets Olga's 'polyvocal' nuances as regret]
>
> [Interviewer]: Are you not pleased that you came back?
>
> [Olga]: Yes I am very pleased but I was overwhelmed that I finally could come back to Auschwitz. (Olga 1998)

Is Olga noting something in the commemorative phase of her trip that obfuscates the epistemological identification she so needs? Why the bolt from the safety of the memorial service to questioning her reason regarding the return? Maybe Olga is experiencing what Eaglestone (2004: 55) refers to as an epiphanic moment in testimony, whereby the speech or writing diverges from the 'comfortable' narratives. Olga's identity is entwined in the solidification of her knowledge and the memorial service seemingly disrupts this identification. Olga can't identify with the dead. It is the emptiness of non-identification, as Eaglestone (2004: 75) suggests: 'identity without memory is empty, memory without identity is meaningless'.

Embodied Encounters II: Sites of Atrocity a Place and a Void

In her testimony, Sonia, the sole survivor in her family sent to Birkenau where her mother and sister were murdered, describes returning to the camp with her husband:

> I just wanted to see the place where my mother and my sister died and for couple
> of years I couldn't think of anything else. Well, I did go back and it shook me up,
> the place that I saw, all the unshed tears came to me then. I was quite hysterical.
> Somehow Auschwitz was so familiar that it didn't make an impression on me
> [in a whisper]. I could recognize everything and it didn't matter. It's very hard
> to explain to somebody when you just show them a place where you stayed; it's
> just not the place itself. (Sonia 1997)

How can Sonia feel 'hysterical' in Birkenau, the place that 'didn't make an impression'? Sonia is in a place where she is affected and unaffected simultaneously. Expressed in this apparent contradiction of feelings is that Sonia is somehow empirically and imaginatively *there* and *not there*. There seems to be a 'tremendous difference' between the 'over there' and the 'back there' (Schweitzer 2010: 62). It is what Spargo (2006: 254) refers to as the 'paradox of post-Holocaust language'. The place that shook Sonia was the same place that 'didn't make an impression' on her. Does the survivor then return to a void, a placelessness (Bernard-Donals 2010)? However, Sonia's testimony, full of complexity, is very much tied to the material landscape. During another part of her testimony she describes standing with her husband on a windy hill reading a plaque at the site of the former labour camp Plaszow in Krakow:

> While we were standing there reading that plaque, it was uneerie how we both
> felt the presence of our nerves. So it's not much you can show, but the way you
> feel about the place you have been in, that makes the difference. (Sonia 1997)

We are reading 'uneerie' here as a contraction of uncanny and eerie, simultaneously saying that the way Sonia feels about the place cannot be expressed in the landscape and yet the way one feels about a place 'that *you have been in*' [our emphasis] dramatically alters how the landscape can be experienced. That Sonia feels 'the presence of [her] nerves' in Plaszow (where incidentally her husband was detained in the camp from 1941 to 1945, but she was not) demonstrates the corporeal effect of place (and not necessarily places of one's own atrocity). For Sonia, the camps are 'uncanny' spaces both familiar and unfamiliar where 'the one seems always to inhabit the other' (Gelder and Jacobs 1998: 23).

There is a void that is encapsulated in the historical lived experience of Birkenau that is not reproduced by simply returning to the site. It may lie in a realm of what Bernard-Donals terms 'forgetful memory', where Sonia, like many other survivors, 'does not experience the presence of [the original] ... event – as if it were ever possible to relive the events of history – but it brought to a nexus, a juncture composed not by a convergence of objects or events but rather by a concavity of experience, a void' (Bernard-Donals 2010: 120). As Bernard-Donals points out, the original experience can never be relived: it cannot be repeated or imitated. If it were imitated, it would be the original experience as Derrida reminds us: 'a perfect imitation is no longer an imitation ... [it] does not correspond to its essence, is not what it is – imitation – unless it is some way at fault or rather in default' (Derrida 1981: 139). The survivor who was unwillingly sent to Birkenau and who willingly (although in some cases reluctantly) returns is not re-experiencing the original event but a new experience that may or may not conjure up the original occurrence. It can never imitate; if the return could, it would be the original experience. Feelings of familiarity and unfamiliarity are also evident in our final encounter: imagination.

Embodied Encounters III: Nostalgia and 'Home'

One reason why the VHA videotestimonies are useful for exploring ideas of mobility is that they are filmed in the survivor's home. Mostly shot in medium close-up (rarely does the camera pan or zoom out or in from this angle), the background scene often includes paintings on walls, a vase of flowers, candelabras, books or trinkets while the survivors are often perfectly groomed. The quiet stillness of home juxtaposes with narratives regarding the return to the camps that are recounted with *disorder*. Bolkosky (2010: 185) writes that 'Auschwitz, in its transformational chaos, disrupted everything' and this is illustrated clearly in Sonia's videotestimony after she wistfully remembers her visit to her former home town Krakow:

> In a way I was glad that everything is the way it was and somehow I sort of felt I wish it was all flattened and all my family went why couldn't that go with them [here, Sonia's voice is low with a tone of resentment]. It's mixed feelings. If I

could go back again, I don't know I think I like to remember things the way they were. (Sonia 1997)

Before this sequence, Sonia recalls returning to her home town in Krakow and, in a contemplative voice that nostalgically describes the sacred landscape of her pre-Holocaust years, she uses such words and phrases as 'love ... regain ... memories ... childhood ... still there it was ... remember ... recapture'. The word 'nostalgia', Hirsch and Spitz (2002: 257) remind us, is 'from the Greek *nostos*, to return home and *algia*, a painful feeling'. Susan's apparent ambivalence regarding her pre-Holocaust home town as 'somehow better, simpler, less fragmented and more comprehensible' (Hirsch and Spitz 2002: 258) is also the place she wishes was 'flattened'. So while the notion of nostalgia is 'comprehensible' it also captures, as Horowitz (2010: 49) explains, 'a sense of rupture and radical discontinuity, the impossibility of a "cure", irretrievable loss, incomplete mourning. Since trauma resembles nostalgia ... there is sometimes a slippage between the two'. Sonia's return visit to Birkenau where 'nearly every hour something happened' (Susan 1997) contrasts with her representation of her return to Krakow. Birkenau *did things to her*; but in Krakow, Sonia desired to *do things to* it.

Nostalgia is also evident in Guta's testimony. She went first to Israel to see her family and then went to Poland with her son, daughter and cousin. She took a took a taxi and had a guide:

because she [the guide] knew everything about Auschwitz, Auschwitz-Birkenau. So, one day, yes, I took another half of Valium [slight laugh] and we went first to Kracow ... [the guide] showed us around and she took us to the Jewish Quarter, running [*sic*] by non-Jews, and there you sit and have a cup of coffee, and the old records are playing with the old songs my mother used to sing. Then we went to Oświęcim, by car. (Guta 1996)

A combination of the visit and the senses of taste and hearing prompt Guta's wistful recollection of Poland. Her self-medication, akin to Szaja's nip of whisky, reminds us of the medical origins of nostalgia. Although there is a dramatic shift from her recollections of Krakow to her journey to Oświęcim, as she walks around Birkenau her nostalgia continues. She:

counted the barracks, and I found the place where I was sleeping. There was quite a lot of barracks left there. But one particular one, on the left hand side, I remember, when we turned the line, I said, I should be here somewhere, and he said, 'what do you mean you should be here somewhere'? I remember it was, in this area here, and I walked in and I found a bed. On the third row down, and there were flowers there, I laid flowers on my bed. And on the chimney where we used to warm ourselves up, where there was hardly any fire. (Guta 1996)

For Guta, Krakow is a particular experience. Born in Poland but not in Krakow, Guta can engage with the tourist aspect of the place and safely engage with a nostalgia that is comforting, ceremonial and helps her lay to rest a haunted past and recall and imagine an idyllic one. For Sonia, this is more difficult. Sonia has difficulty reconciling her home in Krakow with her place in Birkenau and simultaneously has difficulty, in the end, separating them and hence she wants to flatten her birthplace. The issue of belonging no longer exists and hence she feels a desire for both worlds to be 'flattened'.

Conclusion

This chapter has explored survivor returns to sites of atrocity through three encounters. Illustrated by the videotestimonies we examined, each survivor narrative connects ideas of imagination to place. By their very construction, the videotestimonies demonstrate simultaneously categories of identity: host/guest, place/voids and complex notions of home. Returning to 'Auschwitz', the place where either the survivors were incarcerated or their immediate family members were murdered, conjures up these complex notions of identity. The emotional response that physical presence in the landscape generates continues through the recounting of their testimony. That affective encounter continues across spatial and temporal distance, an extreme time/space compression (Larsen et al. 2007), because for Nathan, as for other survivors: 'It's still in your body' (Nathan 1997).

The VHA is a fertile ground for further geographical research on the Holocaust. The focus in this chapter is on Jewish Holocaust survivors. However, further research, via the VHA, will focus on other victims, such as Roma and Sinti, and also liberators of the camps. As the Shoah Foundation's *Witness for Humanity* programme continues – which is collecting a large bank of Armenian, Cambodian and Rwandan genocide survivor testimony – these issues of embodiment and identity can be broadened. And although the archive does not collect perpetrator or bystander testimony we think that this would also add significant nuance to our understanding of embodied engagements with the landscapes of the Holocaust and other genocides.

Acknowledgements

Thanks to Sarah Clarke for her Research Assistance, and Monash University and the Jewish Holocaust Museum in Melbourne for access to the testimonies. Thanks also to the Deakin University's Alfred Deakin Research Institute and Cultural Heritage Centre for the Asia and Pacific for funding. We are also grateful to the International Network of Genocide Scholars for the opportunity to present a version of this chapter at their Third International Conference in San Francisco in 2012.

References

Ashworth, G.J. 2002. Holocaust tourism: The experience of Kraków-Kazimierz. *International Research in Geographical and Environmental Education*, 11(4), 363–7.

Beorn, W., Cole, T., Gigliotti, S., Giordano, A., Holian, A., Jaskot, P.B., Knowles, A.K., Masurovsky, M. and Steiner, E.B. 2009. Geographies of the Holocaust. *Geographical Review*, 99(4), 563–74.

Bernard-Donals, M. 2010. 'If I forget thee, O Jerusalem': The poetry of forgetful memory in Israel and Palestine, in *After Representation? The Holocaust, literature, and culture*, edited by R.C. Spargo and R.M. Ehrenreich. New Brunswick: Rutgers University Press, 120–134.

Bolkosky, S. 2010. 'And in the distance you hear music, a band playing': Reflections on chaos and order in literature and testimony, in *After Representation? The Holocaust, literature, and culture*, edited by R.C. Spargo and R.M. Ehrenreich. New Brunswick: Rutgers University Press, 179–89.

Charlesworth, A. 1994. Teaching the Holocaust through landscape study: The Liverpool experience. *Immigrants and Minorities*, 13(1), 65–76.

Charlesworth, A. 2004a. A corner of a foreign field that is forever Spielberg's: The moral landscapes of the site of the former KL Plaszow, Krakow, Poland. *Cultural Geographies*, 11, 291–312.

Charlesworth, A. 2004b. The topography of genocide, in *The Historiography of the Holocaust*, edited by Dan Stone. Basingstoke: Palgrave Macmillan, 216–52.

Charlesworth, A. and Addis, M. 2002. Memorialization and the ecological landscapes of Holocaust sites: The cases of Plaszow and Auschwitz-Birkenau. *Landscape Research*, 27(3), 229–51.

Cohen, B.B. 2007. *Case Closed: Holocaust survivors in postwar America*. New Brunswick: Rutgers University Press.

Cohen, J. 2003. *Interrupting Auschwitz: Art, religion, philosophy*. New York: Continuum.

Cole, T. 1999. *Selling the Holocaust: From Auschwitz to Schindler: How history is bought, packaged, and sold*. New York: Routledge.

Cole, T. 2003. *Holocaust City: The making of a Jewish ghetto*. New York: Routledge.

Cole, T. 2011. *Traces of the Holocaust. Journeying in and out of the ghettos*. New York: Continuum.

Cole, T. and Smith, G. 1995. Ghettoization and the Holocaust: Budapest 1944. *Journal of Historical Geography*, 21(3), 300–316.

Collins-Kreiner, N. 2009. Geographers and pilgrimages: Changing concepts in pilgrimage tourism research. *Tijdscrift voor Economische en Sociale Geografie*, 101(4), 437–48.

Cooke, S. 1998. Negotiating memory and identity: The Hyde Park Holocaust memorial, London. *Journal of Historical Geography*, 26(3), 449–65.

Cresswell, T. 2011. Mobility, in *The Sage Handbook of Geographical Knowledge*, edited by D. Livingstone and J. Agnew. London: Sage.

Cresswell, T. and Merriman, P. 2011. Mobilities I. *Geographies of Mobilities: Practices, Spaces, Subjects*, 35(4), 550–558.

Danielsson, S.K. 2009. Creating genocidal space: Geographers and the discourse of annihilation, 1880–1933. *Space and Polity*, 13, 55–68.

Derrida, J. 1981. *Dissemination*. Chicago: The University of Chicago Press.

Diekmann, A. and Hannam, K. 2012. Touristic mobilities in India's slum spaces. *Annals of Tourism Research*, 39(3), 1315–36.

Eaglestone, R. 2004. *The Holocaust and the Postmodern*. Oxford: Oxford University Press.

Felman, S. and Laub, D. 1992. *Testimony: Crises of witnessing in literature, psychoanalysis, and history*. New York: Routledge.

Frieze, D.L. 2008. The death of the suffering Other: Responding to Holocaust survivors through the philosophy of Emmanuel Levinas, in *Testifying to the Holocaust*, edited by P. Maclean, D. Abramovich and M. Langfield. Sydney: Australian Association of Jewish Studies, 75–92.

Gelder, K. and Jacobs, J.M. 1998. *Uncanny Australia: Sacredness and identity in a postcolonial nation*. Melbourne: Melbourne University Press.

Gibson, C. 2010. Geographies of tourism: (Un)ethical encounters. *Progress in Human Geography*, 34(4), 521–7.

Golan, A. 2002. Israeli historical geography and the Holocaust: Reconsidering the research agenda. *Journal of Historical Geography*, 28(4), 554–65.

Hartman, G.H. 1996. *The Longest Shadow: In the aftermath of the Holocaust*. Bloomington: Indiana University Press.

Hart-Moxon, K. [1981] 1997. *Return to Auschwitz: The remarkable story of a girl who survived the Holocaust*. London: Panther.

Hirsch, M. and Spitzer, L. 2002. 'We would not have come without you': Generations of nostalgia. *American Imago*, 59(3), 253–76.

Horowitz, S.A. 2010. Nostalgia and the Holocaust, in *After Representation? The Holocaust, literature, and culture*, edited by R.C. Spargo and R.M. Ehrenreich. New Brunswick: Rutgers University Press, 41–58.

Keil, C. 2005. Sightseeing in the mansions of the dead. *Social and Cultural Geography*, 6(4), 479–94.

Kobayashi, A. Preston, V. and Murnaghan, A.M. 2011. Place, affect, and transnationalism through the voices of Hong Kong immigrants to Canada. *Social and Cultural Geography*, 12(8), 871–88.

Larsen, J., Urry, J. and Axhausen, K.W. 2007. Networks and tourism: Mobile social life. *Annals of Tourism Research*, 34(1), 244–62.

Lennon, J.J. and Foley, M. 2000. *Dark Tourism: The attraction of death and disaster*. London: Cassell.

Rojek, C. 1993. *Ways of Escape*. Basingstoke: Macmillan.

Rosen, A. 2010. *The Wonder of their Voices: The 1946 Holocaust interviews of David Boder*. Oxford: Oxford University Press.

Rutland, S.D. 2005. *The Jews in Australia.* Cambridge: Cambridge University Press.

Schweitzer, P. 2010. Death in language: From Mado's mourning to the act of writing, in *After Representation? The Holocaust, literature, and culture,* edited by R.C. Spargo and R.M. Ehrenreich. New Brunswick: Rutgers University Press, 59–74.

Seaton, A.V. 1996. Guided by the dark: From thanatopsis to thantourism. *International Journal of Heritage Studies,* 2(4), 234–44.

Sharpley, R. and Stone, P.R. (eds) 2009. *The Darker Side of Travel: The theory and practice of dark tourism.* Tonawanda: Channel View Publications.

Sheller, M. and Urry, J. 2004. Places to play, places in play, in *Tourism Mobilities: Places to play, places in play,* edited by M. Sheller and J. Urry. Abingdon: Routledge, 1–10.

Simon, R.I. 2005. *The Touch of the Past: Remembrance, learning, and ethics.* New York: Palgrave Macmillan.

Spargo, R.C. 2006. *Vigilant Memory: Emmanuel Levinas, the Holocaust, and the unjust death.* Baltimore: The Johns Hopkins University Press.

Till, K. 2005. *The New Berlin: Memory, politics, place.* Minneapolis: University of Minnesota Press.

Tolia-Kelly, D. 2006. Affect – an ethnocentric encounter? Exploring the 'universalist' imperative of emotional/ affectual geographies. *Area,* 38(2), 213–17.

Uusihakala, K. 2011. Reminiscence tours and pilgrimage sites: Commemorative journeys in ex-Rhodesian diaspora. *Suomen Antropologi: Journal of the Finnish Anthropological Society,* 36(1), 57–64.

Witcomb, A. 2010. Remembering the dead by affecting the living: The case of a miniature model of Treblinka, in *Museum Materialities: Objects, engagements, interpretations,* edited by S.H. Dudley. New York: Routledge, 39–52.

Testimonies

Bronka 1996. USC Shoah Foundation Institute, code 22404.
Chaim 1997. USC Shoah Foundation Institute, code 32061.
Guta 1996. USC Shoah Foundation Institute, code 24384.
Nathan 1997. USC Shoah Foundation Institute, code 32951.
Olga 1998. USC Shoah Foundation Institute, code 42006.
Sonia 1997. USC Shoah Foundation Institute, code 29370.
Susan 1997. USC Shoah Foundation Institute, code 31562.
Szaja 1997. USC Shoah Foundation Institute, code 34520.

Chapter 13

Ready for Takeoff?
Lacerated Fantasies of Caribbean Paradise in the *Décollage* Art of Andrea Chung

Marsha Pearce

Images produced within the arena of tourism and travel are ingrained with the performative role of a travel agent. In one sense, they serve as liaisons, visual links or points of contact between sites of here and there, setting up mental bookings long before credit card details are used to reserve accommodations and suitcases are filled. In de Botton's engagement with a travel brochure, he marvels at 'how a lengthy and ruinously expensive journey might be set into motion by nothing more than the sight of a photograph of a palm tree gently inclining in a tropical breeze' (2002: 8–9). In another sense, as agent, such images act as vehicles for transportation, for instant travel across distances and time. Francisca Kellett (2008), the *Telegraph*'s Digital Travel Editor, insists that 'really good travel photography should … take you there'. Similarly, CNN's Ashley Strickland (2011) divulges that in choosing a travel photograph, she asks: 'Can this one image take you there?' Both Kellett and Strickland intimate a need for tourism and travel images to be built in a certain way that makes transport possible. Such images are most often constructed with specific components to 'take you': rudder, propeller and the fuselage of well-groomed Edenic landscapes or what Hunter describes as 'a symbolic erasure of the untidy' (2008: 364). Yet, the motor of these images, the engine of these vehicles is fantasy or the faculty of imagination.

The images of idyll geographies, which are presented in travel magazines and brochures, trigger fantasy, which constitutes at once mental imaging and mental mobility. They function in a way that makes travel and imagination imbricating notions. Such images exert a force on the viewer that compels him or her to take flights of fancy or fantasy (the word 'fancy' is derived from a contraction of 'fantasy'). With a fuelled engine of imagination, the viewer is obliged to accelerate down the runway of the mind and takeoff. He or she travels and touches down in the destinations charted by the images. Upon arrival, the mechanism of imagination does not stop. It sustains travel as the mind traverses the boundaries of the imaged place. The viewer takes off again, extrapolating from the presented imagery, picturing self beyond the visuals printed on the magazine or brochure page and building his or her own utopic, fantastic narratives.

Figure 13.1 Andrea Chung, *Cut Yai*, 23 × 30.5 cm (9 × 12 inches), magazine
                    ***décollage*, 2009**

Source: Reproduced with permission from the artist.

Many published images of Caribbean islands have and continue to function as travel agents. From images in works like James Hakewill's 1825 publication entitled *A Picturesque Tour of the Island of Jamaica from Drawings Made in the Years 1820–1821* to present-day images in such magazines as *Islands* and *Caribbean Travel and Life*, idyllic images of the Caribbean region abound. They stir takeoff, with mental flights of fantasy, which are, more often than not, destined for island leisure and pleasure, tropical diversion or Caribbean paradise escape. Such images, however, transform 'place into a standardized commodity', they 'serve as a universal medium of commercial exchange and by doing so commit symbolic violence by erasing [a place's] past ... or ... confiscating its history' (Hunter 2008: 361). Mental takeoffs, therefore, are almost always destined for imagined, paradisiacal places with pasts that have been excised.

This chapter pivots on the notion of 'takeoff' in its investigation of the *décollage* artwork by Andrea Chung, an artist born in North America to Caribbean parents. The term *décollage* comes from the French verb *décoller*, meaning 'to take off'. *Décollage* is an art technique that involves tearing away, removing or taking off fragments of an existing image. Chung manipulates travel magazine photographs of Caribbean islands, through a process of gashing, ripping and taking off parts, to reveal images of a colonial past with the faces and bodies of plantation labourers appearing in the gashes (see Figure 13.1). The term *décollage* is also used in French language to refer to an airplane taking off or lifting off the ground – connoting travel. The chapter deploys this term in its dual sense: as art technique and as mental takeoff, travel and fantasy.

The chapter argues that Chung's art lacerates fantasies of an idyll Caribbean or Caribbean paradise. It insists that she commits her own counter-symbolic violence in acts of tearing away and slashing in an effort to reinsert a traumatic Caribbean history of colonial servitude, which has been erased from contemporary tourism and travel images. I posit that Chung's art compels the viewer to engage in uneasy acts of imagination and travel through time, back and forth, between present and past, between the idyll and colonial regimes of enslavement and indentureship. I maintain that Chung's work asks viewers if they are ready for uncomfortable flights of fantasy; her work asks viewers: are you ready for takeoff? First, the chapter establishes a context for Chung's art by a look at visual portrayals of Caribbean destinations, followed by an exposition of *décollage* as a creative strategy of taking off or unmasking within the history of art. Then, the chapter builds on this context through an analysis of some of Andrea Chung's work.

Safe Takeoffs: Caribbean Destinations and the Western Imagination

Safe, comfortable, mental takeoffs and flights to the Caribbean have long been a chief priority. The engine of Western (North American and European) imagination was especially sparked to power secure travel to Caribbean islands by tourism industries operating in the Caribbean in the late nineteenth century. Tourism entrepreneurs set about building sound vehicles, images that could work in tandem with the imagination to guarantee untroubled, pleasant trips. Krista Thompson (2006: 4, 7) observes that 'photographic images played a constitutive role in this process ... photographs of tamed nature ... ensured potential travelers of their safety in a tropical environment'. The soundness of the image-as-vehicle was tied to constructing a utopian picture, a tamed depiction – one that did not betray anything unsavoury. Through her exploration of photography, tourism and the picturesque in the Anglophone Caribbean, Thompson elucidates this effort to create safe flights of fantasy:

> Starting in the 1880s, British colonial administrators, local white elites, and American and British hoteliers in Jamaica and the Bahamas embarked on campaigns to refashion the islands as picturesque 'tropical' paradises, the first concerted efforts of their kind in Britain's Caribbean colonies. Tourism entrepreneurs faced a formidable challenge. Beyond the region the West Indies were widely stigmatized as breeding grounds for potentially fatal tropical diseases ... Despite the availability of preventative medicines for 'tropical' diseases in the 1880s, tourism promoters had to dispel the fear of the islands, which haunted the imaginations of potential tourism clienteles in Britain and North America. They had to radically transform the islands' much maligned landscapes into spaces of touristic desire for British and North American traveling publics ... To create new and alluring representations of the islands, the colonial government and British and American corporations in Jamaica and the Bahamas ... enlisted the services of many British, American and local photographers, artists and lantern lecturers. (2006: 4–5)

I quote Thompson at length here in order to establish a palpable want on the part of tourism operators to create psychogenic takeoffs and journeys to Caribbean destinations, via visual vehicles, that are not fraught with discomfort or, rather, dis-ease.

Purging imagined trips to the Caribbean of dis-ease, however, involves a specific process, that of tropics or tropicalization, wherein the words 'tropics' and 'tropical' take on dual valence. First, the process of tropics or tropicalization pinpoints and idealizes places located in the torrid zone between the tropics of Cancer and Capricorn – creating parameters for what such places should look like. Second, an attendant tropical element is made manifest in the discourse of tourism, in other words, a visual trope comes into being. This process creates, through a semblance of the real, a sense of safety for the Western traveller. According to Hayden White (1978: 2, emphasis in the original): 'tropics is the process by which all discourse *constitutes* the objects which it pretends only to describe realistically'. The trope that is produced in the process is an agreeable illusion or, to use Bloom's (1975: 93) words, 'a willing error'. For Bloom, 'every trope ... is necessarily an interpretation ... tropes ... are necessary errors ... defending ultimately against the deathly dangers of [the] literal' (1975: 93, 94). Bloom makes specific reference here to a poetic urge and the making of tropes in the language of poetry. He speaks from a standpoint where the poet is understood as a person who wields the power of imagination and therefore Bloom sees literal interpretation as a kind of death. Yet, his insight into poetry has strong implications for the visual language of tourism. The tropical island image circulated within the domain of tourism is a visual metonymic trope that uses the attributes of sun, sea, sand and palm tree together as an interpretation that defends the Western traveller against the 'deathly dangers' of literal, unembellished Caribbean realities. What is at risk of death is a desire to travel, for in efforts to market destinations and entice Western travellers, a literal interpretation of a place can potentially kill the imagination and shutdown flight. The tropical island trope therefore works as a psychological mechanism, a comfortable interpretation that facilitates an innocuous passage between temperate and tropical zones. For tourism operators and the device of the Western imagination, a safe, metonymic trope made in the tropicalization of Caribbean places becomes a 'necessary error' or vital fantasy.

Yet, tropes that give comfort are not produced without an element of danger, for 'metonymy reduces meaning through an emptying-out that is a kind of reification' (Bloom 1975: 95). The danger is not, however, one that threatens the traveller but rather, one that puts the destination in jeopardy of reductionism. Visual metonyms in tourism, specifically, the tropical island trope, reify or make real a hollow or shallow interpretation of place. Such tropes empty destinations of their complex histories. Mental trips to tropical places run on this kind of emptiness. Daye (2008: 22) observes: 'the legacy of history ... of countries that are endowed with tropical attributes [is] not necessarily privileged in the Western imagination of Paradise'. Despite socio-cultural and historical nuances, the process of tropicalization renders destinations, like that of the Caribbean, as what Featherstone (2005) calls 'non-places'. Featherstone (2005: 214) uses the tropical beach as an example in his discussion about non-places:

> The tourist beach can be seen as another ... non-place. Stripped of geographical and political specificity and fixed within its elements of white sand, blue sea and clear skies, the tropical beach can be endlessly reconfigured as a desirable tourist destination that is almost independent of social context.

Decoupled from any discomforting actualities, the tropical non-place exists as if in a vacuum and as such, is made a safe destination.

Images of stripped or emptied places, that is, non-places, hail the Western traveller into an asymmetrical relationship between self and destination where he or she can feel secure. With vivid pictures like those of North Americans and Europeans enthroned on chaise longues surveying their loyal subjects of sand and sea, or those of the Euro-American tourist relaxing in a hammock suspended in sovereignty above a tropical kingdom, the Western traveller can imagine him or herself as powerful ruler of the non-place. The Western traveller can be free and comfortable in such places. Echtner and Prasad (2003) refer to this freedom and ease as 'the myth of the unrestrained'. According to Echtner and Prasad, the myth of the unrestrained 'presents a romanticized version of colonial exploitation' (2003: 672). They argue:

> the myth of the unrestrained takes the tourist to the luxuriant lands of the sea/sand destinations (such as Cuba, Fiji, and Jamaica) ... These are places where nature is pristine and never harsh ... In the myth of the unrestrained, the destination ... must be portrayed as open and willing to offer a ... comfortable environment to the tourist. Harsh ... conditions are simply not conducive to paradise. (Echtner and Prasad 2003: 672, 673)

In this myth of the unrestrained, the Western traveller freely enjoys the luxuries and comforts of a constructed paradise while the chains and manacles of image-making practices within tourism discourse, restrain the destination's complexity. It is a myth that draws on the dynamics of colonialism but does not make issues of suppression and subjugation readily apparent. It is a myth that is maintained by 'significant silences' (Echtner and Prasad 2003: 673) – one that couches mental takeoff and travel in the vernacular of safety. How might such a myth be debunked? In her study of the limitations of sun, sea and sand images, Daye (2008: 29) calls for an 'epistemic shift in imagining the [Caribbean] region ... [she espouses] an alternative ontology'. How then, might the silences and emptiness of images of tropical Caribbean destinations be redressed? How might Caribbean realities – beyond sun, sea and sand – be revealed? How might a mask of comfort be removed? For answers we can look at the art of taking off.

Décollage: The Art of Taking Off

Décollage is an art technique with ties to the artistic phenomenon known as *Nouveau Réalisme* or New Realism. Tracing the phenomenon gives insight into the technique. Formulated in 1960 by French art critic and philosopher Pierre Restany and French artist Yves Klein, New Realism was an ideological response to stylistic variants of Abstract Expressionism, which dominated Europe in a post-Second World War era. Abstract Expressionism emerged in the United States after the war but the style also took root in Europe under such labels as Lyrical Abstraction and Tachisme. These abstract styles were characterized by non-representational, highly emotive, uninhibited applications of paint including pouring, throwing and dripping. Paintings in these styles were devoid of depictions of 'reality' in the strict sense of the term. In contrast, Restany and Klein aimed to reinsert images from real life into art. They conceived of a return to the nineteenth-century artistic and literary movement of realism, a creative movement, which sought to portray quotidian life without idealization. Yet, they contended that their notion of realism would be 'new' by reason of its engagement with a new twentieth-century reality distinguished by heightened consumerism and advertising. The world was seen as an image from which the *Nouveaux Réalistes* could take parts and incorporate in their art works. The *Nouveaux Réalistes* took objects and elements from everyday life or, from what Restany referred to as 'modern nature' (1986: 267), which comprised urban and commercial materials.

Restany promoted New Realism as a practice, which eschewed contestation and embraced positivity, one that celebrated a seeing of 'the real perceived in itself and not through the prism of conceptual or imaginative transcription' (1996: 306). Yet, some works being made under the umbrella of New Realism proved to be polemical constructions of a reality produced through an imaginative prism of violence – a violence kindled by a Dadaist philosophy of negation. Indeed, the ideology of New Realism would also be informed by Dadaism, an artistic movement with a genesis that can be traced to the First World War. Restany's art exhibition entitled '40 degrees above Dada' held in May 1961 acknowledges this origin.

Dada works of art mocked social conventions with creative juxtapositions and visual contradictions. Dada was an art of subversion, one that deployed a brand of 'violence' in order to take off or remove social facades. For example, Dadaist, Marcel Duchamp's piece entitled *L.H.O.O.Q.* is a reproduction of Leonardo da Vinci's *Mona Lisa* with the pencilled addition of a beard and moustache. Schneider Adams (1999: 859) calls it a work of art that 'plays with the sometimes fine line between creation and destruction'. Yet, the work accomplishes much more. Through a psychoanalytical interpretation of da Vinci's art, Freud ([1910] 1957) argued that da Vinci was a passive homosexual. Therefore Duchamp's art can be read as an unmasking of da Vinci's veiled sexual orientation. Jones (2001) insists that Duchamp's piece – with the inclusion of the beard and moustache – 'reveals, in a simple gesture, that which the [da Vinci] painting conceals'. Jones adds: 'Duchamp uncovers an ambiguity of gender at the heart of Leonardo's aesthetic – that Leonardo sees the male form in the female' (2001: n.p.). It is this philosophy of uncovering, or taking off – a principle of reinterpretation and recreation through defacement and mutilation – that would be assimilated into the New Realism movement.

Like the Dadaists, artists working in the vein of New Realism made use of everyday ready-mades. The *Nouveaux Réalistes* pulled from the world around them using various strategies of appropriation and violence. César used the strategy of compression, crushing cars and other ready-made articles of consumer society while artists like Jacques de la Villeglé, Raymond Hains and François Dufrêne worked with the strategy of *décollage*, stripping various print advertisements – posters in particular – from the walls of Paris and pasting the ripped pieces in layers on a strong surface. In this first step, these artists made collages (the French verb *coller* means 'to stick'), in other words, art made from various lightweight pieces that were glued together. In their next step, the artists invoked the French verb *décoller*, which translates in English as 'to unstick' or 'to take off'. They engaged in violent acts of taking off, removal, tearing away fragments of material, unsticking elements and lacerating the surface to expose and juxtapose various strata.

Décollage afforded a deconstruction, re-membering and a re-imagining of reality. It was a generative strategy that deployed a nexus of destruction and creation. Artist Wolf Vostell emphasized this nexus through his presentation and use of the word as 'dé–coll/age'. Vostell's dissection of the word is based on his observation of its use in a newspaper account of an airplane accident. The word *décollage* was used to describe the simultaneous takeoff and crash of the plane. His syllabic division of the word highlights this simultaneity. Stiles (1991: n.p.) notes that Vostell's linguistic rendering of the word *décollage* 'inverts the constructive process of collage and deconstructs the binary creation/destruction into semiotic units that transform in time: "dé" and "coll" name oppositions while "age" refers (in French) to temporality'.

Time is indeed a key factor in the re-making of reality through a process of *décollage*. The layering and lacerating of visual fragments, which were collected from the streets at different times, point to the multiple temporalities contained within these works of art. In an interview with Bernard Goy (n.d.), torn-poster artist Villeglé says of the practice of tearing in *décollage*: 'the tear is ... the passing of time' (jca-online.com). *Décollage* therefore imbues a work with history. *Décollage* is 'deconstructive and historical' (oxfordartonline.com). Each laceration is an effort at unveiling the connections and relationships between different instances in time. *Décollage* is 'an archaeological process unmasking the sequential, continuous relation of apparently dissociated images and events' (Stiles n.d.: n.p.).

It is this capacity for taking off a veneer of disconnection between moments; between present-day, paradisiacal images of tropical destinations and past images of colonial servitude – enslavement and indentureship – that the strategy of *décollage* can offer a Caribbean ontology. This kind of taking off allows for an epistemic shift in imagining the Caribbean region. *Décollage* is a strategy that can re-inject history through a violence that counters that which renders Caribbean places as non-places. The appropriation of tidy, idyll travel images and their incorporation into a process of *décollage* makes it possible to hijack mental flights to paradise. The commandeering of the vehicle – the image – and the engine – the imagination – through *décollage*, can disrupt any expectation of safe travel. This is precisely what the art of Andrea Chung accomplishes in her deployment of *décollage* to destroy and re-create imaginings of the Caribbean.

Turbulence in the Art of Andrea Chung

Andrea Chung's artistic practice involves a manipulation and juxtaposition of ready-mades of her choice: archival colonial imagery and travel magazine advertisements and photographs, in order to reconstruct narratives about land and labour in the Caribbean. She mutilates what is seen in the travel image as a means of unmasking the unseen. By tearing into visuals of a Caribbean paradise to expose labourers from a colonial past, she lacerates flights of fantasy. Each artwork bears her violent movements, her slashing and ripping, which make for mental travel that is fraught with turbulence.

In her 2009 piece *The Good Life*, Chung appropriates a photograph, which was published in an issue of *Caribbean Travel & Life* magazine. The photograph served as a visual accompaniment to an article by Christopher Cox entitled 'St. John: Here's to the Good Life'. In the image, a Caucasian woman reposes in a lime green, ring-shaped life preserver. She floats in shallow water where a turquoise sea skirts a sandy shore. The frothy, white break of waves make her appear to rest on small, puffy clouds across a stretch of blue sky, high above an earthly realm as if she is in heaven or rather, paradise. The notion of safety is established by the presence of the lifesaver and the fact that she has not been depicted in deep water. There is no risk of being hurt. All is favourable, secure and 'good'. It is a picture that triggers the imagination and safe takeoff to the island of St. John, which the photograph constructs as an idyll destination.

With this photograph and the power to imagine or see in the mind's eye, the viewer quickly and easily takes flight with a course charted for the good life, despite the fact that Cox includes some historical details about St. John in the magazine article. Cox (2008: n.p.) writes:

> St. John has a history not unlike that of almost every other Caribbean island: a sighting by Columbus, an indigenous people quickly eradicated, marginal sugar and cotton plantations enabled by slavery. Less than 20 square miles of mountains and dry forest, St. John is distinguished by its quirky patrimony: It was settled by Denmark, a third-tier colonial power whose choicest overseas possession was Iceland.

Cox's words do not, however, set up a narrative that conflicts with that of the photograph. His use of the words 'quirky patrimony' and his description of Denmark as a 'third-tier colonial power' dull the edge of servitude and make light of the severity of domination that are a part of a Caribbean colonial past. His words put a smooth finish on the island's history – a surface coating that is enhanced by the photograph. With Cox's words and the accompanying image, the viewer is therefore able to imagine and travel unperturbed.

Chung's appropriation of the photograph (see Figure 13.2) addresses this surface treatment and creates conflict as she tears into the image, taking off coloured bits and pieces to dig deep into a Caribbean past, which she depicts in black and white.[1] Her tears represent the passing of time as we travel from the surface of the image to the interior of each incision; from full colour to black and white; from present to past. In Chung's lacerations we become aware of female

---

1 All of Chung's art pieces are reproduced in this chapter entirely in black and white. For the full effect of her work visit: http://andreachungart.com/collage/tears/.

Figure 13.2 Andrea Chung, *The Good Life*, 46 × 30.5 cm (18 × 12 inches), magazine *décollage*, 2009

Source: Reproduced with permission from the artist.

Figure 13.3 Andrea Chung, *Eastern Hideaway*, 46 × 30.5 cm (18 × 12 inches), magazine *décollage*, 2009

Source: Reproduced with permission from the artist.

labourers carrying loads on their heads. Through strategic gashes, Chung turns the reclining woman in the lifesaver into a load upon the head of the past. What keeps the woman afloat is no longer the coloured ring around her, but the black and white arms bearing her. The viewer of this work cannot imagine him or herself ensconced in the perfect safety of paradise. Instead, he or she can only picture self precariously perched on the weary hands of a colonial servant.

Chung's use of *décollage* makes it possible to take off a commercial skin that hides a continuous relationship between colonial labour and the work involved in serving people within a contemporary milieu of tourism. In cutting and tearing, she subverts a rupture between these moments in time. Her mutilation of the photograph uncovers a connection between a past marked by the trauma and hardship of a subjugated workforce and present vacation leisure. Chung frustrates the notion of 'the good life'. In her acts of taking off, the artist functions as a hijacker. She disturbs the idea of a Caribbean paradisiacal destination and therefore makes mental takeoff and travel uneasy.

In her piece entitled *Eastern Hideaway* (see Figure 13.3), Chung destroys the myth of the unrestrained as she slashes into an image she takes from a 2008 issue of *Caribbean Travel & Life*. The photograph is one that appeared with an article, which focused on such beaches as Cas en Bas, Anse Louvet and Anse Chastanet on the Caribbean island of St. Lucia. The article refers to these beaches as 'hideaways', a term for which the words 'sanctuaries' and 'safe havens' can function as substitutes. Again, the idea of safety is promoted here. The photograph shows a couple enjoying the comfort of a hammock, which has been securely strung between palm trees. Only the line of rope connecting the canvas bed – on which they lay – to the tree trunk, ties them to the place. Otherwise, they remain suspended above and safely detached from the location. Their figures dominate the image such that they can be interpreted as masters – lord and lady – of the setting. It is a romanticized image of power, one in which even the sea does not make waves. Instead, the waters appear calm, still, obedient. At the far right, an empty hammock signifies an invitation to take immediate flight to join this couple in hiding out. Vacant beach chairs in the distance also serve as bait for the imagination. The viewer is stirred to mentally touchdown in this unspoiled place where the restraints of quotidian life dissolve and all is comfortable, luxurious and easy.

Chung creates dis-ease and spoils this picture of Caribbean paradise by violently taking off its rosy lacquer to reveal black-and-white images of Indian indentured labourers. Chung unmasks the so-called hideaway, bringing the faces of an exploited people to light. With two gashes, left and right, she cuts the cords that hold up the hammock and immediately any imagined comfort and security go into a tailspin. Chung inserts another couple into the hammock: two female labourers, but the hammock – now severed from its ties – does not provide rest and relaxation for them. The hammock can also no longer hold the reclining couple. Both couples, from the past and the present, crash-land on the ground and the viewer's flight of fantasy is forced to take a nosedive.

**Figure 13.4 Andrea Chung, *Dry Yaye*, 23 × 30.5 cm (9 × 12 inches), magazine
        décollage, 2008**

Source: Reproduced with permission from the artist.

The wounds that Chung inflicts upon the photograph open portals to what is
suggestive of the moment when indentured labourers arrived in the Caribbean from
India. Her positioning of these labourers on the shore suggests their landing after

a long journey across the sea, which now appears behind them like an ominous blanket that conceals trauma. Their arrival in the photograph is equally painful as their presence is felt with every abrasion Chung exacts on the image. She reinserts Caribbean history with each tear she makes: indentured labourers came to the Caribbean in the wake of the abolition of slavery. They worked under restrictive contracts of employment on sugar plantations, in often poor conditions. Chung exposes the superficiality of the myth of the unrestrained by showing us what lies beneath it. She juxtaposes the carefree faces of the couple in the present with the austere faces of the past.

The artist elevates her aggressive demand for the viewer to face the past in her art entitled *Dry Yaye* (see Figure 13.4). This time she seizes an image of a tropical scene with incredibly blue sky, swaying palm trees and aquamarine sea. It is an image with which the viewer can imagine him or herself in idealized isolation, happily marooned on the island in the background, cut off from a mundane world. Chung, however, rips into this fantasy to reveal the countenance of an African woman – a face from a history of African enslavement in the Caribbean. The viewer is confronted with her scorn and hatred, which are communicated with her eye. The title of the work helps to explain Chung's intent. In the Jamaican context, the term 'dry yaye' connotes a contemptuous, bold look in the eyes. The eye Chung incorporates into the piece conveys a rebelliousness against the viewer's gaze. The woman staring out from the slashes counters any imaginings of being marooned on an island paradise. Hers is the look of maroonage or defiance.

Maroons were enslaved Africans who took flight from the oppression of the plantations on islands like Jamaica, St Vincent, Dominica, Haiti and Cuba. They broke the social order of the day by resisting and escaping conditions of colonial servitude to set up independent, secret societies. In tearing and slashing the image, Chung uncovers this dimension of Caribbean history and enacts her own maroonage as she breaks the order of a trope of sun, sea and sand. The woman she inserts into the photograph functions as a signifier of resistance. Her presence and facial expression – her dry yaye – create a tension that makes mental engagement with the depicted tropical location uncomfortable. With the unflinching, hard gaze of the African woman, Chung facilitates a juxtaposing of flights from sugar plantations with contemporary flights of fancy. Chung (2012) insists that in order to pilot or navigate these conflicting narratives of past and present, her work asks the viewer to question 'the real' – to interrogate the seen and unseen.

Conclusion

Andrea Chung's *Dry Yaye* and her other artworks analysed here make notions of travel and imagination, specifically within tourism discourse, untidy. Her art lays bare the machinations of constructing place within a commercial matrix that elides or glosses over socio-historical details. Chung's art attacks a convenient amnesia built into efforts to stir us to imagine and travel in bliss. She imposes memory with every rip, tear and peel. Using the strategy of *décollage*, she rips open and remakes a Caribbean, that is, she re-members a Caribbean. She simultaneously destroys and creates place, working in a manner that is antithetical to a process of tropicalization in order to re-envision and re-picture islands with depth. In the process of taking off a façade of comfort, she recuperates the Caribbean from paradisiacal constraints and rescues it from a detachment from the past. Paradoxically, her ruptures serve as connectors, linking temporalities so that continuities between colonial and post-colonial eras are called into awareness and sharp scrutiny. Chung tampers with the visual vehicles that can 'take us' to tropical destinations and in doing so she also hampers the workings of the imagination. Her art vexes any attempt at easy, safe takeoff.

References

Adams, L.S. 1999. *Art Across Time Volume II: The fourteenth century to the present*. Boston: McGraw-Hill College.

Bloom, H. 1975. *A Map of Misreading*. New York: Oxford University Press.

Chung. A. 2012. Artist statement. *Andrea Chung Art* [Online] Available at: http://andreachungart.com/about [accessed: 8 June 2012].

Cox, C. 2008. St. John: Here's to the Good Life. *Caribbean Travel & Life* [Online] Available at: http://www.caribbeantravelmag.com/article/St-John-Heres-To-the-Good-Life [accessed: 6 December 2011].

Daye, M. 2008. Re-visioning Caribbean tourism, in *New Perspectives in Caribbean Tourism*, edited by Marcella Daye, D. Chambers and S. Roberts. New York: Routledge, 19–43.

de Botton, A. 2002. *The Art of Travel*. New York: Pantheon Books.

Echtner, C. and Prasad, P. 2003. The context of third world tourism marketing. *Annals of Tourism Research*, 30(3), 660–682.

Featherstone, S. 2005. *Postcolonial Cultures*. Edinburgh: Edinburgh University Press.

Freud, S. [1910] 1957. Leonardo da Vinci and a memory of his childhood, in *Standard Edition of the Complete Psychological Works of Sigmund Freud Vol. XI*, edited by J. Strachey. London: Hogarth Press, 63–137.

Goy, B. n.d. Jacque Villeglé interview. *Journal of Contemporary Art* [Online] Available at: http://www.jca-online.com/villegle.html [accessed: 25 June 2012].

Hunter, W.C. 2008. A typology of photographic representations for tourism: Depictions of groomed spaces. *Tourism Management* [Online], 29(2), 354–65. Available at: http://www.sciencedirect.com/science/article/pii/S02615177070 0060X [accessed: 5 June 2012].

Jones, J. 2001. L.H.O.O.Q., Marcel Duchamp (1919). *Guardian* [Online, 26 May] Available at: http://www.guardian.co.uk/culture/2001/may/26/art [accessed: 24 June 2012].

Kellett, F. 2008. You, the travel photographer. *The Telegraph* [Online, 22 September] Available at: http://blogs.telegraph.co.uk/travel/franciscakellett/5281587/You_the_travel_photographer/ [accessed: 5 June 2012].

Restany, P. 1986. La réalité dépasse la fiction, in *1960: Les Nouveaux Réalistes*, edited by the Musée d'art modern de la Ville de Paris. Paris: MAM.

Restany, P. 1996. The Nouveaux Réalistes declaration of intention, in *Theories and Documents of Contemporary Art: A Sourcebook of Artists' Writings,* edited by K. Stiles and P. Selz. Berkeley: University of California Press, 306–7.

Stiles, K. n.d. Décollage. *Oxford Art Online: Grove Art* [Online] Available at: http://www.oxfordartonline.com/subscriber/article/grove/art/T02 1762 [accessed: 25 June 2012].

Stiles, K. 1991. Thresholds of Control: Destruction art and terminal culture. *Ars Electronica* [Online] Available at: http://90.146.8.18/en/archives/festival_archive/festival_catalogs/festival_artikel.asp?iProjectID=8900 [accessed: 25 June 2012].

Strickland, A. 2011. Top five: Awe-inspiring travel photos. *CNN* [Online, 5 August] Available at: http://ireport.cnn.com/blogs/ireport-blog/2011/08/05/top-five-awe-inspiring-travel-photos [accessed: 5 June 2012].

Thompson, K. 2006. *An Eye for the Tropics: Tourism, photography, and framing the Caribbean picturesque*. Durham, NC: Duke University Press.

White, H. 1978. *Tropics of Discourse: Essays in cultural criticism*. Baltimore: Johns Hopkins University Press.

Chapter 14

Venice, Desire, Decay and the Imagination: Travels into the 'Dark Side'

Russell Staiff

... Venice
Abhorrent, green, slippery city
Whose Doges were old, and had ancient eyes

– D.H. Lawrence, Pomegranate

Never To Be Forgotten

I know precisely when Venice entered my imaginative world. I was an undergraduate in the early 1970s and I went with a group of friends to see Luchino Visconti's controversial film *Death in Venice* (1971), based on the Thomas Mann novella of the same name. There may have been earlier encounters with Venice at school or on television, but I don't recall them. It was the movie that created a rich interior world of images, desire, feelings and strong emotions that became a template for a precession of imaginings and for the embodied experiences (with which they were fused) of travelling to Venice. My Venice was not of picturesque renderings in contemporary tourism representations (with their loose and tenuous threads to populist notions of romanticism) (see the images and videos on Google Image and YouTube) but something darker, and more deeply felt, something that breathed the air of what may be termed a neo-Romantic construction and was a response to what, in the end, I regarded as a city befitting the description dystopian.

This chapter is an intensely personal exploration of my imaginings of Venice, my creation of a place I call 'Venice', a place that is simultaneously of the mind and a material entity that has entangled various selves with particular, and highly selective, representations and performances. My aim is to reconnoitre two ideas that have currency in travel scholarship: 'performing tourist places' (see, for example, Baerenholdt et al. 2004) and 'flirting with space' (Crouch 2010) and in a manner where the personal, affect/emotions/the subjective, is central to my musings.

One could be eloquent about the powerful imagery of Visconti's film, about the enduring legacy it has in Italian cinema history, about Dirk Bogarde's performance, about the *mise-en-scène* and the use of Gustav Mahler in the soundtrack – they are all worthy of comment and I will return to them soon – but for me the potency of this film had everything to do with me, two hours spent cocooned in a dark cinema 'lost' in a secret emotional journey that had a passionate force probably far beyond what Visconti may have, or may have not, intended. For a same-sex attracted male, completely closeted at the time, I had entered into a world all too familiar with its unspeakable yearnings, with a distant study of male beauty, with the seeming impossibility of emotional and physical love between males, with the dire consequences of this forbidden fruit, even down to the protagonist's death by cholera after eating strawberries. Desire, yearning, impossible love, tragic consequences mixed with the most stunningly luscious evocations of place and circumstances that evoked these powerful feelings and intellectual responses. I completely identified with Gustav von Aschenbach as he was unexpectedly awestruck by the beauty of Tadzio, the boy holidaying with his family on the Lido in Venice; I too had worshipped, even loved, from afar. I too dreamed and fantasized about the handsome men in my life, all of them never suspecting they were the object of desire. Trapped in my own imagined world of male love, my emotional and sexual self was hidden, secret and yet, strangely, all the more enticing. At the time I saw the film I was particularly attracted to a dancer with the Australian Ballet: he was my Tadzio, beheld from afar, an aesthetic object into which I poured my secret longings, my secret life. *Death in Venice* was far more than a cinematic experience; I read it and experienced it as a rendering of my own thoughts, feelings, desires, a representation on screen of the possibility and the impossibility of same-sex love, infatuation, sexual obsession, male beauty. The film had externalized my internal fantasy world in a way I had never before experienced except in reading fiction (cf. Morkham and Staiff 2002).

A few days later I returned to the cinema and watched the film again, this time by myself so I could fully engage without the terror of being with friends who knew not my 'secret'. In the second viewing two things became more pronounced: Venice and Gustav Mahler's music, especially the Adagietto from the Fifth Symphony. This impossible city of water and reflections, of decay, of maze-like canals, walkways and bridges, of floating exotic buildings, was infused with love, beauty, melancholy, disease and death. Nineteenth-century Romanticism was writ large across the city-scape and re-presented in a cinematic form that simultaneously evoked a powerfully felt enduring cultural concoction but always at a distance; we, the viewers, were painfully in Venice, but not (cf. Aitken 2011). Could this city be anything other than of the imagination? Aschenbach had travelled there to recuperate from his work-induced collapse in Germany after the death of his daughter. Venice was thus a place to travel to, set in its Lagoon, one had to go there purposely, but once there, it was an enchanted island where beauty, impossible love, fantasies, decay, disease and death awaited the traveller. Venice, the place, Venice of the film, Venice in my imagination was a shimmering destination beyond the grubby reality of the quotidian, beyond a life lived elsewhere. And Mahler's music was perfect for such imaginings. It haunts me still. The Adagietto is forever in my mind associated with the opening sequences of the film; a gradual pink-purple dawn spreads slowly across the Lagoon as a solitary steamboat travels towards the Rialto with Aschenbach rugged up against the cold sitting alone on the deck lost in his inner world. Whenever I hear the Mahler I feel so intensely the yearning, the sadness, the melancholia, the exquisite joy and sorrow of unattainable love and beauty, of sweet sorrow, of the suffering of being and the unbearable depths of unrequited love. In my mind, the Mahler is *Death in Venice*, and I can never stop the immediate imaginative journey into the film/to Venice the music always prompts. There's a video on YouTube that sets the Adagietto to a series of striking black and white photos of Venice. Other YouTube videos bind the music to images of the young actor in the role of Tadzio.

From this precise moment in time the Venice of my imagination was profoundly intertwined with Visconti's re-creation and my own embodied response to the film. It was so elemental that when I later saw Venice depicted in a James Bond movie and an Indiana Jones movie the city was an alien place lacking any of the emotional force 'my Venice' encompassed.

Visit One and Two

My first trip to Venice was mid-winter: grey, bitingly cold, incipient light, misty fogs hovering, short virtually sunless days. My second trip to Venice was in high summer. The heat and the humidity was searing and asphyxiating. The fetid smells of the city were almost nauseating. The constant sea mist made everything shimmer, especially on the Grand Canal where palaces became, seemingly, quite insubstantial entities dissolving into the ripples and reflections of the water. I kept thinking of Turner watercolours of Venice (see Wilton 1982).

These two journeys to Venice came four and six years after my encounter with *Death in Venice*. The first visit was a bonus when an archaeological study tour I had joined took a side trip into Venice. The second was during a long period of travel in Europe and the USA. During both visits I was intoxicated with Visconti's film and during both visits I was still, mostly, in the closet. The wintry Venice replicated every mood I associated with film/place and confirmed every part of the Venice I had imagined as a consequence of the film. Will Aitkin in his analysis of *Death in Venice* describes Aschenbach as a man who lives inside his mind, who is 'exquisitely, tremulously self-aware' (Aitkin 2011: 115). This was I. The Venice I conjured was a type of anti-picturesque aesthetic and hardly recognizable in the tourist guidebooks. Everything our guide told us, and he was following the *Venice Blue Guide* to the letter, was like water running over oilskin, no traction, words and ideas disconnected to my imaginary Venice. For me Venice was sad, saturated in melancholy, discoloured, rubbish-filled, weathered, weirdly moist, drowning, a city slipping away beneath the rising sea and into oblivion. The carefully hidden modernity of the city added to this ghostly spectre and spectral atmosphere. This was especially the case at night when the fog descended thickly and being lost inevitable. I looked in vain for a Tadzio but to no avail, but I left the island city with my imagined Venice in tact.

Venice in summer was almost unbearable and the heat inescapable. So this was the stifling heat of the Sirocco, discussed in both the film and Thomas Mann's novella (Mann [1912] 1998). My travelling companion and I were languid. Venice sapped our energies. The perspiration and dreadful smells were a constant. We ate memorably, but sightseeing was a trial. We took boat trips in the hope the movement of the craft across the water would produce a cooling breeze. And for the first time, I went to the Lido just to visit the Grand Hotel des Bains, to soak up the atmosphere of Aschenbach's encounter with his beloved Tadzio. I wasn't disappointed. The borders between fantasy and reality became very vague, my heart quickened and memories flooded back as we ate gelato looking out over a lifeless, calm and glassy sea. My companion was not at all enamoured with my *Death in Venice* obsession. She had hated the film. But in my embodied self – and thanks to the heat, debate about the film was brief – I could see and feel quite palpably all that had been sparked in that dark cinema some six years before. And, this time, there were Tadzios in abundance: beautiful Italian men at work and at play, lounging in the heat (barely clothed), waiting on our tables, sitting in the bars, working the boats, managing the hotel. We went to hear a Vivaldi concert in a little church along the Riva Ca di Dio. I sat as much entranced by one of the violinists as the music. But like the film, it was adoration of male beauty at a distance, the emotions locked within an imaginary world, a wistful melancholia accompanied by sublime music, this second self, aching for realization.

In the end the heat was too stultifying and we fled Italy altogether, endless train rides through Italy, Switzerland, Germany, Belgium and Britain to get to Edinburgh for the festival and cool days. I left with a heavy heart, but only because of the uninterrupted power of my imagined Venice. And maybe the leaving would have been even more poignant if I had known that I was also leaving behind the Venice of Mann, Visconti, Aschenbach and Tadzio.

An Interlude: Venice as a Dystopia

It was 10 years before I returned and quite another imagined Venice was to arise and, on many levels, supplant the Venice of my youth, although not entirely. This interlude is marked by my studies in art history, a mid-career detour and with a particular focus on Italy from the fourteenth to the seventeenth centuries and on the art of Byzantium. My preference in these studies was for things Florentine and if I was to buy into the 'myth of the renaissance' – where the past and tourism meet – it would be in the urban spaces of the Tuscan capital (cf. Staiff 2010). Venice was something else, and in my mind, even darker than the perpetual agonistic strife of late medieval and renaissance Florence. Yes, both were republics in a sea of duchies and kingdoms, but one, it seemed, embraced the present/future and the other a dubious past of misadventure tinctured with stifling social and political practices.

Of course, the polarity, Florence versus Venice, is a complete construction fuelled by the apologists for both cities, living and dead, but it is a seductive imagining and not entirely fabricated. What can be deduced is that both cities have, over the centuries, busily contrived identities of themselves, layered like sedimentations, for their own edification and for the worlds they courted. These formulations were consciously about distinction, a quality they sanctioned with the authority of the past (however conceived and, mostly, where myth and fact were fused). I already had a somewhat queer view of Venice (the pun deliberate) and my studies reinforced this but in a different register.

The use of the term dystopia is intentionally problematic because for me it is about my imagined Venice and my traveller Venice and possibly far removed from the quotidian Venice of those who live and work there, of those who still call the islands of the Lagoon home, who are still subject to, and the creators of, the rhythms of daily life on the islands and who may still speak the Veneto dialects. For the inhabitants of the Lagoon, to call their home a dystopia would undoubtedly be a step too far. The way the term dystopia has been employed in the twentieth and twenty-first centuries, largely in fiction and the cinema, is of recent coinage: a world pretending to be a utopia but marred by totalitarianism, decadence, environmental degradation and crisis, top-down economies and political power structures, caste-systems, brutal, corporate, segregated and where those in control spend inordinate amounts of time and resources producing and controlling the illusion of serenity, wealth and brilliance (see, for example, Rabkin et al. 1983, Gordin et al. 2010). Ridley Scott's film *Blade Runner* (1982) meets my imagined *Venezia*. Reading backwards, my imagined historically grounded Venice approximates a contemporary description of a dystopia. This imagined Venice is not necessarily referring to contemporary Venice although commentators like Debray have suggested my historically inflected conjuring of a dystopia is pertinent today (Debray 1999, also Davis and Marvin 2004).

In trying to be succinct, a description of my Venice as dystopia is far more stark than it is in my imagination, where it is more fluid and lacks the hard edges and finalities of what I will write, but I want to offer an entre into my mind and offer something of what I 'carried' within me on two subsequent visits to Venice. Also, I want to indicate a shift in my imaginings partly away from the deeply personal towards including a more knowledge-based set of responses. And so I draw a very particular portrait of Venice, *La Serenissima*, the most serene republic.

I still find it difficult to comprehend that what we see in Venice is not quite the whole story. Underpinning those fading palaces, water eternally lapping at their doors, are hundreds of pylons of wood hammered into the wet sand forming the foundations of the buildings, thanks to a process of petrifaction that over centuries has turned wood into stone. But because of the constant ebb and flow of water, expansion and contraction of the sand, the marble facades of the palaces lining the Grand Canal are not tightly tethered to the walls of the palace. They are facades in the strictest sense of the word. But marble is expensive and the number of marble clad palaces in Venice suggests great wealth, as does the Basilica San Marco with its gold mosaics covering entire walls and ceilings. Boatbuilding for fishing was transformed into one of the greatest medieval European industrial enterprises in the historical records, shipbuilding for war and trade and not all of it legitimate. The Venetians were pirates, the scavengers of the Mediterranean. With brute force their navies brought back to the city untold riches/loot which in turn was not only used to build a city in marble, but to build a series of fortress-castles around the Mediterranean Sea. For the veracious Venetians, nothing, it seemed, was sacred, even a great city like Constantinople, which was sacked in 1204 when the Venetians were ostensibly on their way to liberate the Holy Land in the Fourth Crusade. The booty, after a three-day period of rape and vandalism, included a huge fortune in silver and the removal of the famous bronze horses, already nearly 1,000 years old, and now destined for the facade of the Basilica San Marco. They are still in Venice and copies now grace San Marco's exterior.

And back in Venice, the whole operation – shipbuilding and plunder – was overseen by a small and elite group of patrician families who ruled the maritime city-state tyrannically. Their names had been inscribed in the 'golden book' and, after this, all other aspirants to power excluded. A notorious and secretive Council of Ten (representing and consisting of the patrician elite) ruled ruthlessly and the so-called self-proclaimed 'most serene republic' was the product of what today we may call a 'police-state'. Fear, spies, a system to inform on your neighbours, segregation of the population into classes and the 'undesirables' and 'foreigners' confined to ghettoes (the word is Venetian) were some of the modes of control along with exotic torture and dark, wet prisons beneath the Doge's Palace. The Jewish population was quite literally locked, each night, into their ghetto. Homosexuality and fornication were severely and publically punished. The name 'Venice' may hark back to Venus the goddess of love, who, like the city, was born from the sea, but in medieval and renaissance Venice, sexual behaviours were rigidly and harshly regulated.

The oligarchy would elect the head of the republic, the Doge, from among themselves and then imprison him in his palace for the rest of his life. Elaborate state and religious rituals dominated his life (the two conveniently merging, with the spiritual underpinning state secular power). But even religion was peculiar. Venice prided herself in being an apostolic city to rival Rome. If Rome could boast the presence of St Peter and St Paul, then mysteriously, St Mark's remains were exhumed in Alexandria (Egypt) and brought back to Venice (more piracy) and eventually placed within the Basilica that bears his name. Throughout the city, St Mark's presence is marked by his symbol, the winged lion. But what sort of Christianity did the elites of Venice practice? After a sumptuously designed high Mass in San Marco's, the Doge, accompanied by choirs and incense-waving priests, boarded the state barge with its tiers of rowers to be taken to the place near the Lido where the Lagoon meets the sea and there, each year, the Doge tossing a ring into the water, proclaimed the republic as symbolically wedded to the sea.

Then came the decline. Mercantile fortunes were to be made elsewhere as European imperialism spread globally and the mercantile power of Europe shifted west with the arrival of the machine age and centralized nation-states. Stronger navies emerged. By the eighteenth century Venice was broke and turned to gambling, opera, prostitution, tourism and other 'decadent' past-times to maintain, in tawdry fashion, the 'glamour' and prestige they had claimed for themselves.

But like the masks of *Carnivale*, it was an illusion. For many, she had become the 'whore of Europe'. Casanova was her calling card and while gambling houses and the whore houses attracted aristocratic males on their grand tour, Venice was suffering a seemingly terminal illness made worse by the malarial mosquitoes of the Lagoon and the persistence of cholera and other water-borne diseases. Napoleon brought it to an inglorious end. The first army to successfully invade the water bound city-state set off a chain reaction that ended in Venice's absorption into the newly formed nation of Italy in 1866.

If we momentarily return to the characteristics of a dystopia, it is not hard to see how they map onto this very particular and somewhat schematic description of Venice. The utopian idea of a serene republic was merely a rhetorical device that described a surface calm maintained by a harsh autocratic system of oligarchic and corporate control where the life of the many was not matched by the spectacles of state, where ill-begotten gain was a major economic activity and where mastery over the Lagoon's environment was a constant. What sort of society imprisons its head of state or ransacks a grave in far-off Egypt in order to proclaim apostolic status or ransacks a great city purely for material gain? What sort of society profits from a reputation as the 'whore of Europe' at the same time as it evokes the Virgin Mary as its protector (a contradiction exquisitely exploited in Madonna's music video (1984) *Like a Virgin* (see Plant 2002))? If Venice was to be adored, it would be for her paradoxes, impossible beauty corrupted by power, decadence, physical decay, an ignoble past, the home of *Carnivale* where masks hid the true identities of their wearers in the hope of some erotic and sly dalliance. Venice the city was a mask, an exotic, colourful and beautiful mask that attempted to hide her dystopian underside.

This new imagining of Venice made me realize how piquant the place was as a setting for *Death in Venice*. In the final scene as Aschenbach sits on the beach dying, we presume, from cholera, his face, 'youthfully' restored with garish makeup (a piteously comic and ill-fated restoration), he attempts to reach out to his beloved Tadzio who stands, after a fight with his friend, looking out to sea, and away from Venice. Aschenbach is sweating profusely from his disease, the black hair colour running down his face, the mask slipping and revealing what lies beneath. He falls back into his seat and as he dies, Tadzio, forever a distant and impossible 'object' of love and beauty, stretches out his arm to somewhere across the Adriatic just as the Mahler Adagietto reaches its urgent climax, the music's opening serenity giving way to something desperate, tragic, deep and dark.

Visit Three and Four

My next two visits to Venice saw me in the role of a tour leader taking Australians to Italy on art and history excursions. While my tour groups were invariably in the grip of adulation accompanied by excited expressions of awe and romance about the aqueous world of Venice, my responses arose from somewhere beyond the photogenic exoticism of elegant buildings floating on the water.

I know that Venice has often been characterized as the most cosmopolitan city in the late medieval and renaissance periods, bringing a large number of 'foreigners' to the city and acting as a trading conduit between the East and the West (Marco Polo inevitably cited during this observation). And I know that art and architecture historians are enamoured by the fascinating mixture of styles that seem to make up the city's urban fabric – Byzantine, Arabic, Gothic, Romanesque, Classical – but when I stand outside the Basilica San Marco and the Doge's Palace, I see two things simultaneously. Yes, I can observe the strong replication of architectural ideas from Constantinople and in the palace something Arabic and something Gothic, but, at the same time, I also ponder on the strangeness and 'out-of-place' quality of Venice's political and religious centre. Dominating the visual experience are the rounded onion-domes of San Marco; the gracefully thin, but fussy, forest of spires across the roof; and the rounded arches within arches, within more arches of the facade. Inside, the glittering golden mosaics completely adorn the walls and ceiling with the figures of saints hovering, shimmering, across the wall spaces like the ripples on the canal. Nothing is quite substantial, all subservient to dizzying effects. This is so different to the rest of northern Italy. I recall that in dystopian science fiction movies, the architecture of the imagined future cities is also strange, usually off-worldly strange, especially that reserved for the rich and powerful, well above the streets wet with continuous toxic rain and crowded with 'low-life' beaten into submission by law-enforcement agents that have high-tech cars and arms. Isn't Venice similar I ask myself? Strange. Weird. During a king-tide, when the streets and piazzas are flooded, and my tour group has to manoeuvre over boardwalks around the environs of San Marco, I think, 'very strange'.

So is this imitation of styles from elsewhere a conscious emulation, or conscious propaganda, or a conscious creation of an identity that is different, *par excellence*, and exotic? I was thinking about these questions and about strangeness in the famed art museum, the Gallerie dell'Accademia. There have been many attempts to characterize Venetian art, often to emphasize the unique qualities of art made in Venice by Venetians (see, for example, Muraro and Grabar 1987, Brown 1997, Hills 1999, Plant 2002). Of course generalizations are inevitably banal, but tour guiding makes reductionism mandatory, there is a pressing need for an economy of words. I find myself focusing on certain themes in my commentaries: the domineering spectacle of Venice as a stage for human actions (usually dwarfed by the surroundings) and the obsession with *terra firma*. In the paintings of Gentile Bellini and Vittore Carpaccio the Venetian cityscape dominates the vast narratives they painted. The critical part of the stories is not easily discernible in the crowds of people that process through the pictures. The images are disconcerting and disorientating. At the time of my tours, my favourite Venetian artist was Giovanni Bellini. There are a series of Virgin and Child images and a poignant *Pieta* that I'm drawn to. Many of these paintings seem to deny any relationship to the aqueous surroundings of the city in which they were executed. Bellini places his religious figures in meadows and farmland with ornate and detailed cityscapes in the far background. In the *Pieta*, grieving mother and crucified son merge into the red-brown landscape. The more one stares at this picture, the more perturbing it seems to be. It is intensely distracting. The picture no tour can miss is Giogione's *La Tempesta* (1510). What a very strange composition. A near naked woman suckling a child sitting in a landscape stares at us, looking back at her, while a male figure (soldier, gypsy?) carrying a stave looks at her across a small stream. In the background there is a town and above the town a threatening storm, with jagged lightening tearing apart the dark clouds. Between the figures and the town are some ruins, perhaps antique in origin. This frankly weird and unnerving picture offers no clues as to its meaning. Kenneth Clark, the former director of the National Gallery in London, in his BBC television series *Civilization* called it 'mysterious', 'menacing' and 'pessimistic' (Clark 1969: 91). Along with the Giovanni Bellini Madonnas, there was an opus of work that focused not on maritime Venice but on *terra firma*. Hugh Honour, the art historian, sums up Venetian art in the Gallerie dell'Accademia in this way: a 'melancholic sensual strain' with 'sad-eyed Madonnas' and 'introspective' men (Honour 1970: 22). The play of colour and light outside the museum metamorphosed into something introverted and self-absorbed. More recent scholars have contested this view (Brown 1997, Hills 1999), but for me the elucidations of Clark and Honour suit my imagined Venice perfectly.

Both art and history tours occurred in January. The sea mist dampness mingling with the biting cold winds off the snow-covered Dolomites meant we were always well rugged up, faces stingingly cold. After a dinner in a cosy-warm restaurant and walking back in almost empty wet streets, a gondolier hailed us as we crossed a bridge close to the hotel. After haggling a price, the four of us decided that a night-trip along darkened canals matched our wine-induced joviality despite the cold. What was memorable about his night excursion on Venice's canals was firstly the eerie silence except for the slosh of the paddle and then the darkness. It was not late but most of the buildings we slid past were without even a glimmer of light. In winter, Venice was an empty city. The many foreign landlords were elsewhere, perhaps sunning themselves in sultry climes. Palace after palace was dark, and sinister. The decay of the city seemed even more pronounced at night, the continuously eroding walls sitting in the lapping water accompanied by the smells of mould and cold dampness. Our earlier post-dinner conviviality seeped away and we sat silently witnessing this spectre of mortification.

The Last Visit: Reflecting on Imagination and Travel

My last visit to Venice was recent. A colleague and I were at a very unremarkable conference underscored by shambolic organization. In frustration we escaped to Venice for a day. My companion had never been to *La Serenissima* and I had never been for a one-day visit. If I had found Venice strange in earlier sojourns, then on this occasion the baffling and aberrant feelings were accentuated, but in completely unexpected ways. The crowds were suffocating. All we did was jostle with densely packed tidal flows of people, where surviving the crush became the dominant experience. All of my imaginings of Venice were kept distant, just memories of memories. There was no space internally or externally for a bodily flowering of those things that had been so important to me, things that allowed me to conjure/perform my very particular 'Venice'. On this day Venice just seemed to be weird and freakish. Here was the complete triumph of spectacle drained of all the emotional, aesthetic, creative and intellectual investments earlier travellers, myself included, had garnered this very particular landscape. I realized just how dependent my imaginings of a dystopia had relied on its binary opposite, a utopia. As we scrambled about cheek-by-jowl with the multitudes, neither images of a utopia or a dystopia were possible. My imagined 'Venice' was completely inert in these trying circumstances.

There was a moment when the picturesque Venice asserted itself. I have a picture of a canal, sans people, with a boat of fruit and vegetables, the boatman/retailer selling directly from the canal. It was a brief echo of other ways of being in Venice and of the life of the city represented in earlier travel accounts like the 1960 impressionistic portrait by Jan Morris (Morris [1960] 1993). We had purposely gotten ourselves lost in an attempt to escape the crowds, but this respite was fleeting and not enough for me to sustain any of the imaginings I had on earlier visits. It was the Venice, 'most romantic of cities', that appeared in that brief hiatus. My photo replicates the Venice of Google Images, exotic Venice distinctive, delightful and magical. Looking at the photo back home, it reverts: a glimpse away from the pressing hordes to an enchanting veneer that hides something darker.

On this day of managing myself in a crowd, attempting to invest anything into my companion's first visit to Venice was fraught. My tour guide words seemed to me to be empty, lacking desire, passion and the personal, a fruitless attempt to evoke a 'Venice' that was both (physically) present and (yet) absent simultaneously. I felt sad, but not the sadness I had felt on previous visits, just sadness about a travel experience blighted by fellow travellers, each of us compromising the experience of the other. Strange, yes very strange.

We arrived back at the train station too early and had to wait around. The Simplon-Orient express had arrived. I smiled to myself. We, the train and I, both represented an attempt to resurrect a past long gone, to energize and embody an imagined past, to replicate a sort of fantasy about travel and place. As a Venetian encounter, how uncanny it all seemed. I saw a young girl with her backpack sitting outside the station looking at the chaos of people and watercraft on the Grand Canal. She appeared self-absorbed and pensive. It made me wonder what she was feeling and, I pondered, despite humans being social beings, how locked we are into our own embodied imaginings, desires, feelings, past and present experiences. What 'Venice' was she evoking/performing? Our paths had crossed physically but in parallel psychic universes. I knew we would never interact. Our movements, our journeys, had momentarily intersected and this brief dual occupancy of time and place bore no resemblance to what we were experiencing as embodied subjects. Did she think and feel Venice as something strange? Did she arrive with an imagined Venice that shared any aspect of the emotional landscape my first visit had traversed? As she picked up her backpack and headed towards the *vaporetto* landing, and I headed back to join my colleague, I couldn't help but think about all the 'Venices' in play that day. For me, the only one I could know at the most intimate of levels was my own 'Venice' and this 'Venice' was only very vaguely connected to the 'romantic city' concoctions endlessly circulated on the internet. And as I had discovered, my imagined Venice of desire and decay, needed particular conditions to be an embodied experience, that being *in* Venice was not enough.

Postscript

Before I wrote this chapter I re-visited Visconti's *Death in Venice*. I can't recall how long ago I watched the film but it must be over 30 years. When I first saw it, I was only about eight years older than Tadzio. Today, I'm as old as the fictional Gustav von Aschenbach. In the second decade of the twenty-first century I was very conscious of why I was, once again, watching this movie. Several things emerged. The recall of those first emotional responses and the memories of seeing it back in the early 1970s were still acutely vivid. The depths of feelings – images, narrative, controversial ideas and the Mahler Adagietto – have not dimmed, but now they are feelings fused with memories, rather than something fundamental to my existential reality. Indeed, the fervour and the intensity of the desire that saturated my first viewing, the meanings I made of my first cinematic encounter, the secretive emotional turmoil within is, now, only triggered in memory. *Death in Venice* has become a distinctly nostalgic filmic journey. I was no longer the person I was when I sat in a dark cinema some 40 years ago. Curiously though, my imaginings of Venice have not shifted. I know that my imagined Venice is partial; I know it has doubtful historical veracity; and I know it is intensely personal, but all the reasoning I can muster does not easily displace something so emotionally deep-seated. As I write these words Venice is still for me, in my mind's eye, a place of desire and decay, and a dark dystopian city of the past hovering insubstantially in my present.

References

(Specific references are acknowledged in the text where required. Many of the works cited in this list have contributed to my various understandings of things Venetian and are included as influences rather than arising from direct quotation or text references.)

Ackroyd, P. 2009. *Venice: Pure City*. London: Chatto & Windus.

Aitken, W. 2011. *Death in Venice: A queer film classic*. Vancouver: Arsenal Pulp Press.

Aldrich, R. 1993. *The Seduction of the Mediterranean: Writing, art and homosexual fantasy*. London and New York: Routledge.

Baerenholdt, J., Haldrup, M., Larsen, J. and Urry, J. 2004. *Performing Tourist Places*. Aldershot and Burlington: Ashgate.

Brooks, G. 2008. *People of the Book*. Sydney and Auckland: HarperCollins Publishers.

Brown, P. 1997. *Art and Life in Renaissance Venice*. Upper Saddle River: Prentice Hall.

Chambers, D. 1971. *The Imperial Age of Venice 1380–1580*. Harcourt Brace Jovanovich.

Clark, K. 1969. *Civilization*. London: John Murray.

Crouch, D. 2010. *Flirting With Space*. Farnham and Burlington: Ashgate.

Crouzet-Pavan, E. 2002. *Venice Triumphant: The horizons of a myth*, trans. L. Cochrane. Baltimore: Johns Hopkins University Press.

Davis, R. and Marvin, G. 2004. *Venice: The tourist maze*. Berkeley: University of California Press.

Debray, R. 1999. *Against Venice*, trans. P. Wohlstetter. Berkeley: North Atlantic Books.

Dessaix, R. 1996. *Night Letters*. Sydney: Picador.

Fenlon, I. 2007. *"The" Ceremonial City: History, memory and myth in Renaissance Venice*. New Haven and London: Yale University Press.

Gordin, M., Tilley, H. and Prakash, G. (eds) 2010. *Utopia/Dystopia: Conditions of historical possibility*. Princeton: Princeton University Press.

Hibbert, C. 1990. *Venice: The biography of a city*. New York: HarperCollins.

Hills, P. 1997. *Venetian Colour*. New Haven and London: Yale University Press.

Honour, H. 1970. *The Companion Guide to Venice*. London: Fontana.

Jong, E. 1987. *Serenissima*. London: Bantam Books.

Lane, F. 1973. *Venice: A maritime republic*. Baltimore: Johns Hopkins University Press.

Lawrence, D. 1972. *Selected Poems*. Harmondsworth: Penguin Books.

Littlewood, I. 1991. *Venice: A literary companion*. London: John Murray.

Mann, T. [1912] 1998. *Death in Venice*, trans. D. Luke. London: Vintage Books.

McCarthy, M. 1972. *The Stones of Florence and Venice Observed*. Harmondsworth: Penguin Books.

Martin, J. and Romano, J. 2002. *Venice Reconsidered: The history and civilization of an Italian city-state, 1297–1797*. Baltimore: Johns Hopkins University Press.

Morkham, B. and Staiff, R. 2002. The cinematic tourist: Perception and subjectivity, in *The Tourist as a Metaphor of the Social World*, edited by G. Dann. Wallingford and New York: CABI Publishing, 297–316.

Morris, J. [1960] 1993. *Venice*. Revised edition. London: Faber & Faber.

Muir, E. 1981. *Civic Ritual in Renaissance Venice*. Princeton: Princeton University Press.

Muraro, M. and Grabar, A. 1987. *Venice*. New York: Portland House.

Plant, M. 2002. *Venice: Fragile City 1797–1997*. New Haven and London: Yale University Press.

Rabkin, E., Greenberg, M. and Olander, J. (eds) 1983. *No Place Else: Explorations in utopian and dystopian fiction*. Carbondale: Southern Illinois University Press.

Staiff, R. 2010. History and tourism: Intertextual representations of Florence. *Tourism Analysis*, 15(5), 601–11.

Vidal, G. 1985. *Vidal in Venice*. London: George Weidenfeld & Nicolson.

Wilton, A. 1982. *Turner Abroad*. Exhibition catalogue. London: British Museum Publications.

A Final Word

A Final Word

Chapter 15

Travel and Imagination: An Invitation

Garth Lean and Emma Waterton

Post-travel Imaginings: Part I (Garth)

I awoke on my first morning home from southeast Asia to the sounds of ABC talkback radio. I was tired, my eyes refused to open and the strong Australian accent perplexed me. How were we picking up ABC radio in Laos? After a few seconds of utter confusion, reality sunk in – I was home. My mind, however, was not. It found itself tainted by the routine of travel; a self that had become accustomed to performing, socializing, thinking, being and imagining in very different physical, social and cultural contexts. The simple shift of physical location, and the return to a space of 'familiarity', was not enough to inspire a return to a particular way of thinking. This thinking had been forever altered. In saying this, however, one's thinking undergoes continual alteration before, during and after any given physical travel experience, and while my imaginings upon my return had become entwined in my physical travel experience, they had always been influenced by both physical travel and travel/mobilities more broadly.

Upon returning, my memory and imagination took each other hand-in-hand, entering an emotive, sensual and embodied dance. Continued relationships, photographs, documentaries, news stories, books, movies, conversations, smells, tastes, sounds, ongoing travels (both physical and non-physical), conferences and writing (the list could continue indefinitely, and the boundaries between all of these categories are permeable and blurred) all served to stir and influence my imagination in various ways. In some cases, these stimuli simply sparked an imagination of the related spaces, places and landscapes through which I had travelled, either in the past (when I was travelling through them), present (how they may be at the moment of imagining), or even in the future. This included the people met – locals, expats and other travellers – sometimes no matter how brief the encounter. At various times I have imagined where they might be, what they might be doing and wondered about their prospects for the future. These are not just disconnected thoughts, but are often informed by continued contact with the individuals in question via various communication technologies, along with information on happenings within the places they inhabit. Interestingly, I have also imagined those who I did not meet within the places I have (and have not) travelled.

In other circumstances, new information has reshaped my imagination of places, spaces and landscapes. A pertinent example of this is my imaginings of Timbuktu. Before travelling there, this name had been nothing more than a euphemism for 'remote'; I could not have even placed the city in Mali. The guidebook painted its rich history with wonderful colour, presenting Timbuktu as a wonder not to be missed. As such, there was no question about visiting the city while I was in Mali, even though it was a reasonable challenge to get there. When I finally arrived, however, the mystique I had anticipated did not present itself and, through my eyes, I found a dry, dusty desert town with little of the aura I had imagined. It was the people I befriended – who took me into their homes, fed me and told me about their lives – that became Timbuktu for me; this is what would come to mind whenever I heard the city's name from that point forward, evoking a variety of emotions, with palpable physical reactions.

This imagination was tested, however, in 2012, when I began to hear stories of the Islamist militant group Ansar Dine taking control of the city and installing a strict version of sharia law. A part of this was the banning of all music. Had I not travelled to Timbuktu, this may not have even registered, but I could not imagine Timbuktu, or West Africa in general, without music. Everyone I had met in Mali was infatuated with music; it was a core component of life. When I stayed with a local I had befriended and some of his friends, they drifted off to sleep to a blaring radio that I had to turnoff once they had fallen asleep for the sake of my own rest. Timbuktu could not exist in my mind without music. West African music was to become a catalyst not only for remembering the experience but for prompting an imaginary journey back to Africa, complete with embodied and emotional reactions.

After starting to travel, I also began to reimagine myself differently. I had a travel 'self' that was quite separate from my day-to-day, sat at a desk, 'dull' reality. He was adventurous, less fearful, social, resourceful and resilient. In difficult circumstances after these travels, I could turn to this self and imagine how he would handle any given circumstance. A part of this was a reimagining of the place to which I was returning. This included reimagining the notion of 'home', the opportunities it afforded, the people encountered, their attitudes and Australian landscapes. And, of course, these stories represent only a pinprick on the top of the iceberg of my post-travel imagination, and all of these imaginings continue to twist and turn, and invariably inform, and be influenced by, continuing physical (and non-physical) journeys.

Post-travel Imaginings: Part II (Emma)

I've been to Hawaii twice. On my first visit, a family vacation, I was a child of no more than 10 years old. Much of that trip is a blur to me now, but if pushed I can press my nose up against the dusty windows of my memory and glimpse the coarse outline of a volcano and smell the lingering greasiness of the bright but empty Denny's we frequently patronized. There are traces and scatterings of other moments lodged somewhere in there too, but the memory most redolent of that time begins with a sort of murky silence, in which time seems to almost stop. I'm drifting, completely submerged, in the waves of the Pacific Ocean. All I can hear are the muffled, muted sounds of thrumming rain above me, and all I can see are slow snatches of other bodies and their limbs as they drift in front of the floating veil of my hair. I can barely begin to decipher why this memory clings to me so closely, but it evokes the quiet workings of comfort nonetheless. Few other memories are stimulated from that first trip to Hawaii; nothing else sticks in my mind or gets under my skin. Sure, there are other moments and memories that are embodied, but I feel their presence only at a distance, so much so that when I returned to Honolulu, some 20 years later, I felt utterly disconnected. I knew nothing of the city and felt no trace of its familiarity; we were, in all senses, strangers.

My second trip to Honolulu, in July 2012, was for work: I was there to interview tourists at the Pearl Harbor Visitor Center over the course of a fortnight. Each day I would awake early and wait for the #20 or #42 bus to whisk me away. As it turned out, there was never to be any 'whisking'; each bus ride was instead hot, gritty and tortuously slow. With each grinding mile that we lurched and limped along Ala Moana and the Kamehameha Highway, Honolulu's reputation for having some of the worst traffic in the country was impressed upon me with greater ease. As time wore on, I became more and more grateful for my iPhone, which I had preloaded with new music. Given the amount of time I spent on those buses, commuting back and forth between Waikiki and Pearl Harbor, I know I must have listened to close to 500 songs. It's funny, though. I can only really remember one; one song that is now inscribed into the experience and invokes, still, a range of somatic responses and emotions, even after all this time.

When I hear that song now – whether in my mind or literally, out loud – I respond with a number of visceral reflexes. Sometimes I get gooseflesh or the hair stands up on my arms; at other times I feel haunted, displaced. These somatosenory intensities happen because I have effectively invested in the memories of that lived experience. And so they move me: figuratively, emotionally, imaginatively, back to those long bus journeys and my time spent standing on the USS *Arizona* Memorial. As the song plays – in my car, in my present – I see easily the sunken remains of the battleship and the rainbow sheen of her oil slick 'tears', and feel the solemn atmosphere, the sensory mood. I recall the stark, white memorial itself, which hovers over a wreckage that holds together all that is left of the lives of over 1,000 crew members. I sense the heat of the sun beating down on my skin, the occasional stirring of the air, and struggle, once again, with the startling juxtaposition of the beauty of the harbour and the trauma of its history.

Sometimes these mediated memories conjure up a place that is purely of my imagination: the Pearl Harbor Naval Base, on Sunday 7 December, 1941, at 7.55am ... arrested in time. I often position myself within that place and, once 'there', I hear music. Usually it is the *National Anthem*, echoing softly over the Base, which is bathed in early morning sunlight as young servicemen stand by to raise and salute the 'colors' and start a new day. In the distance, my imaginary 'self' can just about make out the darkening outline of 183 fighters and torpedo bombers as they start to fill the sky – the first wave of the attack. Then there is strafing, shooting, fire and panic. Clearly in these moments I am invoking an historical timeframe that I was never a part of, one that is rooted in nothing but my imagination. But they are nonetheless 'memories' that are held tightly by my body and mind.

And so I replay the song often, relentlessly sometimes, as I drive between home and work. As I listen, I wonder about the shock of the attack and how it must have played out for each of those servicemen. I wonder about the fear, the chaos, the carnage. The specifics of my imaginings don't always stay the same. Instead of the *National Anthem*, for example, it might be 1940s jazz or swing, piped through a radio transmitter that has been tuned to a local station. And instead of the first wave of torpedo bombers filing across the sky, my eye might be drawn to the capsized USS *Oklahoma*, the listing USS *West Virginia* or the USS *Nevada* as she slowly, desperately, runs aground. Either way, time always shifts in those moments, stumbles, and I am treading water once again, as a child in the Pacific Ocean. I know that my responses alter each time because 'that world is no longer there',[1] but their emotive and affective capacities never cease to move, unbidden, across my body.

Imagining the Path Ahead

It is no accident that the narratives we have used to introduce our concluding thoughts hold within them links between travel, imagination and *something else*: this was never going to be a project about 'travel' and 'imagination' alone. Indeed, our two vignettes circulate with a much broader array of material, bodily, social and immaterial phenomena, such as memory, place, relationships and emotion, to which the two concepts of travel and imagination are inevitably fused. The point – as our contributors to the volume have been at pains to express – is that these concepts exist as just two of the constitutive elements that make up the broader constellation of everyday life. In our musings above, for example, there is an explicit appeal to the sonic: the echoes of our past travel experiences are archived in music; but just as readily we have also found that particular songs launch or mobilize our imaginations, even upon our return. Hawaii is an obvious case in point on the matter, for it has almost always entered the tourist's imagination through songs and grass-skirts, irrespective of whether those listening or seeing have had (or ever will have) the chance to go there (Connell and Gibson 2004). The same can be said of scores of other cities, places, landscapes and sites, evocatively conjured through music, beat and lyrics (van Dijck 2006, Şenay 2009). We might imagine visiting southern Spain because we once saw the defeat of the Moors captured in the music and dance of the *moresca* (Bithell 2006), or be transported back to a waterfront in Norway because that is where the melody of *Imagine*, by John Lennon, moved us imaginatively (van Dijck 2006: 361). In these particular instances, travel and the imagination interweave at the insistence of song: thus, as it turns out, we have a tourist's ear as well as a tourist's gaze

---

1   O'Brien (2004: 16).

(Urry 1990, Gibson and Connell 2007: 165); and, as would logically follow, a tourist's nose, tongue and touch.

Where we have foregrounded music, other forms of popular/cultural productions work just as well, as shown throughout the chapters of this volume. A souvenir, photo, fairy-tale, myth, poster, movie, fictional character, painting, textured surface, jingle, food, smell, drink or so forth all have the power to evoke memory, provoke fantasy and trigger imaginative travel. Our purpose in this closing chapter, then, is patently *not* to start making a case for the sonic as the specific, and final, third leg in a tripartite relationship; we are comfortable in leveraging together 'travel' and 'imagination' but not within the restricted confines of only 'this' concept or 'that'. Nor do we seek to venture back down that well-trodden road of latching either concept directly, and solely, to that of visuality. Instead, our reflections upon our post-visit imaginings, as well as those on the volume as a whole, serve only as a reminder that the contingency of meaning exists far beyond the epistemological and ontological insularity so often found in texts about 'travel' and 'the imagination'. Both – and the same can be said of the social sciences and humanities more generally – have been plagued by a preponderance of research that favours the 'eye', the visual, sight-seeing and so on, and it has been precisely our intention with this volume to push at this insularity and position the two within a more sophisticated examination that extends well beyond visuality, representation and signification alone. What else, we have been moved to ask, has eluded our theorizations of imaginative travel? Which other concepts are powerful enough to shape the ways we think, experience and write about it? Where else can we turn to flesh out that which is missing? And where are we to look for those entities that might contribute, trigger, force, intensify and 'become' in that imaginative process of composition?

When we started down this road and the volume was still in its infancy, we were certain of only two things. The first we borrowed from Richard Kearney (2002: 366) and his evocative insistence that 'the imagination, no matter how ethical, needs to play'. The second we understood from our own experiences, which had told us that we, as bodies, need to see, hear, smell, taste or touch a world in order to fathom it, but not necessarily as physical bodies in (real) space and time. We were intimately familiar with the concept of travel, and likewise felt that we could put our fingers on what we thought the term 'imagination' might mean in our own academic contexts. After all, it is a concept that has been with us for some time, explicitly referenced in key texts such as Benedict Anderson's (1983) *Imagined Communities* and implied in the equally canonical 'Between Memory and History: Les Lieux de Mémoire', by Pierre Nora (1989), or *Place and Experience*, by Jeff Malpas (1999). But even though all three of us had dabbled with the concepts in our respective fields of tourism, geography and heritage studies, it soon became apparent in our various conversations that there was a third thing we were certain of: we were not yet sure what, exactly, was conceptually made manifest when the two concepts were brought together. It was with this thought in mind that we set about finding contributors who might be willing to push against things like the existing ocular-centrism of recent inquiry or the implied opposition between the 'real' and 'imagined', and move to fill these new, emerging spaces with explorations that paid closer attention to concepts such as the body, the senses, time, space, performativity, emotions and affects from a rich variety of disciplinary perspectives.

What we present in this closing discussion, then, starts from our collective acknowledgement that there exists a rich and complicated mess of multiple imaginations, imaginaries and realities, made all the more complex by the mediated world in which we live. Adopting this sort of positioning allows us to offer due counsel for future scholarship on travel and the imagination, along with an apt reflection of the intentions of this book. As shown throughout the volume, the investigation of travel and the imagination is by no means a simple undertaking: the surfaces of each are already too congealed with the remnants of other experiences and various elements of human consciousness and sub-consciousness for that matter. The themes arising in this edited collection alone (as explored in Chapter 1) are complex, broad and inevitably interwoven. Considering that it was not the objective of this volume to be comprehensive but, rather, to provide a catalyst for a canon of interdisciplinary and multidisciplinary work exploring travel and the imagination, this complexity will only grow as new areas of enquiry are pursued. And, as the above vignettes suggest, there are many more avenues of enquiry to be explored.

It would go against the intentions of this volume for us to suggest a detailed path forward for investigating travel and the imagination; after all, we only represent three perspectives and there is a limitless range of potentialities available within the broader international scholarly community. There are, however, a number of considerations and ideas that have come to us while reading, compiling, writing and pondering the contributions that combine within this volume, and these we would like to share. In addition to the preceding chapters, these represent an invitation for further work on this theme.

Firstly, we believe that careful consideration needs to be given to how the theme of travel and the imagination is scoped and defined. The notions of 'travel' and 'the imagination' by themselves are subject to numerous interpretations (as evidenced within this volume) and have been the subject of scholarly debate for some time. As such, when these two concepts are combined, their resultant offspring become even more complex and contentious. We believe, therefore, that there should not be a focus upon setting an exacting definition or a tight scope of enquiry as so much travel focused scholarship, particularly in the realm of tourism (for critiques see: Franklin 2007, Franklin and Crang 2001, Robinson and Jamal 2009), has tended to become preoccupied with in the past. Instead, we see this as a theme that should be approached with curiosity, creativity and, as outlined in the opening chapter, from a wide variety of disciplinary perspectives. This volume was successful in obtaining such a diverse range of imaginative and disciplinary perspectives, touching on the studies of migration, diasporas, disabilities, cinema, literature, history, the visual arts, gender, creative writing, science fiction and travel from perspectives as diverse as science education, building conservation, philosophy, heritage studies, literary studies, cultural studies, geography, environmental science, performance studies and tourism studies.

In regard to the scope of future scholarship, it is important to recognize that no one text can set forth an explanatory or conceptual framework. In a similar vein to this volume, this theme will instead be coloured by a cannon of work that stimulates further conversation, debate, writing and research. Interdisciplinary works, and multidisciplinary collaborations, are required to delve into alternative perspectives of travel, the imagination and their complex interactions. This volume has covered a lot of ground in adding to the discussion of alternative forms of physical travel, yet some omissions remain, including virtual travel (within *Second Life* and other attempts to navigate a life online), military travels, migration, refugee travel, meditation, historical journeys, collective travel, daily commutes, forced travel and engagement with foreign and familiar objects at home, to name but a few. And while we remain absolute in our efforts to push at the boundaries of embodiment, we are mindful that scholarship also needs to push the boundaries of the often *too* corporeal conceptualizations of travel, towards an incorporation of alternate forms of mobility, which are, after all, often deeply entwined within physical movement. The lens of the imagination is a particularly good conduit for highlighting the relationship of physical journeying to travel more broadly, as imagination is an aspect of being so undeniably linked to travels in the mind sparked through conversation, virtual stimulation and interactions with objects, people, places, spaces and landscapes (again evidenced throughout this volume and our own vignettes). In all of these explorations, however, it is important that the complexity, slipperiness, fluidity and perpetual evolution of the imagination and imaginaries in relation to travel (as touched upon in Chapter 14 by Staiff and the vignettes above) is continually acknowledged.

The majority of work within this volume (with the exception of Adams (Chapter 2) and Pearce (Chapter 13)), and almost all previous work looking at travel/tourism and imagination, has been presented from a Western perspective. We therefore see a need for scholarship on travel and the imagination, and travel and tourism more broadly, that looks beyond these familiar framings towards non-Western imaginings and perspectives. This will undoubtedly require the inclusion of authors from different cultural settings, rather than Western scholars reflecting upon alternative imaginings; there are limits to how well we can access the imagination of others. While attempts were made to incorporate these perspectives within this volume, our success was limited, but as scholarship within non-Western nations continues to grow, the possibility of achieving this will become increasing likely.

Linked to this is the need to incorporate the perspectives of various other groups whose voices have often been muted in considerations of travel and imagination. This list includes the imaginings and imaginaries of a variety of gendered, cultural, religious, sexuality and marginal collectives. In respect to representing perspectives from these alternative voices, the volume has had some success, with Lazaroo (Prelude), Adams (Chapter 2), Bell (Chapter 3), Waitt and Macquarie (Chapter 4), Hall (Chapter 6), Cooke and Frieze (Chapter 12), Pearce (Chapter 13) and Staiff (Chapter 14) all considering travel and imagination through a wide variety of alternative experiential lenses, many of which have rarely been considered both in terms of travel and the imagination, and travel and tourism more broadly.

Further explorations of travel and the imagination will also require methodological experimentation to develop new ways of capturing both the imagination of individuals and social and cultural imaginaries. One of the more common methods drawn upon by the chapters within this volume was authoethnography; after all, when it comes to an understanding of an individual's imagination, who better than ourselves to delve deeply into our own thoughts? Accessing, understanding and interpreting the imagination, both of oneself and of others, however, presents problems that warrant further exploration. Accessing conscious thought processes presents enough difficulties in itself, without even considering the challenge of accessing the subconscious mind (McGinn 2004). This also raises questions about the limitations surrounding how far one is willing to reveal their innermost personal thoughts, along with ethical concerns about the consequences that may come from doing so for both the author/researcher and participants. These debates will need to be fleshed out as further work is conducted. With this in mind, we still point to the success of the authors gathered here in pushing at the boundaries of traditional methods by incorporating those such as imagination diaries (Bell (Chapter 3) and Waitt and Macquarie (Chapter 4)), video testimonials (Cooke and Frieze (Chapter 12)), the exploration of representations of the imagination (Waitt and Macquarie (Chapter 4), Bennett-Hunter (Chapter 5), Hall (Chapter 6), Heynders and van Nuenen (Chapter 7), Robinson (Chapter 10), Williams (Chapter 11), Cooke and Frieze (Chapter 12), Pearce (Chapter 13), Staiff (Chapter 14)), and the critical unpacking of cultural and social imaginaries through examples of representations (Watson (Chapter 8), Calchi-Novati (Chapter 9), Pearce (Chapter 13)). There is of course always room for further advances and critique of these methods.

In addition, following recent shifts within tourism research (see for example: Ateljevic et al. 2007, Jennings 2009), we see a need to push further into a methodological landscape that incorporates the embodied and multisensory performances of travel. Here, we sit comfortably alongside a steadily increasing volume of literature within the humanities and social sciences agitating for the reinvigoration of traditional research methods (see Latham 2003, Simpson 2011). We also feel there is a need for approaches that can better capture and represent travel and the imagination. Methods emerging from mobilities – such as: mobile diaries, the walk- or go-along, mobile ethnography, auto-ethnography, auto-photography – (see for example: Büscher and Urry 2009, Büscher et al. 2011, Urry 2007) and visual investigations – such as: photo elicitation, photographic/ visual essays, video diaries/essays – (see for example: Burns and Lester 2010, Lean forthcoming, Rakic and Chambers 2009, Scarles 2009, 2010) may pose some interesting considerations. Again, alternative disciplinary perspectives to tourism are required.

As always, there is a cautionary tale to tell as well. This is one that has been well-rehearsed by many of our contributors to the volume, who point out that there are relations of power at work, even in our imaginations. Our own post-visit reflections are themselves peppered with intimations of power and subjugation: why else would that narrative from Pearl Harbor call so strongly upon the specifics of an American perspective and not the Japanese? In that particular temporal transport, as with any other, there is a politics at work from which the confluence of memory, history, emotion and place cannot readily escape. The imagination in that context takes up at least a double role, imagining an historical narrative that is projected into a museum and memorial space – by the curators that fashion the narrative – which is then taken up and woven, in multiple ways, through the imaginings of those who have visited it. We feel the memories – they are intensely real – but they are borne of evocations of events that were prepared and imagined by someone else; someone who perhaps paid less attention to the ways in which a Japanese veteran or visitor might conceive of that history than an American.

There is always a risk when we venture onto new theoretical terrain that we will forget some of the important things we learnt elsewhere. In our calls for a re-theorization of the imagination together with travel, then, we want to be explicit with our intentions to bring with us that critical work we have already commenced upon elsewhere that parries with issues of power, ideology, politics and social justice. Those narratives of inequality that we see and deal with in everyday lives can follow us into our imaginative travels, too; those divisions and asymmetries that align and spring from identities defined around gender, sex, religion, age, health, class and ethnicity. It can be, when all said and done, as decidedly undemocratic as anywhere else, as fragile and dissonant. Our invitation to travel and imagination is, then, a cautiously optimistic one.

References

Anderson, B. 1983. *Imagined Communities: Reflections on the origin and spread of nationalism*. London: Verso.

Ateljevic, I., Pritchard, A. and Morgan, N. (eds) 2007. *The Critical Turn in Tourism Studies: Innovative research methods*. Oxford: Elsevier.

Bithell, C. 2006. The past in music: Introduction. *Ethnomusicology Forum*, 15(1), 3–16.

Burns, P.M. and Lester, J.-A. (eds) 2010. *Tourism and Visual Culture*, Vol. 2: *Methods and cases*. Cambridge, MA: CABI.

Büscher, M. and Urry, J. 2009. Mobile methods and the empirical. *European Journal of Social Theory*, 12(1), 99–116.

Büscher, M., Urry, J. and Witchger, K. (eds) 2011. *Mobile Methods*. Abingdon: Routledge.

Connell, J. and Gibson, C. 2004. Vicarious journeys: Travels in music. *Tourism Geographies: An International Journal of Tourism Space, Place and Environment*, 6(1), 2–25.

Franklin, A. 2007. The problem with tourism theory, in *The Critical Turn in Tourism Studies: Innovative Research Methodologies*, edited by I. Ateljevic, A. Pritchard and N. Morgan. Oxford: Elsevier, 131–48.

Franklin, A. and Crang, M. 2001. The trouble with tourism and travel theory. *Tourist Studies*, 1(1), 5–22.

Gibson, C. and Connell, J. 2007. Music, tourism and the transformation of Memphis. *Tourism Geographies: An International Journal of Tourism Space, Place and Environment*, 9(2), 160–90.

Jennings, G.R. 2009. Methods and methodologies, in *The SAGE Handbook of Tourism* Studies, edited by T. Jamal and M. Robinson. Los Angeles: SAGE, 672–92.

Kearney, R. 2002. *The Wake of the Imagination*. London: Routledge.

Latham, A. 2003. Research, performance and doing Human Geography: Some reflections on the diary-photograph, diary-interview method. *Environment and Planning A*, 35(11), 1993–2017.

Lean, G. forthcoming. *Transformative travel in a mobile world*. Wallingford: CABI Publishing.

Malpas, J. 1999. *Place and Experience: A philosophical topography*. Cambridge: Cambridge University Press.

Nora, P. 1989. Between Memory and History: Les Lieux de Mémoire. *Representations*, 26(Spring), 7–24.

O'Brien, G. 2004. *Sonata for Jukebox: Pop Music, memory and the imagined life*. New York: Counterpoint.

Rakic, T. and Chambers, D. 2009. Researcher with a movie camera: Visual ethnography in the field. *Current Issues in Tourism*, 12(3), 255–70.

Robinson, M. and Jamal, T. 2009. Conclusions: Tourism studies – Past omissions, emergent challenges, in *The SAGE Handbook of Tourism Studies*, edited by T. Jamal and M. Robinson. London: SAGE, 693–701.

Scarles, C. 2009. Becoming tourist: Renegotiating the visual in the tourist experience. *Environment and Planning D: Society and Space*, 27(3), 465–88.

Scarles, C. 2010. Where words fail, visuals ignite: Opportunities for visual autoethnography in tourism research. *Annals of Tourism Research*, 37(4), 905–26.

Şenay, B. 2009. Remembering the 'timeless city': Istanbul, music and memory among the Turkish migrants in Sydney, *Journal of Intercultural Studies*, 30(1), 73–87.

Simpson, P. 2011. 'So you can see ...' Some reflections on the utility of video methodologies in the study of embodied practices. *Area*, 43(3), 343–52.

Urry, J. 1990. *The Tourist Gaze*. London: SAGE.

Urry, J. 2007. *Mobilities*. Cambridge: Polity Press.

van Dijck, J. 2006. Record and hold: Populuar music between personal and collective memory. *Critical Studies in Media Communication*, 23(5), 357–74.

Index

Page numbers in italic indicate figures.

Aboriginal culture 54
actor 114, 183
Adams, Jennifer D. 18
affective ontologies 55–6, 57, 63, 65, 66,
    68, 69, 130–132
African-American imagination, *see*
    railroad
Agamben, Giorgio 139, 141, 146
    caesura 140, 142
    thresholds 142, 146, 147
anticipatory travel 14, 25
artwork 19, 67–8, 199, 204–5, 209–10
    Cut Yai 198
    Dry Yaye 208, 209
    Eastern Hideaway 206, 207–9
    The Good Life 205, *206*, 207
atrocity sites 181, 182, 183–4, 185–90, 192
Auschwitz-Birkenau, Poland 19, 181, 183,
    184, 186, 187–9, 190, 191
Auschwitz, Poland 19, 181, 183, 184, 185,
    186–7, 192
Austin, John Langshaw 146

Bal, Mieke 107, 114
Bell, Harriet 18
Benjamin, Walter 140
Bennett-Hunter, Guy 18
Bernard-Donals, M. 190
blogging tourists 104, 115, 153
Bloom, H. 200–201
bodies 17, 65, 66, 69
Bronka (videotestimony) 184, 186–7
Brooklyn Caribbean 25, 26–7, 35
Brotherhood of Sleeping Car Porters and
    Maids, *see* BSCP
Brown, Sterling A. 18, 89, 90, 91, 93, 94,
    98, 100
    'Law for George' 89, 94, 96–8

'Long Gone' 89, 94–6, 98, 99, 100
'Sister Lou' 89, 94, 98–100
BSCP (Brotherhood of Sleeping Car
    Porters and Maids) 89, 93

caesura 140, 142
Cage, John 143, 144
Calchi-Novati, Gabriella 19
Caribbean 18, 19–20, 25–6, 28–31, 35,
    199–200, 201–2
    Brooklyn Caribbean 25, 26–7, 35
    décollage artwork *198*, 204–9, *206*,
        208, 210
    tropical places 25, 26, 27, 28–30, 199,
        201
Caribbean identity 18, 26, 31, 35
Chung, Andrea 19, 199, 204–5, 209–10
    Cut Yai 198
    Dry Yaye 208, 209
    Eastern Hideaway 206, 207–9
    The Good Life 205, *206*, 207
Clark, A. 66
cogito 145–6
Cooke, Steven and Frieze, Donna-Lee 19
Cooper, Gordon 124, 125
Crang, M. 158, 160, 162
Crouch, D. 68, 132
Crouch, D., Jackson, R., and Thompson, F.
    10, 112, 151
Cut Yai (Chung, 2009) *198*

Dadaism 203
dark tourism 182
de Botton, Alain 11, 16, 75, 82–3, 197
de Maistre, Xavier 18, 75–6, 78, 79, 81–2,
    85, 86–7
    room travel 78, 79–81, 82, 83, 84, 86,
        87

System of the World 84–5, 86
Death in Venice (Visconti, 1971) 213–15, 216, 219, 223
décollage artwork 19, 199, 202, 203–9, 210
  Cut Yai 198
  Dry Yaye 208, 209
  Eastern Hideaway 206, 207–9
  The Good Life 205, *206*, 207
Deleuze, G. 56
des Essientes (Huysmans) 76–7, 78–9, 84
diary work 39, 41, 236
  Illawarra Escarpment 60, 65, 66–7
  limited mobility travel 43, *44*, 44–50
Dry Yaye (Chung, 2008) *208*, 209
Duchamp, Marcel 203

Eastern Hideaway (Chung, 2009) *206*, 207–9
Echtner, C. and Prasad, P. 201–2
ekstatic imagination 140, 141, 142, 144–5
embodiment 16, 17, 53, 55, 57, 235
Encounters at the End of the World (Herzog, 2007) 140, 141–2, 143, 144–5, 146
Escobar, Arturo 26, 29

feminist geographers 55, 57, 69
Flickr website 153–8, *155*, *156*, *157*, 159, 160–162
Ford, Richard 119, 122

gaze 53, 106–7, 108, 111, 114, 115
Guta (videotestimony) 184, 191–2

habit 56, 64
Hall, Michael Ra-shon 18
Hawaii 33, 230–232
Heidegger, Martin 83
Herzog, Werner 19, 146–7
  Encounters at the End of the World 140, 141–2, 143, 144–5, 146
Heynders, Odile and van Nuenen, Tom 18–19
Holocaust 19, 181–2, 183–4, 192
  videotestimonies 19, 181, 182–3, 184, 185–9, 190–192, 236

homemaking 53, 54, 55, 57, 61, 65, 67, 68–9
homo ludens 109–10, 111, 112, 114, 115
Hugill, Robert 131, 132
Huizinga, Johan 109, 110, 113, 115
Huysmans, Joris-Karl 18, 75
des Essientes 76–7, 78–9, 84

Illawarra Escarpment, New South Wales, Australia 18, 54, *55*, 57–9
  diary work 60, 65, 66–7
  homemaking 53, 54, 55, 57, 61, 65, 67, 68–9
  Janet 54, 59–60, 61–6, 67, 68–9
  rainforest walking 56, 60, 61–4, 68
imaginaries 10–11, 15, 54, 56–7
  social 19, 57, 61–2, 119
  Spanish Imaginary 19, 119–20, 121, 122–3, 128–9, 130–132, 133
  tourism 11, 150–151, 152, 161
imaginary proximity 104–5, 112, 115
imagination 9–12, 14–16, 41–2, 86–7, 139, 140–141, 142–3, 150–151, 232–7
Ingold, T. 56, 64
Irving, Washington 119, 120, 122–3, 133

Janet, Illawarra Escarpment 54, 59–60, 61–6, 67, 68–9

Kincaid, Jamaica 28, 30
Klein, Yves 143–4, 202

landscapes 13, 31–2, 58, 192
Latham, Alan 30, 43
'Law for George' (Brown, 1980) 89, 94, 96–8
Lazaroo, Simone 11
Lean, Garth and Waterton, Emma 20, 229–32
limited mobility travel 39–40, 41, 42–3, *44*, 44–50
'Long Gone' (Brown, 1980) 89, 94–6, 98, 99, 100

MacArthur, Wilson 127, 129, 130
Man Without a Body, The (Mitchell, 1877) 166–7, 171, 173
Markula, P. 33–4

McGinn, C. 14
Merleau-Ponty, Maurice 40, 56–7, 85, 86
'migrants of identity' 29
Milosz, Czeslaw 108
Mitchell, Edward Page 166–7, 171, 173
mobilities paradigm 151–2
modernism 105, 110–111
Molz, J.G. 159, 162
Morris, Jan 122, 128, 129, 130
MT (matter transmitter) 19, 165–7, 168–75
'myth of the unrestrained' 201–2

Nathan (videotestimony) 184, 186, 192
New Realism 202–3
Nolan, Sidney 68
nomad 111, 113–14, 115
Nomad's Hotel (Nooteboom, 2007) 111,
    113–14
non-representational theory 18, 39, 40–41
Nooteboom, Cees 103, 104, 105–6, 107,
    108, 110, 111, 114, 115
    Nomad's Hotel 111, 113–14
    Roads to Santiago 111, 112–13
nostalgia 191, 192
Nouveau Réalisme 202–3

Olga (videotestimony) 184, 187–9
Orientalism 120–121, 124, 129
otherness 119, 120, 121, 122, 124, 128,
    133

Pacific culture 32–5, 230–232
Pearce, Marsha 19–20
photo-sharing website (Flickr) 153–8, *155,
    156, 157,* 159, 160–162
pilgrim 111–12, 113, 114, 115
place 13, 15, 25, 26, 29, 54
play 109–10, 111, 114, 115
porters (Pullman cars) 90, 91–3, *92, 95,* 97,
    98, 100
    'Law for George' 89, 94, 96–8
portmanteau biota 32, 35
Pritchett, V.S. 124–5, 128, 129, 131, 132
Probyn, E. 56

railroad (US) 18, 89, 90–91, 92, 93,
    100–101
    'Law for George' 89, 94, 96–8

'Long Gone' 89, 94–6, 98, 99, 100
    porters 90, 91–3, *92, 95,* 97, 98, 100
    'Sister Lou' 89, 94, 98–100
rainforest walking, Illawarra Escarpment
    56, 60, 61–4, 68
reality 15–16, 18–19, 104, 109, 114–15
Reijnders, S. 10–11
Restany, Pierre 202, 203
Roads to Santiago (Nooteboom, [1992]
    1997) 111, 112–13
Robinson, Shanna 19
Romanticism 58, 59, 62, 63
room travel (de Maistre) 78, 79–81, 82, 83,
    84, 86, 87

Said, Edward W. 120–121, 131
Salazar, N. B. 11, 150, 151
Scarles, Caroline 160, 162
Scarry, Elaine 140–141
science fiction 165
    MT 19, 165–7, 168–75
    spaceships 167–8, 167–8, 174
    time machines 165, 167, 168
Sheller, Mimi 26, 35
'Sister Lou' (Brown, 1980) 89, 94, 98–100
Sitwell, Sacheverell 124, 125, 128, 129,
    130
social imaginaries 19, 57, 61–2, 119
Sonia (videotestimony) 189, 190–191, 192
spaceships 167–8, 174
Spain 119–20, 126–8, 132–3, 232
    Orientalism 120–121, 124, 129
    tourist guidebooks 123–6, 127–8, 132,
        133
    travel writing 122–3, 128–9, 130–132
Spanish Imaginary 19, 119–20, 121,
    122–3, 128–9, 130–132, 133
Staiff, Russell 20, 150
subjectivities 9, 20, 55, 56, 62, 65
System of the World (de Maistre) 84–5, 86

Taylor, Charles 11, 19, 119
telescopic eye 108, 111, 115
television 150, 172
The Good Life (Chung, 2009) 205, *206,*
    207
Thompson, Krista 200
thresholds 142–3, 146–7

Thrift, N. 50, 55
  non-representational theory 18, 39,
    40–41
time 139–40, 143
time machines 165, 167, 168
tourism 11, 53, 57–9, 106, 109–10, 114,
    132–3, 182, 199–202
tourism imaginaries 11, 150–151, 152, 161
tourist gaze 53, 106
tourist guidebooks 123–6, 127–8, 132, 133
tourist imagination 103, 104, 107, 110, 115
touristic experience 149, 150, 153, 155,
    159, 162
toy mascots, *see* travelling toys
transportation 165–6
  MT 19, 165–7, 168–75
  spaceships 167–8, 174
  time machines 165, 167, 168
travel 9–12, 13–14, 16, 39, 197, 232–7
travel literature, *see* de Maistre, Xavier;
    Huysmans, Joris-Karl
travel photography 106, 197
  travelling toys 153–8, *155, 156, 157,*
    159, 160–162
travel writing 103–4, 106, 108–9,
    122–3, 128–9, 130–132; *see also*
    Nooteboom, Cees; Spain
travelling toys 19, 149, 152, 153

Flickr website 153–8, *155, 156, 157,*
    159, 160–162
tropical places 25, 27–8, 35, 200, 201
  Caribbean 25, 26, 27, 28–30, 199, 201

Urry, John 104, 109
  mobilities paradigm 151–2, 161
  tourist gaze 53, 106

Venice, Italy 20, 213, 215–16, 217–19,
    220–223
  Death in Venice 213–15, 216, 219, 223
VHA (Visual History Archive, Shoah
    Foundation) 183, 190–192
videotestimonies 19, 181, 182–3, 184,
    185–9, 190–192, 236
virtual travel 104, 152, 159, 162
Vostell, Wolf 204

Waitt, Gordon and Macquarie, Patricia 18
walking 60, 61
  rainforest 56, 60, 61–4, 68
Watson, Steve 19
websites 159; *see also* Flickr website
Williams, Sean 19
Wollongong, New South Wales, Australia,
    see Illawarra Escarpment
Wright, Richard 125, 126, 131

For Product Safety Concerns and Information please contact our
EU representative GPSR@taylorandfrancis.com Taylor & Francis
Verlag GmbH, Kaufingerstraße 24, 80331 München, Germany